Images and Echoes

Images and Echoes

An Odyssey of Hope

by

Bianca Covelli Stewart

DORRANCE PUBLISHING CO., INC.
PITTSBURGH, PENNSYLVANIA 15222

ISBN # 0-8059-6558-0
Printed in the United States of America

First Printing

For information or to order additional books, please write:
Dorrance Publishing Co., Inc.
701 Smithfield Street
Third Floor
Pittsburgh, Pennsylvania 15222
U.S.A.
1-800-788-7654
Or visit our web site and on-line catalog at *www.dorrancepublishing.com*

This book is lovingly dedicated to the memory of my mother, Contessa Fara Stella deli Alfani—matriarch, lioness, guardian angel—and to my husband Phil, whose sudden and untimely death prevented him from seeing the completion of this book. I like to think, however, that he who was always my first editor, critic, and fan is with me in spirit and reading over my shoulder as I write.

Contents

Acknowledgments

For their enthusiastic encouragement, honest and productive criticism, and invaluable suggestions, I extend my most sincere thanks to the following fellow writers and friends, without whose generous and patient assistance this book would not have come to fruition:

> Maureen Cannon, Barbara Cismowski, Madelyn Elliot, Sheila Lombardi, and Winnie Walsh.

And a very special thanks to Doris Kernan, whose unwavering and stellar dedication to this project has been the propelling force that has launched this book into print.

"You think you have a memory but it has you."
—John Irving
A Prayer for Owen Meany

"I learned what every dreaming child needs to know—
that no horizon is so far that you cannot get above it or beyond it."
—Beryl Markham
West with the Night

"You may be disappointed if you fail
but you are doomed if you don't try."
—Beverly Sills

Images

If I should see the world again,
perhaps it would not be with the same eyes
as those that clouded over decades past.

So much within ourselves clouds over
and goes dead throughout the harsh, unyielding years,
deep within the soul where seeing truly starts,

that the seeing must be better
locked within the clear-eyed memory
of a bright, untarnished childhood.

For ten years I saw and in those ten
I gathered images that I harvest
and reharvest season after season—

Lake Michigan, dark, compassionate,
straining to reach the wounded purple sky
that was split wide open by yellow sword-speared light;

the angel on the cover of my First Communion book;
a young nun's secret auburn glory breaking bondage,
rippling around her startled, perfect face;

a New York skyline, windows a chain of fallen stars;
our pines offering arms full of virginal, white snow
for dawn to kiss and change into a blush of rose;

the first crocus, the first tulip
piercing muddy ground, flashing love like promises
along a cracked Chicago sidewalk;

my paints, shiny in their jars, impatient to become
sunsets, hillsides of grazing horses,
blond-haired dandelions dancing in the wind;

clouds tangled in the curtains of my room,
sculpting Easter lilies, doves in flight,
an old man's wrinkled face, an infant in a blanket;

our cherry trees in spring, pulsating with life,
each bloom a hymn of praise, an alleluia
that I, wonderstruck and staring, learned to sing.

I have seen and I cherish sights of so much beauty
that my heart could hold no more—except of course,
for the image of your face looking at me with love.

One
Michigan Summer
The First Recognition of Irony

We swooped out of Chicago every June, my mother and I, seated in my father's long, black Cadillac behind a uniformed chauffeur, Mario or Angelo or Salvatore. My father believed in hiring his own people. In his mind it was a kind of giving back to the destiny that had seated him behind the district attorney's imposing mahogany desk.

The annual ride to the country in luxury was another kind of giving back—a bitter reminder to my mother, who had left him, that it might have been wiser not to have returned his roses of apology, wiser not to have left all the jewels he had ever given her on the dresser and walked out of the marriage with a year-old baby in her arms and nothing more.

As I watched the city streets curve into country roads, I'd fall asleep and wake to see Mario or Angelo or Salvatore unloading suitcases in front of my grandparents' summer home in Michigan. Tall, slim pines, like Gothic pillars holding up the deep blue dome of the sky, lined either side of the long driveway. At its end a sprawling white wooden house, cheerful in drizzle as well as sunshine, waited for us, although its owners had been forced to leave it years before.

My grandfather, in the diplomatic corps, had been called back to Italy at the onset of the war and my grandmother had succumbed to cancer within a year of their leaving. I was scarcely three years old when my mother and I accompanied them to the ship for their departure, but I had been very much aware of the sorrow that was engulfing the three adults in my life. After the last embrace, when my mother carried me down the shiny metallic gangplank and we turned to wave our final farewell, the image of my grandparents' faces was etched in my memory forever—my grandmother's delicate oval face, pale as death, framed in soft, dark, undulating hair; large dark eyes luminous with unshed tears; my grandfather's angry, set mouth

1

beneath a gray mustache, steel-blue eyes drilling through the space between us as though his stare could grasp and hold us, could keep the family together. They must have seen and despaired over what I couldn't see or know, the fear and loneliness of their only daughter, divorced, alone with a toddler in the midst of indifferent strangers. We stood silently on the dock and watched as our only family inched slowly away from land and into a war torn future. The festive, loud band music and laughter and merry shouts of waving voyagers at the railings of the ship only accentuated our own grieving loneliness.

For my sake, my mother struggled to maintain the summer house and the couple who had cared for it since before I was born. Carmela and Otto were always outside waiting for us when we arrived—she with plump arms ready to hug me, he with a shy smile and a nod as he lifted the suitcases from the porch and carried them inside.

Their only child, Anton, as reticent as his father, habitually managed to appear in time to stroke the gleaming fenders of the Cadillac before it pulled away.

The final summer we were there before the house had to be sold, he stood silent and sullen, gazing intently into my face with his dark saucer eyes. I knew he was searching for a sign that would let him know if I had changed, had become too much of a girl to be a worthy playmate for another season. His sandaled toe drew a slow design across the wide, swing-bearing porch as he watched and waited. We were both six, but the months since we had last seen each other had added height and breadth to him. He was inches taller than I, stocky, solid, a brick of a boy.

A hint of nervous hostility twitched at the corners of his pursed mouth as he scrutinized me. I was glad the humid Chicago heat had compelled me to change out of a dress and into shorts and a t-shirt for the ride to the lake. I plunged a hand into my pocket, squared my shoulders to assume as masculine a posture as possible, and smiled at him. To my relief, his face softened into a comfortable expression of familiar and accepting camaraderie. We both knew without a word having to be spoken that we would happily share another three months of beach and play.

"I got some tomato seeds, wanna plant 'em?" he asked.

"Sure," I said. "We'll plant them, but first let's go out to the court. I couldn't wait to get here and play."

Old tennis rackets and balls were stashed in a closet in the back hall of the house and Anton ran around the porch to retrieve them. The net had disappeared long before, but we would pretend it was still there and spent hours smacking the ball at each other.

The court glistened in the bright sun. It looked wet. Otto must have hosed it down for me, I thought. He knew how much I liked the game. I blinked at the court's brightness and raised my glance from its shimmering surface to the prairie grass that stretched across the flat land behind the court for miles. The green expanse blended into the horizon like an expertly executed chalk drawing.

Anton ran onto the court and thrust a racket into my hands. We took our usual positions.

"Ready?"

"I'm ready," I said, but his new superior size had already undermined my confidence. Balls whizzed by me before I could take aim. "Don't hit so hard," I complained.

"You really are just a little girl," he said almost disdainfully.

I bit my lip, concentrated, and kept trying to connect with the hard white bullets that skimmed past my head. I was remembering the previous summer and the only argument Anton and I had ever had. The disagreement erupted because of a drinking glass with red flowers stenciled on it. We both wanted the red, although there was an identical glass in blue.

"Blue is prettier," my mother had whispered to me. "It's the color of the Blessed Mother's robes. Red is the devil's color."

I hadn't been convinced but I had acquiesced. Despite my acquiescence, Anton had glared suspiciously at me each time I entered the kitchen for days after the incident. Now I was not eager to begin the season with a new argument that might taint days well into this summer holiday. We played on.

Flanking the stone pond at the left of the house, a peach orchard sent us teasing whiffs of sweetness on the occasional breeze. I was just about to suggest that we stop our game and run for one of the trees laden with sun-warmed fragrant peaches (their goodness worth the itchiness the fuzz always left on my skin) when it happened—my phobia crawled out of the swaying grass and slithered slowly onto the court, inches from my feet. It was small and green, not the coiling black horror with staring yellow eyes that haunted my nightmares, but despite its innocent appearance, it propelled me into mindless terror. My heart banging in my chest, I dropped my racket and raced into the house, abandoning tennis, abandoning the peach trees, abandoning the customary bike rides and hikes on the prairie for the rest of the summer.

"Wanna plant the seeds now?" Anton asked, impatient and frowning. He had followed my terrified scramble through the back door into the kitchen and was holding the packet of seeds out to me. I couldn't speak. I shook my head. "What's a-matter with you anyway?" he asked. "You're not scared of a little snake, are you?"

Still trembling, shaken, I ripped the packet out of his thick, short-fingered hands. Impatient myself now and frustrated at this dull boy's inability to empathize with my terror, I tore the packet open and flung its contents out the kitchen window into the grass that had become for me nothing less than a circle of Dante's inferno. "There," I said, surprised at my impetuousness. "They're planted!"

Anton said nothing. He simply stared at me, an unbelieving bewilderment spreading slowly over his strong-jawed tan face. His round liquid brown-eyed glance seemed to melt into the sunlight. He shrugged, crossed the kitchen, let the screen door slam behind him, and whistled for his homely, rough-haired mongrel. I watched him go, saw his retreating blue shorts, his red t-shirt, his brown hair disappearing in the distance beyond the tennis court. I saw his sturdy, tan, bare legs running through the calf-high grass. Shuddering, I latched the protecting door between me and whatever lay hidden on that forbidding stretch of land.

On rainy days Anton and I amused ourselves with Monopoly or card games. Often his mother sat at the kitchen table helping her son build model airplanes while I read or covered large, creamy sheets of art paper with shapes and colors that shone with my treasured acrylic paints.

But most days were sunny and since I refused to venture very far from the house, the beach was our unfailing destination. My mother drove us in the ancient, square-topped, black Ford down a long narrow lane to a private strip of beach along Lake Michigan. Now and then we convinced her to let us stand on the running board and hold on to the window ledge. The car crept along and stopped at the top of the mountainous sand dune that was our entrance to the beach. Before my mother could step out of the car, Anton and I were tumbling down the steep incline and landing, squealing and breathless, on the flat expanse of shimmering sand at the bottom. Jumping to his feet, Anton sprinted toward the water. "I'll beat you into the lake!" he'd shout, and he always did.

Evenings Carmela and her son joined my mother and me for the half-mile walk down the road to the little pink-and-white parlor that offered homemade ice cream. There we watched the silky chocolate or foaming vanilla swirls ooze out of a shiny silver machine that spouted the ice cream into flat-bottomed cones.

Going and coming I was careful to remain in the middle of the group. I stared straight ahead, my eyes averting the possible horror that might, at any moment, slither out of the roadside grass.

Pleasant days flowed into languid weeks, but my fear remained vivid. I didn't forge onto the tennis court again until the day I saw something red nestled in the grass below the kitchen window. I stepped gingerly onto the court and stood as still as the posts for the missing net. Although I was curious, my feet would not move an inch, but Anton, male and fearless, strode over to investigate. He separated the shielding grass and there, bright and beautiful and the reddest red I had ever seen outside my paint jars, was a host of perfect tomatoes—the tomatoes that had been parented by fear and frustration.

For the rest of the summer Anton and I traveled with salt shakers in the pockets of our shorts. Whenever we felt hungry or thirsty he would stride into the grass and pluck plump, fragrant tomatoes for us. Standing in the hot Michigan sunshine, juice dribbling down our chins, we would devour with the full-hearted abandonment of well-cared-for children the fruit that had flourished on neglect.

"We never even really planted 'em or watered 'em or nothin'," Anton would say every time he popped another tomato off the vine.

"I know," I'd say, walking quickly off the court and onto the relative safety of the sidewalk that led to the house. "That's really weird, isn't it?"

Two

The Attic

The first time I saw the attic apartment I was seven years old and too young to know the meaning of the word *metamorphosis*. I simply could not imagine that such a desperately ill-kept place could ever be converted into a home for my mother and me.

A family of three occupied the five rooms: a melancholy faced man in dingy t-shirt and baggy trousers; a frizzy-haired woman in a partially buttoned, faded blue housedress; and a pale, scrawny boy of about four whose deep-set gray eyes were frightened and suspicious when they finally dared to look at me.

The apartment was a shambles of tossed newspapers, magazines, clothes, used plates, and coffee mugs. A massive, shaggy brown dog, gnawing on a soup bone that bore an uncomfortable resemblance to a skull, lay in the middle of the grimy, linoleumed living room. His large, slanted eyes shifted in our direction as we stood in the doorway, but he continued to work at the bone he held between his enormous paws and didn't move.

I stood at the threshold, wordlessly refusing to enter. My mother shot me an "all right, if you're going to be that way, stay right there" glance and followed the woman across the living room, through the dining room, and turned right into the depths of the apartment. The turn brought her into a large eat-in kitchen. Just inside the kitchen to the right a hallway led to a bath and the single bedroom. To the left an archway opened into a long, narrow alcove with a full expanse of windows along the outside wall. That space was to become not only my art studio but also my reading and thinking room. The view from the wall of windows extended across a trim backyard and what seemed miles and miles of flat prairie reaching to the horizon. In the spring glorious pink and white blossoms on the eight cherry trees that graced the yard bobbed outside the attic windows. In the winter glaring white windblown snow so totally filled the landscape that I would scarcely be able to see where sky and prairie met.

In a few minutes my mother returned to the living room and she was smiling. She thanked the woman, nodded to the taciturn man standing awkwardly beside the dog, and closed the door behind us.

"We're not really going to live here, are we?" I asked as we walked down the flight of carpeted steps to the front entrance hall. "It's such a mess. It's even dirty!"

"The neighborhood is pleasant and there's good fresh air here for you," my mother said in her definite, no-room-for-discussion tone of voice. "We'll make the apartment beautiful, you'll see."

I was more than skeptical. I was horrified. This attic apartment, not only unattractive but unclean, was too much of a contrast to what we had left behind only days before.

My parents had tried to reconcile and we had lived on my father's country estate for the duration of the experiment. His house, a stone colonial perched on top of a hill, overlooked lush grounds, a terrace of flowers, a pool, and a five-dog kennel that boarded the Dobermans that prowled the property at night. A winding road led from the house to the high wrought-iron gate and the caretaker's cottage at the bottom of the hill.

My stepbrother Dan and I spent long afternoons rolling down the gently sloping hillside like two newly unleashed pups. It was the first time we had lived together and we enjoyed each other's company. Although he was years older than I, his great hunger for affection made him more than willing to be my friend. We shared everything—crayons, paints, comic books, records, the last chocolate pudding in the refrigerator, and my mother. His own had died (a suicide) before his second birthday. Since then, he had been living with a series of housekeepers or our aging paternal grandparents and unmarried aunt. Most recently, he had been subjected to a hostile live-in mistress of my father's.

I liked to watch Dan's face glow with pleasure when my mother encouraged him to "Eat your vegetables! Finish your milk! Put on your shoes before you go outside."

I worried daily when he came out of the pool or the shower that his beautiful blond hair, dark with water, would never return to its lustrous gold. "What are you looking at me like that for?" he had asked the first time he caught me staring at the distressing transformation.

"Isn't your hair going to be blond anymore?" I had asked and I had actually been close to tears.

Grinning, he slicked back his wavy, dripping hair with long, slim fingers. "Just watch," he'd said. "My head's magic. As soon as my hair's dry it'll be blond again." I had grown to love him and I missed him already.

My mother knocked at an inner door just inside the entrance and an auburn-haired older woman opened it. She had kind hazel eyes and a slow smile. She resembled the picture of ruddy-cheeked farmers in my European geography book. Her husband, tall and with a full head of steel-gray curly hair, loomed behind her. He looked like what I had always imagined St. Joseph should look like, but his face was stern and his disposition, I came to discover, was nothing like St. Joseph. This man was irritable and difficult. I don't remember seeing him smile in all the three years we lived in his house.

"Vell, you like?" asked the woman and I was not surprised that she had an accent.

"I think it will do nicely," answered my mother. "I'll mail you a deposit tomorrow."

There was a bus stop directly in front of the house and, as we waited for the bus, I gazed up and down the block. A variety of two-story houses, most of them bright white, stood a respectable distance from one another. It was midsummer and the majority of houses were adorned with ample, colorful flower beds and neatly mowed lawns. A border of perfectly shaped hedges flanked either side of the walk leading to the house we would live in, and a towering pine tree dominated a corner of the front yard.

"Perhaps it's not as luxurious as your father's place," my mother said, reading my thoughts, "but it's clean and quiet and see, the country starts right there at the end of the block where the sidewalk stops."

I dreaded moving in. I had stayed with friends at the lake for a few days while my mother prepared the apartment and I didn't know what to expect. For the second time I found myself standing at its threshold, staring. The sun danced through gleaming windows and struck ballet poses on the pale apricot-colored carpeting that covered the ugly, stained linoleum of the living room and dining room. A pearl-gray sectional with a cream-colored plume design nestled comfortably in the living room along with bookcases and a matching coffee table and end tables. On one of the bookcases, two pairs of white porcelain Victorian couples danced, the ladies' long skirts sweeping gracefully into the space around them. I was fascinated by the dancers, the artistry of their still motion, the silent music they alone must be hearing. There was an indefinable but unquestionable affinity between those figures and me that I could not understand, but they immediately became my favorite pieces of statuary.

I walked down the length of the dining room and let my fingers skim the glossy surface of the sleek dining room table. At either end of the table, silver candelabra shone in the sun and between them, a victorious, fierce-faced St. George was slaying a dragon. The delicate but distinct scent of lily-of-the-valley rose from two slender silver vases on the windowsills. Enchanted, I watched the clusters of tiny white flowers sway in the puffs of summer wind. Everything was beautiful. Everything was new except for some furnishings that aroused memories in my mind of my grandparents' home in New York. After my parents' divorce, my mother and I had lived with them until the outbreak of World War II forced them back to Italy.

"It's great," I said in awe. "It's magic!" And, for a moment, the word reminded me of Dan Jr.'s hair and I was suddenly gripped by a sinking sense of loss. More than anything I wanted my newly found brother and friend to share all this with us.

"Could Dan Jr. live here, too?" I asked.

"I wish he could," my mother said quietly. "Your father won't allow it. I asked, but Junior is not my son, you know. He's being sent to a military boarding school—poor boy." A shadow fell over her face and over the moment. I was sorry I had asked.

"Look in here," she said, restored to her triumphant cheerfulness. She led the way into the kitchen, where a canary-yellow and chrome dinette set sparkled in the freshly painted room. Crisp white curtains splashed with daisies framed the windows. My art room was also freshly painted and in the center of the long space stood a table and two chairs. In front of the bank of windows my mother had positioned my easel. Along the far wall an empty bookcase waited. While my mother cooked our dinner, I unpacked boxes of my belongings and filled the bookshelves with books, statues, and photographs of dogs and horses, pastel watercolors, brushes, chalks, and jars of bright oils and acrylics.

After dinner, she washed and I dried the dishes, a seemingly unimportant activity that was to become the focal point of our day, the time for talking and sharing ideas.

I looked out the tall window beside the sink and found the thick branches of a sturdy oak peeping in at us. There would be times when I climbed the tree all the way up to the attic window and looked in at my mother as she prepared the evening meal. Invariably she would motion me down with a shocked, frightened expression and a quick, downward movement of her hands. Of course, there would always be a scolding from her and a promise from me, but I found that promise impossible to keep until the afternoon my mother sat me down and exclaimed in frustration and fear, "If you fall and hurt yourself, your father will say I'm not taking care of you properly and take you away from me, not because he wants you but out of spite because I dared to leave the great Dan Covelli! And then, *Bianchina mia*, you'll end up in a boarding school like Dan Jr." My feet remained firmly on the ground after that.

That first evening we wandered slowly through our tiny castle, my mother pointing out, "Do you remember this painting from Nonna and Nonno's home? This mirror, this statue, this little antique table under the Murano lamp from Venice?"

I looked and listened and tried to absorb the amalgamation of sensations engulfing me. The old objects d'art comforted me with an awareness of family unity and continuity, and the new furniture inspired a sense of hope for the future. We would make it, my mother and I, without father, without brother, without grandparents, just the two of us. We stood in the soft twilight of the living room.

"Look," said my mother, "how do you like this effect?" She snapped on the large rose-colored Venetian lamp that rested on the carved antique table just below a fifteenth-century tryptic. The painting, soft-hewed and framed in gold leaf, almost covered an entire wall. The incongruity of this spectacular work of art's place beneath the sloped ceiling of an attic flat did not occur to me. I watched as the rosy light of the tulip-shaped lamp floated up to the angels, to the Blessed Mother and Child. In the shimmering glow, the figures seemed to come to life. The Infant's eyes seemed to return my look and his mother's soft hint of a smile seemed directed unswervingly at me.

"Magic," I whispered, staring up at the enormous painting. "Pure magic." And that magic was to linger undisturbed and serene in our attic home for the next three fairytale years.

Bianca and Mother, 1943

Three

A Respectable Family

The first and best friend I made in our new neighborhood was Donald (Red), a tall, lean redhead three years older than I. He was the middle child of a German family who lived next door in the only brick house on the block. The house was a long, rectangular, solid, red brick with little, square, curtainless, blind windows from which no one ever looked out and through which no one would ever feel comfortable looking in. Its heavy black roof gave the impression that it was pressing the structure securely to the ground. It was, as my mother often expressed it, a respectable house for a respectable family. And I had no reason to doubt it until the afternoon I saw Mrs. Brockman emerging from her kitchen door with nothing but a bright yellow towel shielding the damp terraces of her bobbing flesh. She slipped one large arm out from behind the towel to reach for a blouse on the clothesline just beyond the porch. Against the bright blue sky her glistening arm looked like a white shark surfacing from the sea. I stared at her from our side of the green wire fence and to my horror, she looked over and saw me watching her. She smiled with her entire round face, brown bovine eyes, and little bright red mouth, all happiness. It was a strange time of day to be taking a bath, I thought, and stranger still that she should have looked so delighted about such a common event, and strangest of all that the mother of a friend with whom I played every day would step out of her house looking like that. In embarrassment I studied a clump of dandelions at my feet and when I glanced up again, she was gliding backwards into her kitchen.

I told no one what I had seen—not my mother, not Mrs. Brockman's son Red, not anyone.

Red was shy, almost withdrawn. There were never any boys from the neighborhood or from school playing with him.

"My mom doesn't want any kids around the house," he had said one day as he slipped into his back door for a baseball. "Wait right here, okay? I can't invite you inside."

12

Surprised, I was about to ask why, but the pained look in his pale eyes discouraged questions or comments. I leaned against the wooden railing of the porch and waited until Red had pulled the door securely behind him. Totally unaware of my inappropriate curiosity, I approached the door and tried to peer through the opaque glass pane. To my disappointment, all I could see was a dark, narrow hallway.

All through the spring we played ball or flew kites on the sprawling prairie behind our houses before my mother and I left for summer at the lake. In the winter we ran through the snowy expanse to throw snowballs at each other. Occasionally we ran to the front of our houses to pursue the game. I knew Red was fond of me, but I didn't know how much until the day that one of the snowballs I aimed at him accidentally smacked the neck of a woman standing at the bus stop. She turned in fury and glared down at me. As she was about to launch whatever volley of words she had ready, Red ran up from the wrong side of the snow missile and said breathlessly, "I did it. It was my snowball. I'm sorry!" At that moment the bus rumbled down the street and the woman had no time to question the logistics of the episode.

Evenings after dinner Red would put on a clean shirt, comb his hair, and come to my art table for an hour of drawing. After seeing his naked mother in her towel, it was difficult for me to look directly at him. I had such a dark and heavy secret to keep from him, from everyone—the woman next door was not RESPECTABLE after all! Was I the only person in the world who knew that terrible truth?

While I merged chalk sunsets and painted stormy oceans and vases of flowers, Red invariably pencil-sketched long-faced horses with sad, half-closed eyes. Now, thinking back, I realize the boy, his drawn creatures, and his father shared the same forlorn expression.

Red's father was a short, slight man. His face was pale and scowling, his balding head was always bent as though he were perpetually searching for something he had dropped at his feet. His dark-blue streetcar conductor's coat hung loosely around his small frame. The only color about him was the fistful of pink transfers he would save for me from his day's work on the streetcar. Every evening just before it was time for me to go inside for dinner, he shuffled into his driveway, walked to the fence that separated our yards, and handed me the pile of pink transfer slips. Wordlessly, he would look diffidently at me and force his drooping mouth into a watery smile. I never knew why he thought I would want his daily gift, but I accepted it solemnly and thanked him. It was as though we were sharing what I felt was an almost spiritual ritual. He never knew that every evening my mother scooped the little pink stack into the trash.

"You don't want these, do you?" she would ask after the lid of the trash can had already swallowed them.

13

"No, I guess not," I'd say, but I worried about the possibility that he might ask to see the collection someday. What would I say then, what would I do?

"He's a good soul, poor man," my mother said one evening as we were finishing the dishes.

"He always looks so sad," I said.

"He has many problems," my mother said, looking at me as if she were not certain that she should burden me with what she was about to confide. "You know Red has a handicapped sister, don't you? She's always inside. They never bring her out. She can't hear or see or walk. She was born that way."

I was stunned. Red had never mentioned his sister. "I didn't know," I said, peering into the glass I was drying so my mother wouldn't see the extent of my distress. Suddenly remembering the merry image of naked Mrs. Brockman on her porch, I said, "Well, if Red's father is sad about his daughter, why isn't his mother sad, too?"

"What do you mean?" asked my mother, stopping her dish washing to look at me.

"Nothing," I mumbled. "Only that Mrs. Brockman looks really happy most of the time, that's all."

My mother looked puzzled and, not wanting her to ask any more questions, I continued with some of my own.

"Will Red's sister always be like that? Won't she ever get better?" I asked, guiding the subject away from the dangerous topic of Mrs. Brockman.

"The doctor comes to see the girl at least twice a week," my mother assured me. "They're doing all they can. Mrs. Brockman told me he stays so long because he does some exercises with the girl's arms and legs. They don't seem to have helped much, if any, though. It's all very sad." My mother scoured the sink and put the can with the bright blue Dutch Boy label back in the neat cabinet.

"Mr. Brockman works hard. He may not be an educated man, a district attorney like your father, but he's an honest, honorable man and they have a united, respectable family."

I didn't respond, but I was beginning to understand the reason for the nightly gift. Perhaps in a small way Mr. Brockman was trying to find in me the glimmer of a daughter who could talk and walk and smile at him. I vowed to save the pink transfers from that day forward. Going into the bedroom, I removed my new shiny tap shoes from their box and set them carefully on the closet floor. "I'm going to keep the transfers in here from now on," I announced, placing the empty box on a shelf in my bookcase. "Please don't throw them away anymore."

In the middle of the winter of the third year in our attic apartment, the For Sale sign went up on the red bricks. "Are you really going to move?" I asked Red one afternoon when we were both too unhappy at the prospect to chase each other with snowballs.

14

"Yep," he said curtly. "Away from here, to some other town somewhere."

"Why?" I asked.

"My dad wants us to get a new doctor for Edie," he said simply, as though we had discussed his sister before.

"Why a new one? What's wrong with the old one?" I persisted.

A slow streak of scarlet started at the collar of his navy pea-jacket and moved across his freckled face to the roots of his red hair. "That's all I know," he said. "I don't know anything else."

"Let's cover the sign with snow," I suggested. "That way no one will see it."

He smiled a patient smile. "Sure," he said. "Why not?" And he bent and gathered a handful of snow and packed it into the frame of the hateful sign.

Afternoons were different after that. Our playtime was dedicated to keeping the sign covered. We had no heart for anything else. As spring rolled across the prairie, snow became more and more difficult to find. Soon even the corners of the yards offered no remnants for our endeavor and FOR SALE loomed big and ugly on the front of Red's house.

As life would have it, fate dictated that I should be the one to move away first, move with the picture of Mrs. Brockman in her towel, with Red's sad face, with his father's forlornness still in my mind.

The box of pink transfers was tossed out along with every other unessential possession when my sudden illness and blindness forced my mother and me to make a hasty escape from our beautiful attic, the cherry trees, and Red before the harsh winter of Chicago would have threatened my life.

Red and I exchanged letters for all of our childhood and adolescence, but he never mentioned his little sister or his father. It was years later that I began to suspect all was not what it had seemed in the Brockman household. As I matured in worldly wisdom, the pieces of the puzzle began to slip into place. I asked my mother about the circumstances of the family's unexpected decision to move, finally unburdening my memory of naked Mrs. Brockman in her towel.

"Oh yes," my mother said. "It was such a shock, such a scandal, the talk of the block. Mrs. Brockman and the doctor...and they looked like such a respectable family."

Four

Ghita's Eyes

*M*argharita (Ghita) had long straight hair, as black and glossy as a raven's wings. Her eyes were dark, too with the profound dynamics of gypsies' eyes, dancing when she was happy and flashing visible sparks when she was angry. Although we had been best friends since we were two years old, very often their fire was aimed directly at me.

My mother and I were spending the summer with Ghita, her sister Lillian, and their mother Valerie in their colonial home in Wilmette, a plush suburb of Chicago.

We had slipped easily into a daily summer routine. Valerie, a dress designer, swirled out of the driveway by seven o'clock three mornings a week for the drive to her office in Chicago. My mother, a school administrator, was free for the summer and watched over us. We rose early, ate breakfast, made our beds, and prepared for the beach. The only clog in the smooth-functioning wheel was the length of time Lillian spent in the bathroom every morning.

Urgings to hurry flew at her in three languages. Ghita would bang on the bathroom door with, "Lill, hurry up! Come on!" If her mother were home, she would stand at the bottom of the staircase and call, "Lillian, *depeche-toi!*" If Valerie were at her office, my mother assumed the same position and called up the stairs, "Lillian, *spiciati.*" Only the French or Italian issuing from one of the mothers prodded Lillian into motion and we would hurry the short distance to the beach for the rest of the morning.

It was on rainy days or after our return home and our lunch that my trouble with Ghita's wrath would begin. "Let's play dolls," Ghita would suggest, just as I had settled comfortably on the porch glider with a book. I was the guest. I had to comply.

"All right," I would say, stalling for time and another page of reading. "Get Pierre and Jacques. I'll wait here."

"You know we can't bring them outside," Ghita would hiss, irritation beginning to smolder in those eyes. "I tell you every day! Pierre's already

16

almost ruined and Lill won't let Jacques out of his cradle. You have to come upstairs and play."

Pierre and Jacques were celluloid treasures brought back from Paris. Pierre had been left too long in the hot sun and had lost his rosy cheeks. Even the blue of his eyes had faded to an indecisive blue-gray.

I made it a point never to bring one of my own dolls to Ghita's house simply because I never wanted to play with one. Unfortunately, Lillian would allow me to play with Jacques if Ghita bribed her with promises such as, "If you let her play with him, she'll make your bed tomorrow." This was not exactly my idea of recompense since I didn't want to play with Jacques in the first place.

Jacques was Pierre's twin, but he still had his beautiful rosy cheeks and bright blue eyes. He looked like a healthy, pompous brat while Pierre looked like a pale, convalescing brat. There was something about their mouths, a definite smugness that irritated me. They were both dressed in long-sleeved silk shirts and pale green knit shorts with matching shoes and caps. I never so much as unbuttoned a button of their fashionable outfits. Lillian's permission was contingent on the order that I never remove her doll from his lace and satin cradle.

Grudgingly I would rise from the swing, still clutching my book, and follow Ghita upstairs. It wasn't fair, I thought. When she came to my house my mother would say, "She's your guest. You have to do what she wants to do," and when I was at her house my mother would say, "You're a guest. You have to do what she wants to do."

Ghita would coo at Pierre, lift him carefully from his own cradle that matched Jacques's and shoot me a burning glance that commanded, "PLAY!" I would rock Jacques's cradle with one finger, still clutching my book and feeling as though I would like to let the Parisian prince accidentally fall out the large bay window onto the flowering shrubs in the sprawling garden below. After a reasonable time, I would venture my usual suggestion in as nonchalant a tone as I could, "Let's put them to sleep now. They look tired. We can wake them up when I finish the next chapter in my book." It was then that Ghita's eyes consumed me with their full-powered fire. Her glare was so full of scorn I would either wither and continue to rock Jacques's cradle or, if I felt particularly brave that day, totally ignore the blazing stare and settle on the floor next to the cradle to read my book as I continued to rock the doll with one finger. I was becoming rather immune to Margharita's flashing temper. It was our second summer together.

Our mothers were best friends, both Italian, both divorced from rich and powerful men. The difference was that Ghita's father was wealthy and generous; mine was only wealthy. It had been Ghita's father who had provided his ex-wife and two daughters with their luxurious home complete with a grand piano, working fireplace, and a cathedral ceiling living room which hosted an enormous, lavishly decorated Christmas tree every year. Valerie, a small, slight woman, had to scamper up a ladder like a nimble kitten to trim the uppermost branches.

Hundreds of red tulips lined both sides of the circular driveway every spring and large stone urns of geraniums graced the steps of the front porch far into autumn.

The girls each had a closet full of designer clothes, including identical mouton fur coats with matching hats and muffs. More important still, they had wonderful and expensive art supplies and a finished third-floor attic playroom just for their dollhouses and enough toys to keep an entire orphanage amused for decades.

Lillian was four years our senior, as pale and blond as her little sister was dark. Actually, Lillian very much resembled the sun-damaged Pierre. All that summer her pale blue eyes were cast down on an autographed photograph of the popular Italian operatic baritone Enzio Pinza. She carried the picture gingerly on her arm everywhere she went, day or night, indoors or out. Ghita and I teased her mercilessly. Lillian just stared over our heads with a distant, knowing smile.

"You're too young to understand," she would sigh and walk dreamily away.

Often Ghita and I came upon her tenderly holding the photograph in her long-fingered hands and staring open-mouthed into the baritone's rather unfriendly eyes.

On one of the typical mornings when Lillian was taking an especially long time in the bathroom, Ghita and I wondered aloud what she could be doing.

Ornate bottles and jars lined a glass shelf along the bathroom wall. All the perfumes, creams, and sprays belonged to Lillian. I often speculated on their purpose. She was certainly not allowed to date yet. There was not so much as a boy's voice coming through for her on the telephone and, true to European custom, she was never permitted to venture out of the house except with her sister and me or under the supervision of her mother or mine, so a clandestine romance was out of the question entirely.

"Maybe Enzio Pinza can smell her perfume through the picture," Ghita laughed.

"Maybe," I said, "or maybe she sprinkles some sweet-smelling something on his picture so she can stand to look at his homely face."

We were still laughing when we heard the scream. The sound pierced the sleepy summer morning and shocked us into a gallop down the long lemon-colored carpeted hallway to the sisters' bathroom. Ghita flung open the door and there we saw her! Lillian was standing above the open toilet. Her hands were crammed into her mouth; her light blue eyes were hooded, half-closed, and mournful, despairing. "I dropped him!" she wailed. "He slipped off my arm! I dropped him!"

18

Ghita and I stared into the watery depths of the toilet and saw it—the photograph of Enzio Pinza floating face up, his unfriendly eyes admonishing us for our uncontrollable volcanoes of giggles.

We were, of course, punished for our unsympathetic response to Lillian's melodrama. There was a list of "no's"—no potato chips, no walks to the village for ice cream cones for a week, and other no's which I can't remember. What I do remember is that Valerie had a difficult time scolding us. The corners of her mouth kept turning up and her little dark eyes kept darting away from my appraising glance as she doled out the sentence.

The only positive result from the entire tragedy was that Lillian absolutely forbade me to touch, rock, or otherwise associate with Jacques for the rest of the summer.

My mother looked at me sympathetically after Lillian's explosive volley of fury had broken over my head.

"I'll buy you a doll you can play with here," my mother offered.

Averting my gaze from what I knew would be fierce, accusing sparks in Ghita's eyes at my forthcoming betrayal, I said, trying not to smile, "Oh, please don't bother, Mom. I'll find a way to keep myself busy. Maybe I'll just walk to the village and get a library card."

Five
Teena

*I*t was Saturday morning. My mother had just put the last of the breakfast dishes away and was heading for the broom closet. I knew what was coming next—our weekly apartment cleaning. My job was dusting. I always started with the two photographs on my bureau—my grandfather in cavalry uniform on his wild-eyed stallion and the one of my stepbrother in his military academy dress grays.

"I miss Dan Jr.," I complained as I picked up my brother's photograph and carefully dusted the glass and brown leather frame.

"I do, too," my mother said, "and I'm sure he misses us. We'll have to write to him more often."

"I guess we'll never live with him again, will we?" It was in the hope of a positive response that I asked the question, although I already knew the answer.

"I doubt it," my mother said. "Don't forget, Dan Jr. is your father's son, not mine."

She was stripping our twin beds. I began halfheartedly running the dust cloth along the top of my bureau.

"Could I have a baby brother instead?" I ventured, pretending to be totally absorbed in my work.

My mother didn't answer. When I finally looked up, I caught her watching me in the large mirror above the dresser. Her deep blue eyes were wide with consternation.

"I doubt that even more," she said. "Your father and I aren't married anymore and you need both parents to have a child."

I was eight years old. I didn't know why that had to be the rule, but I did know enough not to argue. As I pondered the dilemma, I picked up my newest dog book, *Beautiful Joe*, so I could dust under it. As I gazed at the dog on the cover, another idea surfaced.

"How about a puppy then, Mom?"

My mother sighed. She looked worried. "I don't know if Mr. Maise would allow a dog."

20

"The people who lived here before us had a huge monster of a dog," I protested. "Remember that big shaggy brown thing that was lying in the middle of the living room chewing on his bone? We saw him the first time we looked at the apartment!"

"I remember," said my mother. "Let me talk to Mr. Maise."

It was early autumn. The oppressive Chicago heat had given way to dipping temperatures that rode in on a brisk wind off the prairie, definitely an exhilarating change, definitely an outdoor kind of Saturday. The sun shone a coppery gold through the gleaming windows. By playing with the shades, up an inch, down two, I could make the sun spot bounce around the floor and change the pattern on the carpet, lighter, darker, more peach, more blue.

"What are you doing?" My mother had turned around.

Sheepishly I readjusted the shades and went back to the job I hated. While I had been playing with the light effects, I had stolen a glance out the window and had seen Red driving golf balls across his long backyard. I knew he was waiting for me. Maybe we'd ride bikes down the new sidewalk that cut a path across the prairie to as far as we could see. Rumors were that homes would soon be built half a mile into the prairie, big houses with swimming pools!

My mother came to look out the window. "All right," she said, her voice annoyed although her eyes were not. "I'll finish your job. Go out and enjoy the morning. Let me know if you decide to ride bicycles somewhere."

"Thanks, Mom," I said as I handed her my dust cloth and dashed for the back stairs. "Don't forget to ask about the puppy, okay?"

Weeks passed and then, one Saturday as I was dusting the glossy dining room table with slow, languid strokes, my mother said, "The sooner you finish, the sooner we can go into town and look for a puppy."

I looked into her face. She was serious. "Did Mr. Maise really say we could have a dog?"

"I haven't asked him yet," she confessed. "I thought we'd tell him after we've bought it. We'll buy as small a dog as we can find."

The moment we entered the pet shop, I saw my heart's desire in the first cage, a small black-and-white fox terrier just like the dog on the R.C.A. Victor logo.

"How much is that fox terrier?" asked my mother.

"Forty dollars," said the bald, wire-spectacled man behind the counter.

"Oh," said my mother, "that's too much."

I bit my lip to keep from expressing my disappointment. I knew we were on our own and that money was not plentiful. It disturbed me that we were buying the new furniture for the attic apartment on the installment plan. "Is the couch ours yet? Is the bedroom set ours yet?" I would ask from time to time.

21

"Look," my mother said, directing my gaze to the top cage. "That little dog up there is even smaller and it's such a pretty color. It's as blond as you are."

I looked and saw a tiny golden creature with white paws, a white chest, and enormous white-tipped ears. She was standing erect on a stick that traversed her cage.

"She looks like a bird that's ready to fly," I said. "No," I decided, "she looks more like Dumbo except that her ears stand straight up."

"That one's a mix—ten dollars," the shopkeeper told us.

"Yes?" my mother asked, looking hopefully at me.

I studied the tiny animal. Her dark, button eyes stared back at me, not a soft, pleading appeal but a decisive, insistent look that I couldn't refuse.

"Sure," I agreed. "We'll match."

As we left the pet shop, the leaden sky looked as though it were a pulse beat away from letting fall its first snow of the season on the city streets. My mother had worn her navy overcoat with the gold buttons. She tucked the trembling puppy behind the middle button inside her coat. It didn't even make a bulge. No one on the bus we rode out to the suburbs suspected a dog was snuggled inside that slim-lined coat.

As we entered our apartment, my mother put the puppy into my hands. She weighed nothing at all. Her short blond hair was sleek and smooth. Her dark, intelligent eyes swept quickly around the room and back to me. I set her down on the kitchen floor and as she began to move her legs my mother began to laugh. "Oh my, look how bowlegged she is! What a comical little thing!"

My mother took an empty ceramic butter tub, the one-pound size, from the cupboard and filled it with warm, sudsy water.

"We'll give her a bath," she said, swooping the puppy up in one hand and setting her gently into the butter tub. "I'm sure you'll want her to sleep with you and she'll be nice and clean."

After the puppy's bath, my mother dried her and handed her back to me. "Come," she said, "we have to introduce her to Mr. Maise."

The landlord, never smiling, never communicative unless he was complaining or shouting me off the grass, met us at the door that separated our attic apartment entrance from his downstairs home.

"I told you no pets," he said and his head of gray curls quivered in nervous annoyance.

"She's hardly bigger than a mouse," my mother said, looking serenely into this imposing giant's stern face. "It was either this tiny little thing or a baby brother," she said, smiling. "Under the circumstances, tell me, did I have a choice?"

Mr. Maise looked from my mother to me. I was clutching Teena to my chest. Her minuscule head protruded between my fingers. The landlord's

Bianca, age 10, and Teena, a pet

deep brown eyes were angry, then confused, then defeated. He opened his clenched square jaw to speak, but no sound emerged. Slowly he bent his heavy-maned head in an almost imperceptible acquiescence.

My mother nodded. "Thank you," she said. "And don't worry about your yard. We'll walk the dog."

Every day before and after school I clipped Teena's bright green leash onto her matching harness (she was too tiny for a collar) and walked my mouse to the expanse of prairie that began at the end of our block. I held a tight grip on the leash to keep the puppy from climbing into the tall grass, which would have totally engulfed her and hidden her from sight. Once winter came, we'd walk in the other direction where there were houses and clean sidewalks so she wouldn't be swallowed by the mounds of prairie snow.

Teena didn't grow. Perhaps it was because of her genes or perhaps it was because of the whiskey. Valerie, my mother's best friend, had heard that giving puppies a shot of whiskey would stunt their growth. She had bought her daughters Ghita and Lillian a black cocker spaniel pup, Inky, and both mothers wanted to keep the dogs as small as possible.

One night, after we three girls had gone to bed in Valerie's grand house on Lake Michigan where my mother and I were summering, the mothers decided to try the experiment. Hearing unusual laughter issuing from the kitchen, Ghita and I crept down the back staircase to investigate. We reached the landing and peeked over the railing. What we saw could have been a scene from an Abbott and Costello movie—Teena and Inky staggering drunkenly across the tile floor and our mothers sitting at the kitchen table wiping the tears of laughter from their eyes.

That summer Teena brought a new dimension to the boredom of playing dolls with Ghita. Dressing and undressing baby dolls, creating conversations between them was, in my opinion, a waste of good reading or swimming time.

"They're not supposed to talk," I would argue. "They're babies!"

Ghita's dark eyes flashed annoyance. "Never mind. Just play!"

"Let's play dolls with the puppies today," I suggested one afternoon and that introduced the new aspect to the game.

Inky refused to cooperate. She kept jumping out of the doll carriage, toppling it to the playroom floor, but Teena was complacent. I would turn down her tall ears under a tiny bonnet and tie it under her chin, lay her on her back inside the doll carriage and cover her with a doll blanket over which she folded her delicate white front paws as if she were deliberately holding it in place. From under the brim of her bonnet, Teena's bright eyes, accusing but tolerant, stared fixedly at me. I was too guilty to look into those dark pools very often, but soon, even Teena's metamorphosis became a bore and I released her from her new role.

24

"Can Ghita and I walk the puppies to the village?" I asked my mother one hot afternoon. "And can we get ice cream cones for us and for them?" And so it became a ritual for us to walk the few blocks under the canopy of arching elm trees into the village of Wilmette and buy vanilla cones for Ghita and Inky and chocolate cones for me and Teena. We would settle ourselves on the redwood bench in front of the ice cream parlor, Ghita with her long black hair and black dog and me with my blond braids and blond dog. Contentedly, we licked our ice cream and held the dogs' cones out for them. Their quick little tongues slapped nonstop at their treat.

People always smiled at us as they went into the shop or walked by on the sidewalk. One elderly gentleman stopped to watch. "Your hair and your dogs match," he said, grinning. "I wish I had my camera."

The first blustery, snowy day of the winter when my mother and I returned from school, Teena didn't come to greet us.

"She couldn't have gotten out," my mother said. "She has to be here somewhere."

I looked under the beds, under chairs, under the couch, in closets. I even lay down flat on my stomach and peered under my bookcase. Teena was all too familiar with that bookcase. Twice, when my mother and I had been late getting home, Teena had gnawed corners of my books as a reminder that she didn't like being kept waiting for her walk. After the second time I found a favorite book with ragged edges, I moved the books off the bottom shelf, but I thought Teena might have decided the couple of inches between the shelf and the carpet would be a good hiding place. I exhausted every possibility in the apartment and eventually had to admit there was nowhere else to look.

"I'm going to search outside," I told my mother, "just in case she did get out somehow."

The snow was falling hard and fast. The front yard, sidewalks, driveway, backyard, and even the prairie beyond were disappearing beneath a blanket of immaculate white fluff. It was beautiful, a Christmas card picture, but I worried that this lovely cover of freezing snow might be covering Teena, too. I looked around the backyard, under the front yard hedges, in the mailbox at the front door, but all I could see was snow, snow, and more snow.

Despite my boots and snowsuit, wool mittens and hat, I was soon chilled and miserable. If Teena had somehow been able to get out, she would be frozen by now, especially without her wooly red sweater on. Disheartened, I climbed the back stairs into our apartment.

My mother was at the stove. A steak sizzled in the frying pan and the aroma was more than a little inviting. As I entered the kitchen, I saw something crawl out from under the radiator in the corner, something gold with tall white-tipped ears and dark, sleep-hooded eyes. From that day on, we knew where to find her throughout the snowy winters.

25

Gnawing books was not Teena's only misdemeanor. Soon she began to display her lifelong weakness for feathers. Although she loved to attack the feather duster or chase bird feathers that might be floating around the yard on the prairie winds, her obsession with feathers never created a problem until the fateful afternoon my mother invited a guest to our apartment.

Miss Rose Clark, the principal of my school and my mother's boss, had befriended us. She picked us up for school, drove us home, invited us to dinner. My mother decided we had to acknowledge her kindness with a Saturday afternoon of Italian music and food. We lifted the heavy 78-rpm opera records off the closet shelf and set them spinning on the record player. My mother stirred and stirred the simmering pasta sauce in our biggest pot. She pounded veal cutlets until they were paper thin and then dipped them in eggs and flour, folded them around dark green spinach leaves and rosy prosciuto strips, and slid a tray of them into the oven. Frying zucchini and artichoke hearts sputtered and popped on the stove. They were a scintillating mix of greens and golds with toasty brown edges.

"I could paint a picture of those," I said, looking longingly into the frying pan, "but I'd really rather eat them. What time is she coming?"

"She'll be here soon," my mother assured me. "Did you set the dining room table properly? Go and check. Make sure the silverware is correctly placed, fork at the left, knife and spoon at the right."

"That's not Italian, is it?" I asked as I watched my mother frost a chocolate cake.

"No," she admitted, "but it's Miss Clark's favorite dessert."

When Miss Clark arrived, Teena was banished to the bedroom. My principal slipped off her overcoat and lifted a round hat made of gray fur and purple feathers off her head. My mother took the coat to the closet and Miss Clark handed me her hat.

"There you are, dear," she said, smiling at me. "My, it smells so good in here!"

"Come and sit down, Rose," my mother said, leading the way into the dining room. "Everything's ready."

I was left holding the hat and I didn't know what to do with it. Being too short to reach the closet shelf and thinking it would not be a good idea to lay it down on the coffee table or the couch, I decided to bring the hat with me when I slipped into the bedroom to give Teena one last pat before my mother called me to the table.

"I'll be back in a little while," I told my dog as I set the hat down on a chair and left the room. I was unhappy having to shut Teena away for the entire afternoon simply because my mother was afraid she might snag Miss Clark's hard-to-get wartime nylon stockings. Teena must not have thought much of being closed into the bedroom alone with nothing to do because she soon created her own amusement.

26

I hadn't noticed when I put down the hat that some of the longer feathers hung over the seat of the chair, but when it came time for me to retrieve the hat for Miss Clark's departure, I saw that Teena HAD noticed. I stared in horror at all that was left of my principal's hat—a scattering of purple feathers on the bedroom carpet and, in the midst of them, the gray fur crown on which Teena was blissfully sleeping.

I went to the bedroom door and called to my mother, "Mom, can you please come in here?" Teena lifted her head, pricked up her ears, and dove under the bed. I would have loved to follow her, especially when I saw the expression on my mother's face as she surveyed Teena's handiwork. Picking up the fur crown and holding it gingerly in her fingers, my mother went out the bedroom door.

"Rose, I'm so sorry," I heard her begin and I, instead of going out to say goodbye to Miss Clark as I knew I should, indulged in an act of pure cowardice. I hid behind the bedroom door that I had quietly shut behind my mother.

"That tiny thing's a terror," my mother said as she came into the bedroom after seeing Miss Clark to the door with abundant apologies. "Take her out for a long walk now before it gets dark. By the way," she continued, "the minister at that church on the next block has a new big black dog. Teena wanted to chase it when I took her out last night. She's not afraid of anything. That dog is a hundred times her size."

She was kneeling now, gathering feathers from under the bed. Teena, thinking that my mother was reaching for her to administer her just punishment, growled a lion-hearted, mouse-sized growl.

"Take your tiger and go," my mother said.

I coaxed Teena out from under the bed with a bite of dog biscuit, snapped on her leash, and put on my jacket. I picked up my special cards from the nightstand and slipped them into my pocket. They were my delight, my pride and joy. I never left them anywhere. The new fad at school was the trading of playing cards. Some girls collected pin-ups to send to their brothers in the service. Some girls collected flower cards, some collected cats. Mine was a fabulous collection of dogs and horses.

My mother saw me putting the cards into my pocket. She frowned. "Leave those home so you can concentrate on Teena if there's a problem with the minister's dog."

"I'll be careful," I promised, but as soon as I crossed the street, I took the cards out of my pocket to admire them again. With Teena's leash hooked on the index finger of my left hand, I walked along looking at the magnificent galloping black stallion; the grazing chestnut mare with her colt beside her; a rearing palomino; two pinto ponies standing at the rim of a canyon; a soft-eyed collie; a perky terrier; an alert, pointing English setter; an elegant white poodle in a red velvet collar; and my favorite, the noble head of a kingly, serious-eyed German shepherd dog. The cards held my entire attention.

Suddenly, my left hand jerked, cards scattered everywhere, and worse still, Teena's leash flew out of my hand. I sprinted after it, but Teena was already charging across the street, furiously yelping at the big black dog who was placidly watching her approaching fury from the church steps.

I heard the screech of brakes and saw the old brown car all at the same time, but I couldn't see Teena. I ran to the front of the car just as that tiny tiger, both front legs smashed and bleeding, somehow managed to roll out from under the front tire and collapse on the street. She looked up at me with clouded but piercing eyes. I picked her up and held her against my jacket. I was crying so hard with horror and remorse that I could scarcely see. Standing beside the car, staring at the bloody mass of torn flesh and points of protruding bone that had been Teena's legs, I became aware of a man's angry voice shouting in my direction. I could see the driver's mouth moving and I forced myself to tune into what he was saying.

"Not my fault!" he was yelling. "The damn dog ran right out in front of me. I couldn't stop. You saw that I couldn't stop!"

His rage was so intense that it frightened me and I found myself apologizing. "I know. I know," I sobbed. "I'm sorry! I'm sorry!"

I looked into the car. The man had subsided into a sullen teeth-clenched silence. He had graying brown hair and dull gray eyes. Even his glasses were framed in gray. Beside him sat a woman in a gray dress. She was ghostly pale, her mouth a thin tight line, her head bent so low that her chin almost touched her chest. She didn't speak. She didn't look at me. Her eyes were fixed on her hands that lay folded on her lap. She seemed a statue, a figure of stone, not moving, not even blinking, a being turned inward onto herself. Despite my agitation, she made me think of Medusa in the book of Greek myths I had borrowed from the library a few days before. What kind of Medusa had this woman looked at, I wondered, that she should be so stone-like?

Behind the man and woman were two thin, chalk-faced children, a boy and a girl with such huge bewildered eyes that I suddenly felt a great pity for them, for what must be a family tragedy enveloping all these people in this shroud of grayness. The scene might have been a charcoal sketch, a grouping of sculptured beings depicting a profound despair, a terrible, unquenchable sorrow. It must have been only a moment that I stood staring at this granite family, but the eeriness of the tableau has remained in my mind's eye for half a century. With a wave of his hand to move me out of the street, the man revved the motor and the car roared away.

Teena was limp in my arms and silent. Not a whimper escaped her. Still crying, I started for home. All at once, from one of the houses I was passing, a middle-aged woman in a bright morning glory print apron over her dress, a blond crown of braid around her head, appeared and put her arm around my shoulders. She spoke in a quiet, reassuring voice.

"It's all right, honey," she said. "I'll walk you home. Your mom or dad can take the dog to the vet. Don't cry." I just looked at her but I couldn't answer.

With her arm still around me, we came to the curb and stopped beside one of the large placards that stood on posts every few blocks around town. Printed on the placard were the names of the service men and women from that neighborhood who were serving in the war. Next to some names was a gold star. Everyone knew what that meant.

"Look," the woman said, tapping her finger on one of the names that was followed by a star. "See—Arthur Dennison. He was my son. He was killed in the Pacific. Your little dog is just wounded. She'll be fine, but my boy is gone forever."

I heard her words, but at that moment, overwhelmed by my own grief, I couldn't absorb the significance of them. I just held Teena tighter to my jacket.

We crossed onto my block and I saw Mr. Maise in the front yard pruning the hedges. When he saw us coming, he stopped his work and disappeared down the driveway. As we approached the house, his old rust-speckled black car was lumbering out of the garage and toward the street.

"Let me have the dog now," the woman directed as she untied her apron and wrapped it around Teena.

The next moment I saw my mother running out the front door. She seemed to skim the porch and the steps in one fast, fluid motion. The woman handed her the little package wrapped in an apron of blue morning glories.

"I'll never be able to thank you enough," I heard my mother say and then to me she said, "Get in the car. Mr. Maise knows where there's a vet. Just pray that he's still there."

I sat on a bench in the waiting room for what seemed hours. The picture of the brown car, the family inside it, and Teena's mangled little legs played over and over in my mind. And the memory of the woman, the kind, calm, compassionate woman in the morning glory apron kept surfacing, too. Had she said her son was dead? Really dead? I passed those placards every day and never realized before that the names belonged to real people and that those people belonged to real mothers, mothers who wore aprons, who had blond braids like mine. Suddenly my tears were not only for Teena and for what I had allowed to happen to her, but also for the enormity of suffering that was all around me and that I had never been aware of before. The reality of pain, of loss was overpowering. Everything in the waiting room tilted, spun before my eyes. I stared as the orange tile floor began rising to meet me and, to escape it, I shut my eyes and leaned back against the wall.

When my mother came out of the examining room, she was alone. "He'll do his best," she said, "but he can't promise anything."

29

When we were home again, she slipped my bloody jacket off my shoulders and bundled it into the trash. "The vet's going to cost a fortune. You'll have to ask your father for the money. We'll go to his office on Monday."

We took the bus to my father's office, which was in a large, red-brick building in the heart of Chicago. The engraved brass plate above his door read DANIEL A. COVELLI, DISTRICT ATTORNEY, COOK COUNTY. We stepped inside the waiting room, where an attractive young redhead was seated at the reception desk. Without a word, she left her post and glided down a corridor. When she came back, she nodded and we took the same path and passed into an inner office.

In the middle of the room was a long conference table with several tall chairs around it and, to the far left, almost against the paneled wall, sat my father behind the massive mahogany barricade that was his desk. He was scowling. It was impossible for me to focus on his fiercely frowning face and I was grateful I could rivet my attention on a small photograph of Dan Jr. that stood on a corner of the desk. My brother must have been four or five years old in that picture. He wore a sailor suit, his blond curls a halo around his head, his pale blue eyes serious. It never occurred to me to question the fact that there wasn't a photo of me on the desk as well. Intuitively I knew that in my father's world there was only one child—a son.

My mother touched my shoulder with a nudge that meant, "Say something, for heaven's sake," but I just stood beside the desk, totally tongue-tied. With an exasperated sigh at my ineptitude, she explained the situation.

"So," began my father, leaning back in his leather throne, "the dog has internal injuries and two smashed legs." He took a thick, dark cigar out of a box on the desk, slipped off the band, and opened a drawer for the cigar snipper. His hand looked small under his heavy ruby ring and as white as the shirt cuff that peeked out from the sleeve of his suit jacket. He snipped the end of the cigar and reached for a lighter before he spoke again. "Why don't you just let this dog die and buy another one?"

I looked away from my brother's photograph and into the man's cold, pale blue eyes, the same eyes as those of the little boy in the sailor suit. "Because," I said stubbornly, "I love the dog I have."

He was not pleased. I knew I should be asking politely, even begging, but all I could do was return his steady, hard look without another word. Finally, he unlocked his gaze from mine. "Tell the vet to send me the bill," he snapped. "I'm too busy to argue the point."

On the way home the bus stopped at a small shopping center that housed a drugstore, a bank, a café, and Sears & Roebuck. I was surprised when my mother rose and motioned me to follow her off the bus.

We walked into Sears and she led the way to the sports equipment area. "Pick out the baseball bat you've been wanting," she said. And from there we went to the boys' department and bought the blue jeans and the wool

30

red-and-black-checked lumberjack shirt I had been nagging her for. I walked out of the store that afternoon with the three treasures I had previously been denied because "they're too tomboyish." I knew my mother was trying to compensate for my father's harshness, for Teena's injuries, but her attempt only confirmed my fear that my most treasured possession of all was in terrible peril.

We telephoned the vet every day and every day the news was the same—Teena's condition was still hazardous. One afternoon my mother came into my art room as I was working on a painting assignment for my Saturday art school class and said, "I just spoke to the vet. Teena's not doing well. She won't eat. The doctor thinks she could benefit from a visit from you."

Teena seemed smaller than ever in the veterinary hospital cage. Her two front legs were encased in hard, thick, white casts from her shoulders to her toes. She looked at us with dull, unresponsive eyes. "Talk to her," the vet coaxed.

I knelt down at the cage and poked a finger through the metal bars. Forcing the words from a throat that was so tight I could scarcely make a sound, I whispered so that only she could hear. "I'm sorry," I said, "really sorry. I lost some of my cards in the street and I gave the rest of them away, so get better, okay?"

Slowly, laboriously, Teena propelled herself forward on her casts and pressed her nose to my finger.

"She looks so unhappy," my mother sighed.

"They both do," said the chubby, round-faced vet, who looked like a young, beardless Santa Claus. "I'm going to send the dog home with you. I think that'll be the best medicine. You'll have to bring her back every few days for me to check her."

And so my mother and I and Teena made the bus trip to the vet's twice a week for the next month. Fellow passengers smiled and nodded when they saw us and, if the bus was crowded, at least one person rose to offer Teena and her caregivers a seat.

The legs that finally emerged from the casts were scarred, misshapen, discolored sticks but Teena was alive and walking, cautiously, stiffly, but walking.

Gradually Teena regained her weight and her mobility, but she remained listless and uninterested in our games. Would she ever be the quick, perky little dog she had been? I wondered. And then one afternoon, coming in from school, we found a trail of feathers on the kitchen floor, blue feathers belonging to my parakeet. Jitterbug was an intelligent, curious, and comical bird. He always danced a lively little dance after he had eaten. He enjoyed watching me at my art table, often balancing himself on my wrist as I sketched or painted. Not being aware of Teena's fondness for feathers, he had been attempting, of late, to open his cage door. Obviously, he must have accomplished the task that day.

31

"What did you do to Jitterbug?" I gasped when Teena trotted up with a welcoming tail wag. The look she gave me was not in the least apologetic. Her head was up and the expression in her eyes was steady, confident, even smug.

"I'll miss Jitterbug," I told my mother, "but I'm glad the old Teena's back."

Wednesday's War

It was 1944
with catechism Wednesdays after school.
The nuns said to each other, "With the war,
we needn't be concerned about the rule
forbidding gum on First Communion Day.
The children couldn't buy it anyway."

Question—What did Christ die for?
Tall Eddy Blake with frothy, pale blond hair
always cut boys' line a pace before
Sister waved dismissal in the air
so he could race across the yard and meet
the girls' line where it broke up at the street.

Every Wednesday was the same.
We'd walk along not talking much until
we'd come upon that corner where the name
of every serviceman from Oak Park Hill
was printed on a placard; next to some
a small gold star where Eddy'd press his thumb

And say, "This week this one died."
Died? We saw no pain, no blood, no bruise;
we lived in safe cocoons where no one cried.
The war to us meant stamps for meat and shoes.
We'd hurry home to change our clothes and play—
The war? No gum on First Communion Day.

Six

Grandmamma and the New World

She arrived in July—all five-foot-nine, broad shoulders, perfect posture, short gray hair, and ice blue eyes of her—Grandmamma Renata!

It had been a bad summer for polio that year. A boy a block away had fallen ill and died. That was too close for our mothers. We were restricted to the backyard when we were not on the beach. No more movies on rainy days, no more shopping trips into the village, no more activities with neighborhood children. I'm not offering our boredom as an excuse for what we did to Grandmamma, but it might have played a significant role in shaping our resistance to temptation. If we hadn't been confined with Grandmamma as much as the polio scare dictated, we might not have grown to dislike her quite so much.

It was the middle of our second summer at Mother's best friend Valerie's house when Grandmamma arrived. After fifteen years of separation, Valerie's mother had decided to leave her life of gentility in Trieste and join her daughter in what she never ceased to call "the New World." The expression on her stern jawed face was one of chronic disapproval.

"Where are the cook and the maid?" she asked her first day in the house.

"A cleaning lady comes once a week, Mother," Valerie explained. "As for the cooks, you're looking at them."

"You eat in the kitchen?" she asked incredulously her second day in the house. "I shall arrange at least the evening meals in the dining room." And every evening, a fresh tablecloth, the fine china, sterling silverware, and crystal stemware blazed on the table.

"Children should not be boisterous at meals," Grandmamma mandated. She glared menacingly at us as we three girls chatted and giggled through the first formal dinner. After a few days, even our mothers found the new atmosphere stifling. They scarcely spoke at dinnertime except to reply to Grandmamma's questions. Any scrape of fork or knife on a plate rang through the tense stillness like a Chinese gong and was met with a raising of Grandmamma's perfectly arched eyebrows. She so intimidated me that I was afraid to swallow my food for fear the sound might bring her wrathful stare down upon me.

"Is it true that a Russian countess lives next door to you, my dear?" Grandmamma inquired one evening.

"Yes, Mother."

Ghita, the spunkiest among us three girls, lifted her dark-eyed gaze from her plate and volunteered, "She's the skinny lady with the two ugly little dogs."

"Countess L is a lovely lady," Valerie admonished, "and her Pomeranians are show dogs."

"I don't care what they are or what they show," Ghita persisted defiantly. "I think they're ugly. They're mean, too, always yapping."

Lillian's pale blue eyes widened in astonishment at her little sister's audacity. I held my breath, but Grandmamma chose to ignore her outspoken granddaughter.

"Certainly the Countess speaks French and German, possibly Italian," Grandmamma continued. "I feel a need to speak a language with which I am truly comfortable now and then. English is not so pleasant a tongue to me." The matriarch looked steadily at her daughter and carefully rolled her linen napkin into a silver napkin ring. "I really must meet her soon," she said, and it was not a comment but a command.

"I'll arrange it," said Valerie. "We'll invite her to tea."

It would have been easier if we three girls had been banished to the backyard or to our bedrooms the afternoon of the tea, but we were forced to abandon our shorts and t-shirts and, although it was Tuesday, dress as though we were going to church. Our mothers set out fluffy pastel dresses and lace-trimmed white socks. Valerie French braided ribbons into my hair with such a firm hand that tears rolled down my cheeks. Our patent leather shoes not only squeezed feet that had grown accustomed to sandals, but they felt as though they were cramping the whole summer afternoon, now wasted, between our toes.

"It is good training for the girls to learn how to serve gracefully," Grandmamma had decided. "The little ones will bring the food. Lillian will pour the tea." We had practiced carrying in trays of every imaginable variety of foods, placing them on tables, retrieving them, retreating inconspicuously.

"I don't want to see a drop of broth spilled on the tray, girls."

"No, Grandmamma."

Poor Lillian spent hours pouring steaming water from the heavy silver teapot into fragile porcelain teacups.

"This is totally stupid! I'm not planning to be a waitress!" Ghita snarled one morning as we walked back into the kitchen from one of our many deliveries. We were both convinced we had left Grandmamma seated on the settee in the den.

"*Ca va sans dire, ma petite*," (That goes without saying, my little one) Grandmamma's voice commented dryly just behind us.

We continued to carry, place, retrieve, retreat. Lillian continued to pour.

Finally we were deemed ready and the afternoon with Countess L had arrived.

Ghita and I balanced silver trays of tiny tea sandwiches, clusters of grapes, sculptured cheeses, and petit fours. We placed them carefully on the coffee table before the skinny countess and beaming Grandmamma.

We girls had discussed it and were fairly certain they would leave some of the lovely food for us simply because they wouldn't consider it good form to polish off the entire contents of the plates, but we were graciously thanked and dismissed from their presence without so much as an offer of refreshment. We retreated, altogether disgruntled, into the kitchen. But there on the marble top table were three plates of tea sandwiches and the box of petit fours left open with an abundance of remaining pastries at our disposal. My mother slipped into the kitchen and nodded. We ate. We ate as much as we wanted and we talked as much as we wanted as we ate. What a double treat!

When the reciprocal invitation from the countess arrived, a genuine smile skirted across Grandmamma's pale lips. She bent her head over the invitation and looked thoughtful.

"The countess has a fabulous collection of paintings and objets d'art, Mother," said Valerie. "You will love it."

On the afternoon of the countess's tea, Grandmamma came to Ghita and me and said in a tone of confidentiality that she had never bestowed on us before, "It is a delight to converse with the countess in the European tongues we cherish, but I would be pleased to share with her my knowledge of my new language from 'the New World'."

Her cheeks were rosy with anticipation, her blue eyes bright and animated. I had to admit to myself that she looked truly regal and handsome in a champagne colored silk dress with a hint of lace at the neck. She pulled on her white gloves and picked up her small pocketbook as she continued, "It is important to me that I make a good impression on the countess with my English. Be kind enough to tell me some appropriate compliments for when I look at her art collection."

Ghita shot me a flashing glance and we both knew she had instantaneously decided to retaliate for the silent dinners, the hours of waitress training, the Sunday dresses on a hot Tuesday afternoon, and the beds that had not only to be made but stripped and the mattress turned every morning of the world under Grandmamma's sharp and critical eyes. I couldn't guess what Ghita was going to say, but it was her house, her grandmother. I would have plunged a friendship begun when we were two years old into unreconcilable ruin if I had intervened. Besides, I wasn't sure I wanted to save Grandmamma from whatever fate Ghita had in mind for her.

"Tell her," said Ghita evenly with as innocent an expression as anyone could find on a nine-year-old's pretty face, "'Oh but they are lousy'."

There was no place we could hide when we saw Grandmamma coming home, walking stiffly up the walk and onto the porch. I thought briefly of running for the train station, but there was no time. Grandmamma's face was purple, a deep blotchy shade like the interior of a plum.

We dove for Ghita's room and quietly closed the door behind us. We leaned against it, hearts pounding.

Grandmamma was far too civilized to lay a hand on us, but we knew something terrible was about to happen. The house was as still as death. We waited. And we waited. We whispered about the possibilities before us—running away, being sent away to that boarding school in the sky that was a constant threat for misbehavior. Suicide? Why bother? Our mothers would probably kill us anyway.

It was nearly dinner time when my mother and Valerie came to the bottom of the winding staircase and called us downstairs. They didn't speak. Both mothers nodded toward the living room couch and we sat obediently down to wait. I was expecting to see a pamphlet from St. Someone-or-Other's School for Girls in one of their hands, but there was nothing. When Valerie had divorced and come from Paris, the girls had attended a boarding school until Valerie had settled into their home and into her profession as a dress designer. I had visited the school just once but I still shuddered at the memory of a maze of dark and shadowy corridors, nuns in long black habits, unsmiling, gliding soundlessly through those endless hallways, speaking in whispered tones as they escorted the girls to the sitting room. *Please God*, I prayed, *not that place. There has to be another school somewhere that's not so gloomy.*

Our mothers stood before us. Grandmamma, still slightly purple and for the first time stoop-shouldered, stood between them. I suddenly felt sorry for her and remorseful.

"What you have done," began Valerie, her dark eyes flitting from her daughter's face to mine, "is inexcusable! You embarrassed not only Grandmamma, but our entire family. You will have to be punished."

I stared at this small dynamite of a woman and at my more placid mother. They must have been discussing our transgression for hours. What was about to befall us?

"There will be no movies for the rest of the summer!" continued Valerie.

What was she talking about? We hadn't been to a movie since the boy down the street contracted polio.

"You will not be permitted to attend any birthday parties or any other kind of party. There will be no shopping trips, no train rides to Chicago for museums or the ballet—nothing. You girls will be confined to the house, to the backyard, and to the beach."

So? We had been living that routine for weeks. We must have looked confused. Was that a smile fighting for recognition around Valerie's mouth?

"And," she went on, "you will spend one hour a day studying French with Grandmamma!" The confusion was gone. Punishment had come, but after lesson two, Grandmamma decided that the disparity between Ghita's Parisian French and my textbook language skill was too great to make mutual lessons feasible. After all, Ghita had lived three years in Paris while I was just a Chicago girl, a product of "the New World."

"They shall have to forego their mutual French lessons," Grandmamma announced. "Margerita will practice conversing with me. Bianca will practice the piano during that hour."

But that wasn't all. Grandmamma made an appointment for us with the countess. Again, we were hair-ribboned and patent-leather-shoed and Grandmamma marched behind us up the walk to the imposing house next door. I felt a bayonet in my back as I hesitated at the bottom step of the porch, or was that Grandmamma's manicured fingernail poking through my dress?

Grandmamma lifted the heavy brass knocker of the front door and let it fall.

Almost immediately the skinny countess opened the door. The two tiny tan-and-white Pomeranians were still on their double leash at her feet. They must have just come back from their daily walk to the village.

"The girls have come to explain and apologize, my dear," purred Grandmamma.

Ghita and I exchanged glances. Who would be first to speak? I waited. The prank had been HER idea! The victims were HER grandmother, HER neighbor. I continued to wait, but Ghita's lips were set in a tight stubborn line. Finally, I murmured a scarcely audible, "Sorry."

The countess actually smiled at us. She drew us inside into the cool, flagstone entrance. Trying to be discreet, I let my eyes sweep the walls for a glimpse of the infamous art work, but from my position, I could see only two large mirrors in ornate gold frames and a portrait of a handsome man in military uniform, rows of medals across his chest. Below him, on a small, carved table, stood a tall crystal and silver vase overflowing with such deep red roses they looked like velvet. Were they real? I would have loved to touch just one petal, but I knew better than to move.

"You were good to come," the countess said gently. Her voice surprised me. It was soft and deep. It should have come from a plumper, younger woman, I thought. Somehow it didn't match her rather pointed nose and thin white hair.

She reached into the pocket of her dress and brought out two gold-wrapped chocolates.

"For you," she said, as she put one in my hand and one in Ghita's. "Thank you for coming. Perhaps another day you will come back and see my art pieces and find a more suitable adjective for them. In the meantime, do be kinder to Grandmamma Renata."

We thanked her and walked slowly out of the house. It was only when we reached the sidewalk that we broke into a run. The slickly wrapped candy fell out of my moist palm, but I was not about to stop to pick it up.

That evening at dinner, Grandmamma recounted the episode to her daughter.

"She gave them sweets for their misbehavior," she said in disbelief, taking a long sip of white wine. "Sweets! Can you imagine? I shall never understand this 'New World'."

Seven

Red Dot, Black Dot

*I*t was early June, fourth grade, when a heavyset woman in a pale green dress was standing beside our teacher as we filed into the classroom. Disciplined by routine, we stood at our desks, dutifully clamped a hand over our hearts, faced the large American flag that occupied a corner of the room, and recited the Pledge of Allegiance.

"Good morning, children," Miss Delarco began as we settled into our seats and looked with undisguised curiosity at the imposing stranger. "This is Mrs. Fay," she continued. "She has come today to tell you about Chicago's public school art competition."

Mrs. Fay stepped forward. "Hello, boys and girls." Big smile, big teeth. "Every child from the fourth through the eighth grade in the public school system is invited to enter the Art Institute's talent search contest. Winners will be awarded a five-year scholarship to the institute. One child from each grade level will be chosen. Some of us from the institute are visiting art classes to encourage you young artists. So, just work hard now and I'll come around to examine your drawings. Keep in mind that this is just a practice session and that the entries in pastels or acrylics can be entered any time before August fifteenth." Mrs. Fay carefully arranged herself on a small chair beside Miss Delarco's desk, smoothed her skirt, and folded her plump hands on her wide lap to wait for our masterpieces.

"Take out your colored pencils," Miss Delarco instructed. "Today's project is going to be such fun! You're going to draw a jungle. So," she went on, "make the picture look as wild as you can."

Art had become one of my passions two years before when my mother and I had stepped into a craft shop. As my mother browsed in search of a gift for the hostess of a dinner to which we had been invited, I spotted a beautiful young woman, her long blond hair tied back with a blue ribbon. She was kneeling before a huge pottery urn that stood to my waist. The woman, a tiny paintbrush in her hand, was painting abstract geometric designs onto the clay. Effortlessly she exchanged one minute brush for another and shapes of blue, red, green, gold, and purple appeared on the urn. I was totally enraptured and stared awestruck at the beauty that was appearing under her swift but careful fingers. She shot a glance at me, smiled, and continued her work without a moment's hesitation.

"I'm going to do that design painting when I'm big," I had told my mother as we left the shop.

"Why not do it now?"

"How? I don't have a big pot like that," I protested.

"You have paper," my mother pointed out, and that was the beginning of my almost daily application of colored pencils, crayons, and acrylic paints to paper in imitation of the young woman in the shop.

I drew flowers in vases just to decorate the vases with squiggles, lines and circles of contrasting and blending colors. Eventually, I stopped drawing the flowers and vases altogether and just covered sheets of paper with converging lines, linking circles, triangles, and diamonds filled with dots or tiny aimless patterns. I drew other things as well—sunsets or sunrises, serene landscapes. Now and then I attempted a stormy sea, but only occasionally did my ocean have some semblance to the agitated reality. Drawing motion was a difficult perspective for me, but perhaps I could draw a jungle. How hard could it be?

I took my colored pencils from my desk as Miss Delarco handed out the art paper. Where to begin? Probably the bottom of the sheet. I should start creating a jungle at its roots with thick, dark strokes of green. Crayons would have been a better choice, I mused as I penciled in tall grass. Too light! I pressed harder on the pencil. The point broke off. Sighing and glancing quickly at Mrs. Fay who, fortunately, was not looking in my direction, I raised my hand. Miss Delarco nodded. She had seen my clumsy attempt. Her soft brown eyes turned a sympathetic look on me as I rose and made my way to the pencil sharpener at the window sill. She was well aware of my artistic style and its limitations. On my way back to my desk I glanced at my classmates' papers. Several were filling with high, wild-looking grass, tangled tree roots, and dense foliage. One or two drawings already looked as though something savage could be crouching in the umbrage.

I sat down to try again, but try as I might, I knew my drawing was still totally inadequate. It was too neat, too tame. There was nothing remotely resembling a jungle anywhere on my page.

From time to time I looked up at the big round wall clock. Would we be given the entire art period to work? No matter how much time we would be allotted, I knew that for me there would never be enough time to accomplish the assignment.

My desk was the first in the row nearest the door and Mrs. Fay decided to begin her appraisal at my side of the room She stepped to my desk, adjusted a pair of black-rimmed glasses on her rather blunt nose, and peered at my pathetic effort.

"Oh, my dear," she said loudly enough for the entire class to hear, "your jungle looks like a badly mowed lawn. All that's missing is a white picket fence. You really must try to be more forceful, more imaginative," and she moved on down the row. The fact that she was altogether correct in her assessment didn't make her commentary any less humiliating. With the tittering of my classmates echoing in my ears, I shrank into my seat and sulked. It was the first time I ever wanted art period to hasten into geography.

"Don't let a jungle set your limits," my mother advised when I told her of the morning's disaster as she washed and I dried the dinner dishes. "Not all of life that's worth painting is wild grass and lions. You can paint whatever pleases you for the competition. Why not try? You may not have anything to gain, but you don't have anything to lose. You could always submit one of your designs."

In spite of my mother's encouragement, the experience with Mrs. Fay left me not only disheartened but also totally disinterested in the contest. Besides, the school year was grinding to an end and I was eagerly looking forward to another summer in Valerie's home on the Lake Michigan beach. As we packed our bags, however, I noticed that despite my apparent disinterest, my mother tucked my art supplies into my suitcase. Soon we were on the train chugging out of Chicago for what I hoped would be a normal and unstressful summer, but a nagging apprehension made me ask the question that was plaguing me.

"He won't come to Valerie's, will he?"

"Oh no, I doubt it very much," my mother said. "Don't worry about it."

"You got here just in time," Ghita told me excitedly as my mother and I emerged from the taxi that had delivered us from the train station. "Mom's going to have a party tonight."

"What kind of party?"

"For some man in town who wants to be mayor or something like that," she explained. "I'm not exactly sure. It might be boring unless his son Doug comes. He's kind of old, sixteen I think, but he's a lifeguard at the beach and he's really cute."

Lillian stepped down from the porch to greet us and frowned at her little sister. "I'm sure the party will be boring for the two of you," she said. "You might as well not even bother to come downstairs."

Over my head as she hugged me, Valerie reminded her daughters, "Don't forget that the party is for adults. You may stay only if you behave."

As the guests began to arrive, Ghita and I positioned ourselves beside the staircase near a glass top table that held a pair of silver candelabra whose eight candles bestowed a soothing amber glow onto the lively, milling crowd. Lillian had taken her place dramatically poised against the grand piano in the living room.

"This isn't any fun at all," grumbled Ghita after more than an hour of watching the guests filling the room with increasingly loud chatter, laughter, and cigarette and cigar smoke. "Let's go outside."

"I can't," I said.

"Why can't you?"

"It's dark out," I mumbled. "I can't go out after dark."

"I'm not talking about going to town," Ghita argued, "just outside in the yard."

"Sorry, I'm not allowed."

"Since when?"

To my relief, Ghita's persistence was interrupted by the approach of "old" Doug. He was tall, slim, tan, and blond, dressed in navy slacks and a pearl gray blazer. His pale blue shirt matched his deep-set, friendly eyes. Ghita was right, I thought. He looked like someone you'd find on the cover of a movie magazine.

"Hi, girls," he said. "You look as bored as I am. Let's have some fun." He approached the candelabra and extended his hand. "Can you touch the flame without getting burned?" he asked, reaching for the candles.

"Probably not," said Ghita. "Why, can you?"

"Of course, watch," he said as he brushed his finger across each of the flickering candles. "Just do it fast. That's the secret. Try it."

We just looked at him. His demonstration didn't seem like much of a revelation or a tantalizing game. Neither of us wanted to be the first to try and when he didn't get the applause he was expecting, he turned away and wandered out the front door and onto the porch. Ghita beckoned me to follow. As carefully and inconspicuously as possible, we wove our way through the clusters of perfumed ladies and cigar smoking men and reached the door. I hesitated at the threshold, but maybe it would be all right to go just on the porch. There was so much light inside and there were so many people, and Doug and Ghita would be with me so I wouldn't be alone.

Doug smiled down on us. "I guess I'll be heading home," he said as he ambled his long-legged exit down the steps. "See you on the beach."

"Bye," Ghita and I said in unison, both disappointed at his quick departure.

It was when we had approached the railing to watch him go that I saw it—the familiar dot of glowing red light. Sheltered by a clump of trees across the street, it was scarcely visible, but I recognized it immediately and drew in my breath. Instinctively I stepped backwards toward the protection of the house. I was trying to decide if I should disturb the party to warn my mother when guests began drifting onto the porch. Some stood and chatted beneath the porch lanterns, some strolled down the sidewalk to nearby homes. Some climbed into cars parked along the curb and skimmed away. Valerie or my mother escorted them to the door and when the last guest had left I looked again and the small red glow was still where I had seen it.

"Look," I said breathlessly, turning to my mother. "He's here. He DID come!"

My mother grasped my hand. "It's hours past your bedtime. Come inside right now." I recognized the fear in her voice and it made my own heart begin to pound. I needed no coaxing and in a second I was in the brightly lit foyer, safe.

"What's wrong?" Ghita had seen the exchange between my mother and me and had followed us inside.

Uncertain as to whether or not I should divulge the information, I looked at my mother for guidance but she was closing the heavy oak door. When she turned to face us I saw that she was as pale as her white dress, but she managed a weak smile. "I told you not to worry," she reassured me. "Just follow the same rules as at home and you'll be fine. Go to bed now. I'll help Valerie straighten up and then I'll come."

Valerie came into the foyer carrying a tray of glasses she had been collecting. She saw my mother leaning against the closed door and understood immediately. "Don't tell me!" she exclaimed.

"Yes, he's followed us!"

"Are you sure it's really him? Maybe somebody's just smoking out there."

"I'm sure. I'd recognize that cigar anywhere. You know what he's trying to do—catch me in some behavior that he can take to court to prove me an unfit mother, or he's after Bianca."

"Or he's just doing a wonderful job of tormenting you," Valerie commented dryly. "He knows very well there's no man in your life, for God's sake, and we all know he doesn't want his daughter."

The two women moved into the kitchen and their conversation evaporated behind the swinging door.

Ghita followed me into the bedroom I shared with my mother. "Okay," she said as she dropped down on the bed. "What's it all about?"

"It's my father," I said reluctantly. I knew she had heard my mother's words so I wasn't betraying any family secrets. "For some reason he's been spying on us lately. My mom's afraid he might be trying to snatch me away or maybe he's just checking up on her. We've seen his cigar outside the house a few times and now here tonight. That's why I can't go out after dark or any time of day by myself."

Ghita's dark eyes were bright with excitement. "Gee, this is better than a Nancy Drew mystery." She hopped off the bed. "That reminds me. There's a new book out and I have it. Want to read it?"

"Thanks," I said. "I brought my own copy. Anyway," I went on, feigning drowsiness, "I think I'll just go to sleep."

Ghita ran off into her room and I stepped into the adjoining bathroom, switched on the light, and quickly pulled down the shade. I slipped out of my dress and into the pajamas my mother had hung on a hook just inside the bathroom door. I was too uneasy to sleep, to read, to do anything but sit on the bed in the dark and wonder if he was lurking among the trees, watching. Although I knew there was no possible way he could or would come into the house, I couldn't rest until I was sure he was gone. Perhaps I could sneak downstairs undetected if the mothers were still in the kitchen and peek out of a front window to look for the glowing red dot.

I stepped into the hallway. The living room chandelier had been dimmed to a soft glow that merged with the candles still burning on the table. Silently, scarcely breathing, I made my way slowly down. As I reached the landing, I gripped the oak banister and leaned precariously over to stare across the foyer. It was too far from the staircase to the front windows to be able to see out. I would have to go farther.

I was one step from the bottom when the kitchen door swung open and light flared into the foyer.

In an instant my mother had a detaining hand on my shoulder. "Bianca! What in the world are you doing? Where are you going?"

Answers flashed through my mind—I was getting a drink? No, there was a glass in the guest bathroom. I was looking for the dogs? No, my dog Teena and the family dog, Inky, had been bedded down in the kitchen hours before. Why lie?

"I wanted to see if he's still here. I was just going to look out the window."

"This is ridiculous," Valerie cried furiously. "The child is petrified. If you don't go out there and tell him to stop his nonsense, I will."

My mother approached the window and, edging the drapes apart a fraction, looked out into the darkness. "You don't realize who we're dealing with. He would fabricate anything just for spite if I make him angry and he would get away with it, too."

"And I can have him arrested for voyeurism," responded Valerie. Her dark eyes, so like her daughter's, were flashing. "I have more influence in this town than he does. This isn't Chicago! Come, I'll go with you."

I dashed for the front door and blocked it. "You can't go out there," I gasped in terror. "It's dangerous!"

"Not for us," my mother said, easing me away from the door, "and in a minute it won't be for you either. Sit right there," she said indicating the staircase. "I'll be back soon," and she swooped out the door, Valerie following in her wake.

I climbed to the landing and sat on a window seat to wait. The tall grandfather clock in the den struck eleven and I knew when it rang again it would be half past the hour. I hoped the mothers would be back long before the notes of the clock began to sound. My face was burning, but my hands were ice cold against my cheeks. I glanced out over the banister into the living room. I had always loved that expanse of elegance, the fireplace snapping and glowing in winter, the tall vase of fresh flowers atop the grand piano in summer. I had often thought it was a beautiful enough scene to paint someday.

The front door banged open. "Done!" said my mother as she and Valerie rushed back into the house. "Let's all get some rest. Tomorrow should be a beautiful beach day."

Nestling between the cool, fresh-smelling sheets, I drifted off to sleep with the image of the gleaming candles, the stately grand piano hosting a massive bouquet of red and white roses, and the circular, ornately carved staircase suspended in my consciousness. Yes, the scene was beautiful enough to paint someday.

As my mother had predicted, the next day was a beautiful beach day, as were many more that followed. And the evenings were filled with the joyous abandonment of fear where the only dots of light were the tiny sparks of the flitting fireflies Ghita and I chased, occasionally caught, and always released. In this calm, fairyland existence, weeks slipped into one another like a perfectly woven summer tapestry.

One rainy evening in early August Valerie came into the den, sat at her desk, and removed some papers from her briefcase. The three of us had been reading on the long leather couch. "Sorry, girls," she said. "Our next mayor is coming over to go over some campaign strategies with me in a few minutes. You'll have to relocate."

"I hope it's not going to rain tomorrow," Lillian sighed as we tucked our books on the bookcase shelf reserved for us and made our way into the kitchen for a snack. "There's not much to do when you're stuck in the house."

It did rain the next day and the next and the next. It continued to rain for a week. I had finished all the books I had brought with me and some of Ghita's. I had become saturated with reading and then, suddenly, curiously, my fingers began to tingle for the feel of a paintbrush, a crayon, a piece of chalk, anything I could direct into creating a drawing. The feeling was familiar, visceral, like being hungry or thirsty. Later in life, when my sight was gone, the impulse would surface as a call to the piano, typewriter, computer, or knitting project.

I went to my paint supplies, carried them upstairs to the third floor playroom, and spread them out on the discarded picnic table that served a multitude of purposes. Paints? Crayons? Chalk? What did I want to draw? The subject would determine which tools might be most effective in portraying the concept in my mind's eye. I closed my eyes and concentrated. Here it was again, the living room scene! I realized it would haunt me until I had captured it. I removed a large sheet of art paper from its roll and anchored down the corners with small jars of paint. The decision was simple—acrylic tones would be the only choice, rich brown for the staircase, glossy black for the grand piano, silver and warm gold for the candelabra and candlelight, vivid red and bright white for the roses. Best of all, I would deviate from the crystal vase that always adorned the piano and create a tall pottery vase I could cover with intricate designs of many colors. I decided to depict the image from above as I had seen it the night of the campaign party. By doing so, the entire sweep of the staircase would be visible.

I worked feverishly, driven by the joy of seeing what was in my mind appearing on the paper before me. Time had no importance, no substance, and there were no interruptions since Ghita and Lil had lost themselves in a board game.

I thought I heard my mother's voice calling, but I looked around and saw that Ghita and Lil were not responding. I went back to my painting. The staircase was complete and the piano was quickly taking shape. I was eager to finish all but the vase. I would leave that for last so I could savor every tiny brush stroke of color and design.

I didn't hear my mother's approach as she climbed the carpeted steps and, all at once, she was in the doorway. "It's almost lunch time, girls," she announced. "But you know it's Friday, so no meat. Grilled cheese? Tuna fish? I'll take a vote."

She glanced over at me. "Oh, you're painting again! How great! Let me see!" With two quick steps she was beside me. "Oh, my! How lovely! This is going to be the most beautiful painting you've ever done! You're going to submit it to the contest, aren't you? We have a week to get it in. Will it be finished in time?"

Ghita was at my elbow. "Why are you painting a picture of the living room?"

"Do you suppose it's because she likes it?" Lillian asked. "I vote for grilled cheese."

Ghita turned to glare at her sister. "I want tuna fish this week. You had grilled cheese last Friday!" Turning back to me she demanded, "What do you want? Your vote will decide it."

I couldn't vote. I couldn't speak. In all the noise and confusion I had let my brush tip forward and a blob of black paint had dripped onto the oak staircase and was slowly spreading across a step. I stared at it, too stunned to blink, to move, to respond.

My mother saw my overwhelming dismay. "You can fix it," she urged. "We'll get some turpentine! It's really just a dot. It's not very big."

Speechless, I pushed away from the table. Hot tears were streaming down my face.

"What are you crying for?" Ghita wanted to know. "You can do it over. What's your vote for lunch?"

I didn't answer. Blindly I made my way down the stairs and into the bedroom where I closed the door behind me, threw myself face-down on my pillow, and abandoned myself to sobs of real grief. As the initial storm of frustration abated, I heard Ghita's words again. "You can do it over." Perhaps I could try, but the fervor wouldn't be the same and I knew myself well enough to realize that I would not be content with a pale replica of what my first attempt had been able to accomplish. As the painting took on form, I had begun to consider the possibility of actually entering the art competition despite Mrs. Fay. Utterly discouraged, disheartened, and dejected, I dozed off to the steady beat of raindrops against the window.

My mother was wise enough to understand that once the emotional outburst had calmed, I would be embarrassed and need private time to collect my thoughts and compose myself before I could face the world again. It was late afternoon when she opened the door. "The rain's stopped," she said. "Wash your face and change your shirt. You have paint on both. Valerie's going to be delayed in Chicago. I'm taking all of you to town for an early pizza dinner."

Whether the girls had been warned or felt instinctively that my distress was not an appropriate subject for teasing or even for discussion, they were as quiet as I was. We walked the few blocks to the village in silence, avoiding puddles we would have normally splashed in. Pizza was followed by double-dip ice cream cones from the town's popular ice cream parlor, but neither the treats nor Teena's and Inky's happy greetings and playfulness at our return home could dispel my moroseness. It clung to me, an unwelcome but intractable presence throughout the evening and into the night until I finally fell asleep.

I woke with a jolt, an idea tugging at my mind. I opened my eyes and glanced out the window beside my bed. "It looks like it's still gray out," I offered happily. "I guess we can't go to the beach today either." The enthusiasm in my negative weather report must have surprised my mother, who was already preparing to go downstairs. She looked at me quizzically. I knew she had been as unhappy as I had been the day before so I felt I owed her an explanation for my delight in the unpleasant weather. "I know you wouldn't leave me alone in the house if it was a beach day and I want to stay home and work on the painting. I think I can fix it."

Hurrying through orange juice, cold cereal, and toast, I flew back upstairs to the playroom. I had to attempt my possible remedy before anything else. If my skill failed, there would be no point in trying to finish the painting. I chose a tiny brush, removed the top of the black paint and dipped the point of the brush into the jar.

Slowly, painstakingly, I moved the brush along the smear on the step, filled in the blank spots, extended two thin lines of black from each end, revolved the brush to create a round shape with a pointed extension at what was to be the front end, attached a flat, drooping flap to the round section and there she was—Inky, lying on the step, looking through the rails of the staircase into the living room.

The Art Institute of Chicago's letter arrived in late September. Comments like "good sense of depth and color, creative detailing on the vase" gave some clue as to why I had been chosen, but I knew what had truly won the scholarship for me—"A unique and well crafted touch—the cocker spaniel on the staircase."

Eight
Jack — In Memoriam

The Hendrix family was already comfortably installed in their neat little yellow house when my mother and I moved into the attic apartment next door.

Owen and Margaret Hendrix were both short, both plump, and both blond. Actually, they looked very much alike, although his hair was reduced to a narrow ring around the crown of his head and hers was in an ample bun at the nape of her neck.

Their eldest son, Bud, somewhere in his late teens, was tall and extremely thin. In his long green jacket and matching knit cap, he reminded me of the Jolly Green Giant on the labels of cans on supermarket shelves. I didn't see much of Bud. He was either zipping in or out of the driveway on his bright blue motor scooter. A quick smile and a thrust of his wavy blond head in my direction and he would have disappeared around the corner or into his house.

Baby June was just learning to walk when we moved into the neighborhood. She was plump and blond, a perfect replica of her mother except that her hair bobbed in a pixie cut and her round cheeks were rosier, her blue eyes bluer and livelier.

The first time I saw her, she was toddling along beside a lean-faced boy of about twelve. He was holding her hand and steadying her staccato paces around their yard. They stopped before a flower bed and the boy sat her gently down on the grass while he examined the soil and plucked a weed away from the blooming flowers.

This boy didn't resemble the rest of the family in its unrelenting blondness. His hair was darker, a rich chestnut color, and his eyes were a soft hazel with prominent flecks of green and gold.

I had watched from my side of the driveway and waited for him to say a welcoming hello, but he said nothing. I wondered if he had even seen me.

June scooted along on her lilac overall bottom to the edge of the grass and waved a chubby hand in my direction.

Encouraged, I spoke first. "Hi," I said. "What's your name?"

At the sound of my voice, the boy spun around from his concentrated effort at the flower bed and reached a protective arm out to corral his sister.

"Her name's June," he commented in a flat, disinterested tone. "Mine's Jack." He turned back to his flowers.

I waited for him to ask my name, but when minutes passed and he hadn't asked, I felt too self-conscious to offer the information. Obviously he didn't care what my name was.

"I guess you like flowers, Jack," I said, trying to begin a conversation.

"No," he said. "I hate them."

"What?"

"Of course I like flowers," he said irritably. "Doesn't everybody?"

Getting up from his knees, he took June by the hand, steadied her on her little white shoes, and began walking toward their house.

"What kind of flowers are those?" I asked, hoping to get another glimpse of his beautiful eyes.

"Snapdragons and marigolds," he said with a sigh. "Don't you know anything about flowers?"

"I know something," I said in my own defense. "I know roses and daisies and tulips and Easter lilies."

"Keep trying," he said without turning around. "Someday you might be a horticulturist."

"I will not," I snapped. The limitation of my vocabulary convinced me I had just been insulted. "And," I hurled at his back, "I know lily-of-the-valley and violets, too. We have some on our window sills."

Jack lifted his little sister onto the step at their back door and they disappeared into their yellow house.

Jack's attitude discouraged any further attempts at friendliness from me for the remainder of the summer. From time to time I would see him sitting on a redwood lawn chair in his backyard, a book in his hand and June playing contentedly at his feet or splashing in a little orange rubber pool he positioned beside his chair. Most of the time I saw only the back of his head bent over the flower bed.

One golden afternoon, as I was painting at an easel I had set up on our side of the driveway, he called to me, "Want to see how snapdragons snap?"

His previous unfriendliness made me cautious. I put down my paintbrush and walked slowly across the driveway.

"I'm going to hold the flower very lightly," he said. "Watch what happens," and he positioned thumb and forefinger around a snapdragon. As I watched, the flower petals closed like a miniature pink mouth snapping shut.

I stepped closer to him and caught the scent of soap and freshly ironed shirt. June toddled over and pushed between us.

"Can I try?" I asked eagerly.

"Go ahead," he prompted. "Be sure you don't squeeze the flower too hard."

I slipped my thumb and forefinger around one of the snapdragons. The petals were so soft and silky, so fragile I was almost afraid to apply any pressure to them. "Go ahead," commanded Jack.

I pressed my fingers in place and stared as the flower curled itself shut. "It worked," I cried excitedly.

"Of course it worked," said Jack. "You saw it work for me. Are you slow or just skeptical?"

Not wanting to ruin the moment, I didn't lay claim to either the description of me I understood or the one I didn't.

"Me now, Jackie," crooned June. "Me now."

"Okay, but let me help you," said her brother and he held her fingers around a flower. Again, the snapdragon performed its magic and June squealed with joy. Jack swooped her up in his arms. "Time for supper," he said and they were gone without so much as a nod or a goodbye.

Autumn blinked in and out with a swirl of wind and brisk temperatures. My new school, dancing and art lessons, and new friends—especially Red, the boy who lived on the other side of us—occupied all my time, but every now and then I glanced over to the Hendrixes' yard for a glimpse of Jack. Weeks passed. When I finally saw him, he was working in his flower bed, digging up bulbs and putting them into a canvas sack. What was he going to do with them? I wondered. I wanted to ask, but I knew he would give me the same response as he had given me before—"You really don't know anything about flowers, do you?"

As the winter roared in, Jack and his little sister were seldom outdoors. The howling winds and stinging snow that rushed across the open prairie behind our houses kept inhabitants inside except for the most essential traffic of daily living.

It was during one of these snowy and blustery afternoons that my mother exclaimed, "Oh, I don't believe it. There's not enough butter in this tub for the cake I'm baking for Miss Clark! We're giving a surprise birthday party for her in the teachers' lunchroom tomorrow!"

"Let me go to the dairy and buy some for you," I pleaded.

All that afternoon, stationed at the windows of my art room at the back of the apartment, I had been watching the marvel of the snow dance, delicate angel wing flakes spinning and pirouetting across the prairie and finally stopping to rest on the backyard cherry trees. The thick clumps of fresh snow balancing on the tree limbs resembled clusters of springtime cherry blossoms. I had been waiting and hoping for an excuse to join the wonder and excitement of the snow's silent music.

"Don't be silly," said my mother, dismissing the suggestion immediately. "In this weather!"

"I love this weather," I insisted. "You know I do and I can wear your old ski hat! Please! Please let me go!"

The dairy was only a three-block distance from our house and my enthusiastic nagging finally wore down her resolve.

"All right," she said. "But hurry back."

I pulled on my snow pants, boots, and parka and the peaked ski helmet my mother had worn skiing the Alps. The helmet was brown leather lined with fur. A thick leather strap reached around under the chin and a flap of fur-lined leather snapped across the face just below the eyes. I was ready for any snow adventure Chicago could offer and wished I had a pair of skis to buckle on for the trek to the store.

My mother smiled as she handed me my mittens and the money. "You look like you're on your way to Cortina," she said. "Be careful."

The cold and swirling snow exhilarated me. My boots crunching into the thickly covered sidewalk created my own winter music, bright and quick and free. I was tempted to release the face flap of the helmet so I could tilt my head back and catch a taste of the cascading blizzard on my tongue, but I would have to remove my thick mittens to accomplish it and the cold was too severe. Besides, I had been told to hurry.

At the end of our block the sidewalk and the homes ended and the equivalent of two blocks of open prairie stretched to the little group of stores at the corner that met the highway. When the wind, no longer restrained and muted by homes, unleashed its fierceness on me, I picked up my pace, lifted my arms, and seemed to fly to the big chrome-and-white dairy. I pushed open the door and stood a moment to catch my breath.

"My, my," said the pleasant-faced woman behind the gleaming counter. "Look at the little snowman that just blew in here! Close that door, quick!"

"I'd like a pound of butter, please, the one in the blue-and-white marble tub," I said, fighting off my mitten and retrieving the money from the pocket of my parka.

"That's all you came out for, a pound of butter?" asked the woman. "Why didn't somebody drive over for it? This isn't weather to send a youngster out in!"

"I like this weather," I said defensively, annoyed at her meddling. "And anyway, we don't have a car," I added and, pressing the marble tub firmly to my parka, I dove back into the wind and snow.

I had just reached our block when I noticed a figure approaching. Something in the stride and the slump of the shoulders looked familiar. The figure wore a knit cap pulled down to the eyebrows and a scarf that covered nose and mouth. It was only when we drew close enough to see each other's eyes that I knew it was Jack.

"I thought that was you," he said through his scarf. And then, focusing his gaze on the marble tub in my mittened hands, he asked, "You eat butter?" and it was not so much a question as a criticism.

"Sure, don't you?"

"We're not that rich," he replied. "We eat margarine."

"What's margarine?" I asked.

"You really don't know anything about anything, do you," he said and, ducking his head against the blast of wind, he sped past me.

I ran home and climbed the back staircase into our attic apartment. Sitting on the top step, I pulled off my boots and slid into the kitchen on my thick wool socks.

"You remind me of myself when I was a little girl in Italy," my mother mused. "My brother and I had special socks that fit over our shoes so that we could slide around the house and keep the marble floors shiny." I ignored her nostalgic commentary.

"What's margarine?" I asked, handing her the snow-covered tub of butter. I began peeling off my snow pants, parka, and helmet.

"It's a substitute for butter. Why do you ask?"

"I met Jack when I was coming home from the dairy and he said they eat it at his house because they're not rich."

My mother laughed. "They have their own house, a car, and a father who goes to work for them every day, so I imagine they're doing just fine."

"Why is he so nasty?" I asked, more a question to myself than to her.

"Maybe he's just unhappy," my mother said quietly. "He doesn't have much time for himself or for making friends." She glanced at the kitchen floor and the trail of snow I had tracked in. "Get the mop," she said. "It looks like you've brought most of the storm in with you."

Every now and then over the next few months my mother's comment about Jack surfaced in my mind and actually evoked a trickle of pity for our unpleasant neighbor with the beautiful eyes. As spring slowly emerged through the mounds of grimy leftover snow, and Red and I resumed our afternoons of baseball or kite flying, I resolved to include Jack.

"Want to play catch with me and Red?" I asked as I slipped my hand into Red's outgrown baseball mitt.

"No, I can't, Miss Tomboy," Jack said, looking at me disapprovingly.

I tried again another day.

"We'll be hitting golf balls. Red's uncle gave him an old club. We can take turns. Want to do that with us?"

"No, I can't," Jack said, turning to his book, and I knew I had been dismissed.

One afternoon I gathered the courage to try again for the last time. "There's a good wind up today, want to fly kites with us?"

Jack turned an exasperated look on me. "Are you stupid or just stubborn?" he growled. "You know I have to watch June."

Hurt and frustrated, I began to walk away, but casting a glance behind me, I caught sight of June pulling up a fistful of grass and shoving it into her mouth. I called over my shoulder. "If you're going to watch her, then watch her. She's going to choke on that grass she's eating."

Perhaps Jack was trying to apologize for his rudeness or perhaps he was trying to thank me for calling his attention to June's muddy snack, but whatever the reason, the next afternoon he was waiting for me as I came out our back door. "I'm going to plant some gladioli bulbs. Would you like to help?"

"I suppose," I said in as bored a tone as I could generate. I wandered over to the flower bed. A bunch of bulbs, a watering can, and some gardening tools lay in front of the freshly raked soil. I looked around. Something was missing.

"Where's June?"

"My mom took her to the nursery school across from the dairy," he said. "She's going to register her there for a few hours a week. She's old enough now.

"Here," he said, handing me a metal triangular hand spade. "Start digging holes for the bulbs just about four inches apart."

I knelt down at the edge of the flower bed. The thought flickered across my mind that my jeans were new—brand new. I proceeded to dig into the ground. The sun was warm on my back and as I broke into the soil, a breath of unearthed springtime floated into my face. "This is fun," I said as I plunged the blade deeper and scooped out another heaping spadeful of moist, dark soil.

"That's enough," said Jack. "I'll pour water in and set the bulb down."

His lean fingers curled around the bulbs and carefully set them into each space we prepared for them. We worked steadily without a word passing between us until a dozen bulbs were securely in the ground.

"You did all right," said Jack, but he wasn't smiling. I tried to remember if I had ever seen him smile.

I stood and tried to brush off my knees but the deep-set stain of mud and grass was well embedded in the denim. I looked forlornly at my jeans.

"What's wrong?" asked Jack. "A little mud won't hurt anything."

"These are brand new," I said. "I had to talk my mom into buying them for my birthday."

"When's your birthday?" he asked and he seemed truly interested.

"Next Saturday," I said, and then reckless with the rush of our newly acquired camaraderie, I ventured, "I'm having a party. Will you come?"

He began picking up his planting tools and didn't look at me. "Me go to a ten-year-old's birthday party? That's not going to happen."

"Why not?" I persisted. "Kids your age don't eat cake?"

"Not little girls' birthday party cake," he said and walked away toward the garage to store his tools.

On the appointed afternoon I stood at our living room window and watched my guests hopping out of sturdy sedans or sleek convertibles. I would not admit to myself that each slick-haired boy and party dressed girl was a disappointment. Even before the invitation had left my lips I had known that Jack would not come, but I was still hoping nonetheless.

Finally my mother called me away from the window. "I think everyone is here," she said. "Come and open your gifts."

I turned to see a flurry of pink and yellow and blue dresses and I wondered if my mother was disappointed that I had chosen to bypass my aqua taffeta dress and wear a pale green skirt, a long-sleeved white blouse, and "the belt." The belt, a wide white elastic band with a two-inch red plastic heart buckle, was covered in black writing. I had recognized the English and the Italian words the moment I had spotted the belts on the department store counter—*I love you, Io ti amo.* There were other languages, too: *Yo te quiero, Je vous aime, Ich liebe dich.* I had studied the belts so long my mother had grown impatient. "Let's just buy one and you can translate it at home," she had said, snatching a belt off the top of the stack and marching off to the cashier.

Now, looking at the cluster of girls, the effect of the rainbow frills and hair ribbons almost made me dizzy and I was glad I had opted for my outfit.

"Open my present first!"—Linda, with the jet-black sausage curls and the pout.

"Now mine."—Walter, with the starched white shirt and bow tie tucked under his double chin.

"My mom bought this."—Richard, one of the slick-haired boys, embarrassed.

One by one I unwrapped packets of stationery, bubble bath, books, and costume jewelry. And then we were seated around the dining room table and I was about to cut the cake.

"I want a sugar rose."—Lois, with the brown bangs.

"Me, too."—Annette, with the pierced ears.

A chorus of "me too's!"

There were more children than roses. I looked to my mother for help. She intervened. "The girls will get the roses," she said simply. "I'm sure the boys don't really care about flowers." The roses dilemma was settled and everyone was happy, pampered girls and ego-strengthened boys, but my mother's comment reminded me of Jack and the fact that he had refused my invitation.

As I sat at the head of the table watching my friends stuffing their mouths with gooey cake, dripping ice cream on their chins, I was beginning to be grateful Jack hadn't come.

56

The back door buzzer pierced through the high-pitched clamor. I jumped up more from the need to escape than from curiosity. I opened the door and there, in brown windbreaker and tan slacks, unsmiling as always, stood Jack.

"Happy birthday," he said and held out a small square cellophane box. I stared. I couldn't move or find my voice.

"Well," he said, "don't you want it?"

I reached out my hand and he placed the box on my palm. Inside it a small white flower on a pale green stem lay on a soft pink tissue paper bed. Beside it was a long straight pin—my first corsage.

I was spellbound.

"It's beautiful," I managed to whisper. "Thank you."

A moment of awkward silence hung between us as I studied the flower and when I looked up, I met his beautiful eyes. Jack shifted on the step. He was about to leave.

"What kind of flower is it?" I asked, more to prolong his stay than for the information.

"You're hopeless," he said and grinned. *Jack actually grinned*! "It's a gardenia," he said, starting down the steps, but halfway down the staircase he turned around.

"Neat belt," he said. "I can read the English, but what's the rest of it?"

"It says the same thing in all the languages," I explained. Then, pointing to each phrase, I said, "This is Italian. This one's Spanish, this French, and this one's German," and before I had time to deliberate I added, "You really don't know anything about anything, do you?"

Jack laughed. *Jack actually laughed out loud!* He bounced away down the rest of the stairs. "Touché," he flung over his shoulder. "And don't ask me what it means," he said, still laughing. "Look it up."

He stopped and hesitated a moment before he said, "My dad gave my mom a Victrola and some records for their wedding anniversary. Want to come over later and hear them?"

"I don't know," I said, confused. Unexpected events were happening too quickly. "I'll ask my mom."

"What do you have there?" my mother asked as I returned to the table. I held out the box.

"From Jack," I said.

"Oh, really?" she said and looked questioningly at me. "Would you like me to pin it on you?"

"Not now," I said, walking into the living room and laying the little box down on the corner of a bookcase. My classmates left the table and scampered after me.

"Wow!" exclaimed Annette. "A real corsage. Wow!"

"Who's Jack?" demanded Linda.

Again I looked pleadingly at my mother.

"Who wants to be first for 'Pin the Tail on the Donkey'?" she asked, and the games began.

"I can't see! I can't see!"—Richard, eyes covered with one of my mother's silk scarves, staggering around as if he were not only sightless but intoxicated.

"Ooooo, I'm dizzy!"—Lois, trying to peek beneath the scarf.

"Somebody can have my turn."—Portly Walter, sacrificing his place in line to take another Dixie Cup off the tray on the dining room table.

Finally, after what seemed an interminable afternoon, the horns of the sedans and convertibles began to beep outside the house and the rainbow girls and rather rumpled boys streamed out.

As I helped my mother clear the messy table she asked, "Why so quiet? Something wrong?"

I picked up the plate that held the remainder of the birthday cake and headed for the kitchen.

"Mom," I said, hiding my head behind the refrigerator door I had just opened, "Jack invited me to listen to some new records at his house. Can I go?"

My mother waited until I had emerged from the shelter of the door. She looked at me with a mixture of surprise and concern. Without a word she walked into the dining room and glanced out the row of windows that overlooked the driveway. I followed her to see what she was looking for, but there was nothing to see except the Hendrixes' black Ford.

"All right," she said, "but be home in an hour."

> "Peg of my heart, I love you.
> We'll never part, I love you.
> Come be my own,
> Come make your home
> In my heart."

I sat perched on the Hendrixes' living room couch, a rough-textured, dull tan-and-green tweed affair. Across from me Jack was adjusting knobs on the Victrola.

"Peg is my mom's nickname," he explained.

"Oh," I said and waited. I looked around. The room was clean and neat but bare. No paintings, no statues, no silver candelabra, no gracefully carved tables hosting ornate lamps graced the room like those in our apartment. Maybe the Hendrix family really did have to eat margarine.

"Do you know how to dance?" asked Jack, not looking at me.

"I take tap and ballet lessons."

"Not that kind of dancing, silly, I mean regular dancing."

58

The music stopped and Jack removed the record from the Victrola. He slipped another record out of a paper jacket and set it carefully on the spindle of the turntable.

"O, how we danced on the night we were wed,
we vowed our true love
though a word wasn't said."

"This is the 'Anniversary Waltz'," said Jack. "Stand up and I'll show you the waltz step."

"You can dance?" I asked as I slipped off the edge of the couch.

"We had a couple of dances at school and my mom taught me some basics," he said.

Jack took both of my hands and, holding me at arm's length, began to move his feet.

"You make a square, a box shape on the floor," he said.

When I didn't respond he dropped my hands.

"Look," he said patiently, "watch my feet," and he glided smoothly into the steps.

"Now put your left hand on my shoulder and follow me," he said, and with his hand on my belt and holding my right hand stretched up to a comfortable height for him, he guided me around the living room floor.

I held my breath. I couldn't believe this was happening. His eyes, when I stole a quick glance at his face, were gazing at me with an expression I had never seen in them before. Suddenly overcome with an unfamiliar shyness, I concentrated my attention on the small checked pattern of his shirt.

We didn't speak. Each time the record stopped he started it again.

Time passed. Pots and pans began clanging in the kitchen and Bud's motor scooter sputtered into the driveway.

All at once, above the lilt of the music came an insistent tapping at the living room window. Startled, we looked toward the sound and saw my mother standing outside, beckoning me with a quick motion of her hand.

"You did great," Jack said softly as I darted breathlessly toward the door. "I'll show you some other steps next time."

How could we, in the shimmering delectation of our youth, have suspected there would never be a next time for dancing or even a next week for Jack?

"Maybe I could invite Jack to our house sometime," I suggested as I followed my mother home. "I have some Bing Crosby records and you have those old opera records up on the closet shelf."

"Enrico Caruso? I doubt that a young boy would like my records," said my mother. "But," she continued more thoughtfully, "knowing Jack, he just might."

Sunday came and went. Monday after school I changed out of my school clothes and hurried outside. Red came to the green wire fence that separated our yards.

"Coming over?" he asked. "I got some more golf balls."

"No," I said and searched quickly for an excuse. "I can only stay out a few minutes. I have some art work to finish."

Red looked puzzled. "Okay, see you tomorrow, I guess," he said and walked away whistling and swinging his golf club.

I walked around to the front of the house and in a few moments Jack, books in hand, came into view. I met him as he reached his house.

"I've got some records, too," I said. "Want to come over and hear them?"

He looked surprised. "Not now," he said, going up his front steps. "I have to go to the nursery school to pick up Junie, but I'll be over later if that's okay."

I went back into the apartment. I would draw while I waited for him. Taking out my charcoal sticks and a large sheet of soft, creamy art paper, I began planning how I would approach the project due at the Art Institute the following Saturday. I sketched a vase. Eventually I would fill it with snap-dragons. As I worked I heard a siren wail past and fade away. I continued trying to achieve a Greek design on the empty vase.

Suddenly, another siren blared and wound to a plaintive, trembling halt just outside the house.

Dashing to the front windows, I saw a policeman slamming his car door. A second later Mrs. Hendrix ran across the sidewalk with the policeman and almost fell into his car. They roared away, siren screaming, red light flashing.

"Something's wrong!" I cried, running into the kitchen. "That police car stopped at Jack's house and...."

My mother was ironing. She didn't wait for any more explanation. She jerked the iron's plug from the socket and we ran outside. Mrs. Maise, our landlady, and Mrs. Brockman, our neighbor, were already on the sidewalk. There was no sign of the Hendrixes.

"Jack was going to the nursery school to get Junie," I said, my words issuing on shallow gasps of air, the way one breathes in a nightmare.

"I'll take the car and go up there," said Red's mother. "Maybe I can help."

The rest of us waited on the sidewalk. No one spoke. I could feel my heart thumping in my chest, in my head. Mrs. Maise made the sign of the cross on her old gray sweatered chest and stared up at the sky.

Vaguely I noticed the girl who lived down the street swagger by with her perfectly groomed prancing collie. She had never allowed me to pet her dog and I had always felt not only envious but inferior in her presence until the day Jack had asked her, "Is your dog a purebred?" and she had respond-ed, nose tilted up and lips pursed, "No, he's a collie."

60

"Collie or no collie, she's a dimwit," Jack had mumbled and his pronouncement had made me feel better about myself.

Red's mother had a jolly, round face, but it was dissolved in tears as she pulled up to the curb. She sat sobbing, crumpled behind the steering wheel. My mother opened the car door and helped her climb out. And then, her heavy chest still lifting and falling in huge spasms, she told us, "It's terrible! Unbelievable! I can't believe it! Oh my God, my God, Jack was hit by a car, killed instantly. He...."

My brain, refusing to absorb the information it was processing, shut down. Mrs. Brockman's voice evaporated. Her face swam in a dark red haze, an undistinguishable blur before my eyes. My blood turned to ice inside me and I began to tremble, to shake so violently I could scarcely stand. I was sure I was going to be sick.

My mother put her arm around my shoulders and guided me up the steps and back into the apartment. She was crying. Neither of us could speak. I went into the bedroom we shared and closed the door. My mother didn't follow me. She knew I had to be alone, to be quiet, to steel myself in my own way against the tragedy I could neither change nor accept. I don't know how much time passed, but daylight faded outside the bedroom windows and twilight deepened into blackness.

"Why did Jack die?" I asked.

My mother had come in and found me, rigid and cold as death itself and still fully clothed, lying on my bed.

"You heard what happened," she said, slipping off my penny loafers. "June darted out onto the highway and Jack pushed her out of the way of an oncoming car. There was no time to save himself."

"That's not what I'm asking," I said. "I'm not asking how he died. I'm asking why. He was only fourteen."

"You're asking a question I can't answer," said my mother, her voice husky with sorrow. "Only God knows those answers. We'll never know."

She helped me stand and pulled back the spread on my bed. Retrieving my pajamas from under my pillow, she began unbuttoning my shirt. Mechanically I undressed, put on the pajamas, and slipped under the covers.

"Try to get some sleep," she said softly. "I'm making a lasagna for them. They'll need some food when friends and relatives come for the funeral. I'm sure Peg needs all the help she can get."

Mercifully, she left me in the sacred privacy of the darkness and I began slowly to surrender to my grief. Drawing up my knees and turning to the wall, I curled into my pain. Tears I had not been able to shed until that moment began to flow onto my pillow.

"You're right, Jack," I whispered to my neighbor with the beautiful eyes. "I really don't know anything about anything."

Nine
Donna Rafaela and the Piano

My mother told me that on her walk down the aisle to the altar, my grandfather whispered repeatedly through a tight-lipped smile, "There's still time. You can turn back." Unfortunately, she kept on walking. Within the year, she realized the only walking she should be doing was out of the marriage. Consequently, I knew little about my father while I was growing up except that he was District Attorney of Cook County; that he rode around in a long black (always black) Cadillac; that he was blond and balding; that his rather small blue eyes stared a cold, expressionless stare; that he wore conservative dark suits; that he smoked foul-smelling cigars; and that his perfectly manicured hands were never without a thick gold ring set with a large, square, deep red ruby. The ring had been a gift from his mother upon his graduation from law school.

My earliest memories of him revolve around a large, oak-paneled office where the huge portrait of his mother occupied nearly an entire wall. She was young and strikingly beautiful in that painting. Her pale blond hair cascaded around a delicate oval face dominated by calm, serious blue eyes. From her post she surveyed her son where he sat at his desk and every time he glanced up from his papers, he could see her watching him.

"Your grandmother is a highly intelligent, strong woman," my mother told me more than once. "She raised her children with an iron hand inside a velvet glove." Through the years many stories about Donna Rafaela filtered down to me in direct or overheard conversations. She was a combination Dear Abby and psychologist to the community. Women flocked to her door for tiny cups of steaming espresso and sessions of revealed confidences, complaints, and tears over:

An unfaithful husband—"Can your son have him followed?"

A teenager in trouble—"Can your son help him? It wasn't his fault."

Elderly parents languishing of loneliness across the sea—"Can your son do something to expedite their visa?"

Donna Rafaela seldom burdened or compromised her son's law practice with impossible causes, but she always offered words of consolation and wise counsel.

My favorite story about her concerns her encounter with the Chicago mob. In the early days of my father's practice, he was approached on a delicate matter having to do with a member of a high-ranking Mafia family. My father had as many faults as any man, many more than most, but his professional integrity was impeccable. He refused to represent the mobster. That evening he didn't arrive home for dinner. For two days and nights he was missing.

Donna Rafaela made a few phone calls to her lady friends and was ultimately told in a frightened whisper that my father was being detained in an attempt to force him to change his mind. Armed with maternal fury as well as with information gleaned from one of her sessions with a tearful supplicant, she stormed, all five-feet-four-inches of her, into the office of the perpetrator and demanded her son's release. "And I want him home before his dinner gets cold tonight or you may be very much embarrassed when the newspapers print an account of your shameless behavior with Miss X." My father arrived at his mother's home that evening while the pasta was still simmering on the stove.

My relationship with my paternal grandmother was casual, pleasant, impersonal. My mother brought me to visit her the first Sunday of each month and we always found a formal table laid in the dining room. A bottle of champagne waited on ice if a holiday or my birthday were approaching. Donna Rafaela herself ceremoniously poured my portion of the sparkling wine into a tiny shot glass and held it out to me with her blessing.

The only aspect of the visit that disturbed me was having to confront a monumental stuffed owl perched on a tall, mahogany table at the top of the steep staircase that brought us from the street door to the upstairs entrance hall. That bird was eerie, his big eyes staring and engulfing. He looked as though he were about to pounce on us with every approaching step we took. Once I had scampered past the menacing bird, I crossed the threshold into a high-ceilinged foyer. Although the rooms of the house were adequately spacious, their somber decor seemed to exude a palpable gloom. The furniture was massive and dark and the carpeting across the entire front of the house was a deep cranberry floral I found oppressive.

There were always five of us at the table—my grandmother, my father's stepfather (his own father had died of pneumonia just before my father's birth), my unmarried aunt, and my mother and me. The conversation around the table was quiet, civil, and seldom included me. I amused myself by studying the paintings on the walls and the patterns on the plates and silverware.

A real source of amusement—no, fascination—with which I also occupied my dining time was my aunt Mimi's hair. It was fuzzy and the ugliest color orange I had ever seen, somewhere between the color of a rusty bicycle chain and a dying pumpkin. Her complexion was only a shade or two lighter than her hair and every time I looked at her, I wondered if there could be some truth in the fable that some babies were born in a pumpkin patch rather than under a cabbage.

After the meal, the women settled in the heavily draped living room for hours of hushed conversation. I was sent to join my stepgrandfather in the den, where we sat silent and attentive on straight-backed chairs before an enormous brown radio. Sunday afternoons he dedicated to "The Shadow," "Perry Mason," and "The FBI in Peace and War." His round, pleasant, baby-smooth face was solemn with concentration, his head slightly tilted so that he could catch every word of the programs with his better ear. Now and then his finger moved to his lips as a reminder that I should remain silent.

Just before we were ready to leave and walk past the owl and down the staircase to the street door, my grandmother would suddenly focus her attention on me. Reaching into the pocket of her dress or sweater, she would bring out two rolled-up dollar bills. Without a word she pressed them into my hand as though the money were a secret between us. She knew her prestigious son was attending to his familial responsibilities with ten dollars a week, the minimal support the law would allow. She also knew my mother and I were alone since my maternal grandparents had been compelled to return to Italy at the onset of the war.

Although Donna Rafaela was not an outwardly affectionate grandmother (no hugs and kisses, seldom a smile), somehow I knew she was concerned about my mother and me and disappointed in her son's personal life.

"I don't know what his problem is," I heard her say at every visit when my attention escaped the radio in the den and eavesdropped on the more interesting dialogue taking place in the living room. Phrases like "that devil woman" and "those kind turn a man's head away from the decent ones" tugged at my ears.

As soon as we arrived back home, I would slip the two rolled-up dollars into a tall red barrel bank which had originally held brightly wrapped Atlantic City taffy, a gift from vacationing friends of my mother's. The only times I unplugged its cork stopper and removed some bills were to buy an extra dog, horse, or Nancy Drew book. My mother furnished one new book a payday, but often, as I perused the bookshop shelves, I found more than one volume I absolutely could not leave behind. As I approached my tenth year, my reading expanded to include an occasional movie magazine if it featured a star I particularly liked. The last one I remember buying had Cornel Wilde's wistful, sensitive face on the cover. He and Cary Grant were my nine-year-old idea of perfect manhood.

"Cornel Wilde is starring in a movie about Chopin's life," my mother told me one Saturday as we were vacuuming and dusting our apartment. "I think you'll like it. We'll go tomorrow afternoon."

On the Sundays when we were not subjected to the owl, my mother and I sometimes took the bus to the neighborhood movie. So, on that fateful Sunday, we set out for the Bijou Theater and Chopin. What had begun as a slow drizzle on our way to the theater exploded into a harsh, wind-driven March downpour. I was still shivering as I, popcorn and Milk Duds in hand, settled into the theater seat.

The moment the film began, my wet shoes, my dripping hair, my chill, my favorite candy, even where I was—everything vanished. The haunting, poignant, melancholy melodies of Chopin's music transformed the time, the place, and my whole being. I was totally immersed in the incredible beauty of the music and the tragedy of his illness and early death. When Cornel Wilde's straining, perspiring face and suffering eyes looked over the piano keys directly into the camera and, consequently, at me, I bit my lip hard so as not to do anything as degrading as cry in public. I begged my mother to stay through a second showing and we did. Finally, I walked out of the movie theater and into the rain in a daze. Only sheer habit kept my feet moving to the bus stop. The real me was still lingering in Poland and Vienna and Paris, in dark flats and luxuriously chandeliered concert halls.

"Why so quiet?" asked my mother on the rumbling ride home.

"Because I have to have a piano," I said. "I have to learn to play Chopin's music."

She just smiled. I'm sure she thought my passion for Chopin was actually the aftermath of an afternoon spent with Cornel Wilde and that my desire to learn the music would soon fade. When I continued to press her week after week, she eventually told me, "The only way you're going to get a piano is if you ask your grandmother."

The next Sunday was the visit Sunday and everything proceeded according to routine: the staircase, the owl, the dinner, the radio programs. My mother glanced at me from time to time to encourage me, but I couldn't get up the nerve to intrude in the adult conversation, much less bring up the subject of the piano. At the last moment, when the time came for my grandmother to slip me the two dollar bills, I looked into her appraising blue eyes and announced, "I'm saving the money you give me for my piano. I have to learn to play Chopin's music. I just have to."

She looked intently at me. She had never heard such a torrent of words issuing from my mouth all at once. Her calm gaze probed and penetrated mine. "I believe you really do," she said. "You shall have a piano. Your father will buy you one."

My aunt Mimi reported to my mother some days later that my father's response to his mother's request was, "How the hell am I going to find a piano? It's war time."

And my grandmother had replied in her serene, indisputable way, "I don't care how you find one, just find one."

Years later my father related the details of the quest. His secretary had phoned every music store in Chicago in search of a piano that would be immediately available but had not found one. My father, knowing his mother would not accept defeat, walked along the business districts until he found a shop that sold musical instruments. A shiny black spinet stood in the window. He walked into the shop and asked the shopkeeper, "How much is THAT piano in the showcase?"

The shopkeeper quoted the price. My father removed some bills from his gold money clip and handed them to the shopkeeper, who quickly put them into the cash register and wrote out a receipt.

"I want it delivered on Saturday morning to 6265 West Gunnison Street," said my father, tucking the receipt into his pocket.

"Oh," laughed the shopkeeper nervously, "that's impossible, sir. The piano in the showcase is not for sale. It's just a sample. We won't have delivery on a piano like it for at least a year. It's war time, you know."

"When I came in," my father began, "I specifically asked you how much is THAT piano. I didn't ask you how much is a piano like that one. I gave you money for it and you accepted it. Therefore, I have just bought THAT piano. That's the law. I will expect delivery on Saturday morning at the address I gave you. Good day."

Every Friday afternoon a peevish, perpetually angry German piano teacher came to our apartment and sat with a look of smoldering martyrdom on his stubbled face as I crawled through Thompson Book One and Thompson Book Two. "Here We Go Up the Road to a Birthday Party" gave way to "The Moccasin Dance" and "Waltz of the Flowers." Although my musical steps were slow and laborious, I knew I was inching my way to my goal, to Chopin.

And then, abruptly and unexpectedly, the journey was dramatically interrupted one afternoon in May when Fate dropped a black velvet hood over my head. I could no longer see the music, the teacher, the piano. For days I lay semiconscious, trembling between life and death, and when I woke, the hood was still on and the world was forever dark. That darkness would eventually be lit by many candles, lanterns, flares, and spotlights of friendships, loves, family, my studies, and music, Chopin's music. Slowly and with great patience on the part of my teachers who dictated the piano scores to me note by note, the bubbling laughter of his waltzes, the eloquent sadness of his preludes and nocturnes, the grandeur of each polonaise, and the disciplined playfulness or nobility of his études would eventually ripple under my fingers on the spinet Donna Rafaela had ordered the district attorney of Cook County to buy his daughter.

My grandmother never heard me play. There was no piano in her home and she never came to our apartment. I had only been studying a year when my illness struck and I was forced to flee Chicago before its brutal winter could threaten my deeply compromised health. By the first week of September my mother and I were stepping off the train in Tucson, Arizona.

For many months I was not well enough to attend the school for blind children in town. The days were long. I could no longer read or paint. I had no new friends and I soon tired of the radio.

"I need my piano," I announced one day after we had settled into our new little house.

"Write to your grandmother," suggested my mother.

I had always enjoyed toying with a variety of scripts, penpoints, and ink colors. My penmanship experiments had often irritated my classroom teachers. "Your handwriting is too flowery; the squiggles make me dizzy." "Why has your handwriting suddenly become so tiny? I can scarcely see it." "Where in the world did you ever find such a hideous shade of green ink? It's almost worse than the purple you were using last week." It felt strange now in my new darkness to be forming letters I couldn't see or be sure were even legible.

"Dear Nanna, please, I need my piano," I wrote and signed my name. That was all, but I knew Donna Rafaela would understand and force my father to transport my instrument.

Just before Christmas a truck stopped in front of our house and two men carried a packing case inside. They pried the wooden crate apart and carefully slid my piano out.

At the door one of the men turned to ask in a rich basso, "Can you play that thing, honey?"

"Sure," I said, and although I had no idea at that time how it would come about, I knew I had just begun the long and arduous but loving journey to Chopin once more.

The El-Train

The first Sunday of every month,
except for summers at the lake,
my mother and I rode the elevated train
to visit my paternal grandmother.

I always brought a book along,
not only to amuse myself
but to focus my attention on
something other than the swaying, creaking train

that lumbered higher and higher
over Chicago's shabbiness—junk car lots,
factories, run-down neighborhoods
with not a flower, not a blade of grass,

not a backyard swing in sight,
but only grimy tenements,
tall as the highest el-train track,
where, even in the depths of winter,

wash hung from pulleys outside
dingy, curtainless windows. The clothes
seemed always to be gray, always
big and little shapeless garments mixed together.

What I remember most is underwear,
men's sleeveless, hollow undershirts,
hanging stiff with icy covering
or limp and lifeless, ugly, anonymous.

The dark green fabric of the train seats
was ugly, too, and harsh against
seven, eight, nine-year-old bare legs.
I was glad my shiny patent leather shoes

couldn't reach the crinkled paper cups
and butts of cigarettes on the floor
in front of the seats. I'd make a face.
My mother'd read my look. "Just don't touch anything."

Buried in my books, I could avoid
looking out into that unprotected, plunging sky
as we lunged and swayed and tipped toward
the tenements and their anonymous laundry.

And then, one day, I shot a glance
out into that great expanse of space and saw
something else—a little girl's lean and solemn face
pressed against a dirty window pane.

The moment came and went in a single beat
of clicking train wheels, but there had been time
to see her dark, enormous eyes
staring at the train, staring at me.

Beside her stood a man who wore
a no longer anonymous, sleeveless undershirt.
Why could I not forget them as I sat
at my grandmother's formal table,

as I looked at my grandfather's shirt,
soft and snowy white, a shield of privilege,
And why, scores of train rides and decades of years later,
do I remember still?

Ten

Amidst the Blaze of Noon

Total eclipse, no sun, no moon,
all dark amidst the blaze of noon.

　　　　　　　　　　　　　—*Samson*, Oratorio, Handel

I opened my eyes and looked over to my mother's bed. It was empty and neatly made. My glance shifted to the windows beyond. The shades were still pulled down. As I focused my gaze on them, their creamy sheen changed, became bright with splotches of color. Gradations of pinks and greens danced and merged like melting marbles on the once smooth, patternless surface. I rubbed my eyes and sat up. The large mirror above the dresser at the far end of the bedroom returned a blur where my face should have been. I lay back on my pillow and closed my eyes. It was Saturday and I didn't have to get up early to walk Teena before school. Maybe the colors on the shades, lovely but puzzling, would have disappeared by the time I opened my eyes again. And why, I wondered, hadn't I seen my face in the mirror? Maybe I was just sleepy.

The phone jangled loudly in the alcove off the dining room. I heard my mother's voice, but I couldn't make out her words. In a few moments she was in the bedroom.

"Are you awake?"

"Yes."

"You're going to be so surprised and pleased," she said, and I could hear the pleasure in her voice. My eyes were still closed. "Dan Jr. is coming to visit and show us the new car your father bought him for his birthday."

I hadn't seen my half-brother since the summer my parents had tried to reconcile years before. The only communication I had received from him was a brief note and an eight-by-ten photograph of him in full military academy uniform. He looked different, older, his blond curls tamed into a sleek wave that lifted from his forehead. Of course, I had taken his picture to

70

school and the eighth grade girls who monitored our lunchroom wanted to know, "Can we write to him?" Their eyes were wide as they stared at the photograph. "He's gorgeous! When is he coming home?"

"He'll be home for Christmas," I had lied so they would think we lived together. I still missed him.

I jumped out of bed. My vision was clear, but my mother looked at me with concern. Since I had swiftly and mysteriously lost the vision in my left eye three years before, she had become an obsessed caretaker not only of my health, but most particularly of my "good eye."

"Your eyes are a little bit red," she said. "Do they hurt you?"

"They're fine," I reassured her. There was no time to try to describe the dancing colors I had seen on the shades or the fog where the reflection of my face should have been. I had to get ready to see my brother. "Do you think Dan would take me to the fair?"

On the way home from school the afternoon before, we had seen men setting up game booths and rides on a strip of prairie that began at the end of our block. A sign crammed into the ground announced St. Andrew's Memorial Day Fair and Bazaar.

"I hope it won't be here after the weekend," my mother had said. "I don't like the looks of it or of the men setting it up. You're not going alone."

She didn't seem to have a problem with my going with my brother, though, because she said, "I'm sure he'll take you if you ask him. Come and eat some breakfast now. It's a perfect spring day, warm and sunny. You can wear your new blue outfit."

I was excited and timid, joyful and worried. What would he be like? So much time had passed since we had been together. There was no boyishness in the face that looked back at me from the photograph he had sent, only a thin, serious, unfamiliar image with impenetrable, expressionless eyes. I didn't even like the picture. It was a ghostly representation of someone I had once known.

Within the hour a tall, thin teenager with angry bullet-points of acne across his cheeks and forehead came shyly into our living room.

My mother hugged him and said warmly, "Junior, so good to see you! You look wonderful!"

I didn't think he looked wonderful at all. In fact, I was disappointed, but my heart still raced at the sight of him.

"Hi, honey," he said, ruffling my hair with the long, slim fingers I remembered. His voice was different, deep and grown-up. "Ready to go for a spin in my new car?"

I nodded.

"Look out the window," he told us. "I parked in front of the house, right by the bus stop. We'd better get out of the way before I get a ticket."

We looked out. A glistening red Cadillac convertible stood at the curb. "Wow," I breathed. "Is that really yours?"

"Sure is," he said, jingling his keys. "Come on, let's go for a drive." He turned to my mother. "You come, too," he said affectionately.

She smiled at the invitation, but refused it. "Maybe before you go home you can take me around the block," she said. "You two need a little time together to get reacquainted."

As he started down the flight of stairs that led from our apartment to the entrance hall, my brother said, "I saw a carnival at the end of your street. We'll come back and spend the afternoon there, if that's okay with you."

"That's fine," my mother said. "Just be careful." And she added, "Why don't you come back here for lunch?"

"Thanks anyway," said my brother. "We'll fill up on cotton candy and hot dogs. What's a carnival without a stomachache?"

The car smelled of new leather and looked sensational, sleek and gleaming and beautiful. Dan turned on the motor and we zoomed away from the curb. Sidewalks quickly disappeared and vast stretches of prairie ran along both sides of the road. We passed the big chrome and white dairy, the lush golf course, the nursery school, and more prairie.

The day sparkled. Sunshine hopscotched across the dips in the road, tangled and glistened in the tall grass beyond, bounced off the cherry red paint of my brother's car. As we rode along I couldn't help looking up at the sky for that strange conglomeration of pinks and greens and fog. It was completely gone. I stared as far into the distance as I could, but there was no trace of it.

"You haven't said a word since we got into the car," said my brother. "Is everything okay?"

"Yes," I said, forcing my gaze back from the wide expanse before me where I had been searching uneasily for the puzzling images of the early morning. "Everything's fine. This car is like something you'd see Clark Gable driving in the movies."

He smiled with appreciation and pride. Then he said, "I never saw your apartment before. Your mom made it really nice with all the paintings and statues and things like that, but gee, it's so small, really just an attic."

"It's big enough," I said. "We like it."

He darted a quick look at me. "Oh, it's great," he said, "really pretty! A lot of the stuff looks antique. Where'd you get it?"

"My grandparents," I told him. "When they went back to Italy, some friends kept everything in their house for us." And, not wanting him to think we had only old things, I added, "Mom bought some new furniture, too."

"It's all really nice," he assured me enthusiastically, "really nice." Then he smiled and said, "I've got an idea! How'd you like to steer this baby?"

I stared at him. "What?" I gasped. "You mean steer your new car? How? I can't drive! I just turned ten last month."

"I know how old you are." He laughed as he pulled over to the side of the road. "We always shared everything when we were little," he said and stroked my cheek. "We'll share the car, too. Sit on my lap and take the wheel. I'll work the pedals "

I didn't move.

"Old moneybags sprung for an automatic transmission so I don't even have to shift. It'll be easy," he coaxed. "Don't be afraid."

I was not as much afraid of steering the car as I was shy of sitting on his lap, but I shifted my skinny frame onto his bony legs and put my hands on the smooth leather steering wheel. Dan pumped the pedal and the car motor changed from a purr to a roar. We skimmed down the road, miles and miles of prairie on either side and a clear passage ahead to the horizon. Perched high on his knees, the breeze caught my long hair and whipped it back into his face. He laughed. "It's a good thing you're steering," he said. "All I can see is blond hair."

Steering was simple. All I had to do was keep the wheel straight and steady. There were no other cars in sight, not even a jackrabbit crossed our path.

Here and there a narrow dirt road snaking in from a distant group of new homes or a farmhouse intersected our road. Suddenly, out of nowhere, from one of these side roads we heard the grinding motor and saw the huge brown truck, almost entirely rusted to a dirty orange, swing onto the road just in front of us. Its great bulk, swaying and snorting, was swooping down on us with a blast of horn, gears and fumes.

"HOLY COW!" Dan gasped in my ear and his hands grabbed the wheel and turned frantically. We flew onto the shoulder of the road just as the enormous truck rattled past. I looked up to see the driver, his mouth working, his face contorted, shaking an angry fist at us. I slid off my brother's lap and back onto the passenger seat. For a moment we couldn't speak. We sat motionless, suspended in a stunned silence. When Dan finally turned his head and looked at me, his pale blue eyes were dark with fear. "Don't tell your mother," he said breathlessly. "She might tell the old man. He'd take the car away from me for sure."

"I won't," I said, knowing that if my mother ever found out what had just transpired she would never allow me to ride in this magnificent movie star car with him again.

"Promise?"

"I promise," I said, and I kept my word for over half a century.

We eased back onto the road. Dan pushed a blond curl that was undermining his maturity off his forehead. His hand was trembling.

"Did you ever tell anybody about the gun?"

"No, never."

"You're a good kid," he sighed and patted my knee.

I had forgotten about the gun episode until he mentioned it. Now I remembered that summer at my father's country estate, the summer our parents had tried to reconcile.

73

One afternoon while my mother was occupied in the kitchen, my brother had slipped into our parents' bedroom and motioned me to follow. He had opened the deep bottom drawer of a bureau and unfolded some sweaters until he exposed an ugly, black, blunt-nosed revolver.

I had drawn instinctively away at the sight of it and he quickly made the drawer neat again, carefully folding the sweaters back over the gruesome weapon.

"Dad does his own detective work sometimes," he had confided in a hushed whisper. "Pretty great, huh?"

When I didn't answer, he looped his forefinger around my wrist and stared earnestly into my face. "Don't tell I showed you. Promise."

I promised and I had put it out of my mind until this moment.

The near-collision with the truck and, perhaps, old memories reawakening the disappointment of that summer, had shaken and subdued both of us. We drove back to the fair in silence, but as we strolled around the hastily assembled festivities we were caught up in the clamor of the barkers and the grinding music of the merry-go-round.

"I'm too tall and too old to ride that thing," Dan said as we watched the horses pumping up and down, going round and round. "But you can ride if you want to."

Horses were my passion. Books about horses, statues, and pictures of horses lined one of the shelves of my bookcase. I would have ridden even the wooden carousal creatures, but I was shy before this unfamiliar, mature brother.

"That's just for babies," I said. "I started riding lessons this year. I had to ride in the inside arena during the winter, but twice now I've gone out on trails with a group of older kids."

"No kidding!" he said, and the surprise and approval on his face convinced me I had made the right decision not to mount the merry-go-round.

"Want some cotton candy?" he offered and as we stood together beside the vendor's stand, our chins bearded with the sticky cloud of sugar, it occurred to me that the pink of the candy matched one of the gradations of color that had appeared on the window shade. Dan produced a clean white handkerchief for our faces and we set off in high spirits for the next adventure.

"Let's ride the Ferris wheel," he suggested, drawing a clump of bills from his pocket and buying our tickets. We waited in line for the tall circle to come around and stop.

As we settled into the seat I began to feel a strange dizziness and a fluttering in my stomach. We went around once, twice, three times and I began to relax, but after a few more revolutions, the ride stopped and all the riders, on various levels of elevation, were left dangling in the air. Our seat was topmost. From our swinging perch we could see to the horizon, or almost to the horizon. Along the edge of the prairie where it met the sky, a fog was rolling in with splotches of pink and green bobbing in the empty air before me. I was too frightened to take my hands off the bar in front of us so I could rub my eyes. I blinked and shook my head, but the mist crept closer and closer. In a matter of seconds the thick gray cloud streaked with the now-familiar shades of pink and green blotted out everything beyond the immediate fairground. A wave of weakness swept over me.

"Too much candy and too much height for you, eh?" Dan laughed. "We'll be down in a minute. You scared?"

"A little," I admitted.

"You're pale as a ghost," he said in alarm. "You're not going to be sick, are you?"

"No," I said, "but look at the fog coming across the prairie! And what are all those pink and green things floating around?"

"I don't see any fog," said my brother. "Pink and green what? I don't see any pink and green anything!"

The Ferris wheel began turning again and we were soon on the mounting platform. He held my hand as we descended the little wooden steps.

"You look kind of shaky," he said, concerned. "Did the ride bother you that much?"

I couldn't respond. I was too busy looking past the concession stands; the noisy, laughing children; the merry-go-round horses standing still, waiting for the "babies" to mount. Beyond all the activity, I watched the fog closing in, darker, more menacing. A chill sliced through the warm sunshine and I shivered.

"I don't feel right," I said. "I'm freezing. I think we'd better go home." I was close to tears, angry at myself. How could I be ruining a precious afternoon with my brother like this?

"I think that's a good idea," he said and added thoughtfully, "You can't be sick from anything we ate. We haven't even had one hot dog yet."

As we slipped into the car he said cheerfully, "Don't worry, honey, we can come back later if you feel better. I've got all day."

The moment we stepped inside the door my mother put her hands on my shoulders and studied my face. "What's wrong?" she asked, but before I could answer she put a hand on my forehead. "You're hot," she said. "Your cheeks are very flushed and your eyes are so bloodshot, worse than this morning!"

"I just feel really tired," I said, "and cold. My eyes are weird, too. There's a lot of fog and colors floating around me."

"It's Memorial Day weekend!" my mother cried. "We won't find a doctor anywhere. I'll call your father. He'll have some connections."

She ran to the phone.

My brother bolted for the door. "I just remembered! I've got a date," he said. He sounded terrified. "I have to leave!"

"Bye," I said miserably. "Sorry...." But he was already gone. My mother hadn't even said goodbye to him. She was flipping through the red leather telephone book she kept next to the telephone. On the wall above the phone table was one of my favorite paintings, two bluebirds alighting on a bare brown branch painted on a tall, narrow panel of glass. I looked for the delicate little birds. They had been there when I left with Dan just a couple of hours before, but now they were gone, blotted out by this fog that was erasing everything.

I walked into the bedroom and picked up a new book I had been reading when I fell asleep the night before. Somehow I knew my sight was running out and I wanted to read as much of the book as I could, but the words merged into one another. They looked as though they were drowning under water. I set the book down. It was too late for reading.

I walked to the back of the apartment to my art studio. The outer wall of the room was all windows. Normally it was a bright room with a backyard vista of cherry trees and the wild prairie beyond, but there was nothing outside the windows now except the fog that was quickly growing darker and darker.

I took out my art portfolio and my paints. For days I had been working on an intricate design, a textile of many colors and shapes, tiny triangles of purple and rose, minute squares of forest and lime green, dime-size circles of gold and copper, miniature diamonds of sky and robin's egg blue, abstract lines and squiggles of many contrasting tones that intersected, connected, surrounded the shapes. The design was too small, too fine. I couldn't see details enough to finish it. It was too late for painting, too.

For the first time since the onset of the colors on the window shades and the fog in the mirror, I felt afraid. Familiar shapes, my own paintings on the wall, my horse statues, even my little dog curled up on a patch of sun on the floor, were all being swallowed up by the relentlessly approaching fog.

I had to make one last attempt to capture something visual. I took out a new sheet of art paper and spread it across my work table. Dipping one brush after another into my jars of brilliant acrylics, I stubbornly began shaping a new textile design, large configurations of red, yellow, orange, royal blue. Trying to keep each color distinct, I outlined each shape in black to separate it from the rest, but the colors defied the thick black lines and melded into a hodgepodge of patternless paint. It really didn't matter, I thought, the painting had been bold and coarse and too ugly to finish. I began to cry hot tears of frustration and helplessness as I snapped the lids onto my precious paint jars and cleaned my brushes. If this was the only kind of painting I would be able to do, it was not worth pursuing. I would just have to wait until my sight returned to normal.

A terrible fatigue overwhelmed me. I leaned my arms on the table and rested my chin on my hands. The ugly painting was inches from my face and I was almost glad that it, too, was disappearing before my eyes.

I wanted to sleep, but my mother's voice pierced my stupor. She sounded frantic. "I know you're Mrs. Covelli! So am I! I was Mrs. Covelli before you were! Let me speak to Dan. It's an emergency. His daughter...."

I stood up, placed the jars of acrylics, so new, so beautifully rich in color, carefully back on the shelf and sat down on my chair again. Sleep, I wanted only to sleep, but I could still hear my mother's agitated voice.

"She hung up on me again, the bitch!"

Brushing away the last of my tears, I smiled to myself. I had never heard a swear word issue from my mother's mouth before. I listened. She was talking to herself, praying aloud, and those words were more familiar to me. "*Madonnina, aiutami!*" (Blessed Mother, help me!)

She dialed again. "Valerie," she cried, "something's wrong with Bianca. I've tried to call Dan but he won't come to the phone. I have to get a cab and take her to a doctor immediately, but I don't know where to find one today. You do? You will?... Oh, thank God for you. We'll be waiting."

Everything would be all right now. Valerie was coming. I walked slowly through the mist-filled kitchen, down the shadowy hall and into the bedroom, and fell onto my bed.

When they woke me, Valerie was with my mother. The two women sat me up on the side of the bed and stood me on my feet. I could scarcely stand alone.

"She's burning up!" my mother exclaimed. "My God, what's happening to her?"

I tried, but I couldn't open my eyes. The effort was too immense. My mother and Valerie helped me through the apartment, down the stairs and into the rear seat of Valerie's car, where I lay down and, with the car motor roaring in my ears, fell immediately back to sleep. When the car screeched to a stop, I opened my eyes, but the gesture was scarcely worth the effort. There was nothing left to see in my world. With my mother and Valerie on either side of me, holding my elbows as much to guide as to support me, we walked onto a porch and rang the bell.

A woman opened the door. I could make out a blur of white that must have been her dress. "Come right in," she said kindly. "Doctor's expecting you."

At the top of a staircase the indistinct figure of a man deep in shadow was waiting and beside him I thought I saw the outline of a large dog, but I couldn't be sure. It was already too dark. The fog was dense and now there were no more lovely pinks and greens mingled in, just dark gray fog.

I sat in a big leather chair while the doctor held an instrument to my eyes and told me to follow the light. The space before my face swam in a yellow haze. I didn't know where I should be looking, where the light started or ended. I couldn't distinguish any movement. All I could see was a pale yellow mist.

"She must be hospitalized immediately," he said. "Take her to Michael Reece. She has a fierce, wildfire infection. I'll call ahead. They'll be expecting you."

"Will she lose her sight permanently?" I heard Valerie's voice asking what my mother could not ask.

"She'll be lucky to come through this alive," the doctor's voice responded, "very lucky. I'm sorry to be so blunt, but her sight is the least of our problems. Just pray that the infection doesn't reach her brain before we can stabilize her."

We walked back down the stairs. If the dog was there, I couldn't see it. I slipped back into the car and fell asleep.

When I woke up again, I was lying on a hard, high table and several men, doctors, were around me. My head was throbbing.

"We're losing ground," one of them said. "Do you want to call her father?"

"He won't come to the phone for me," my mother answered. She was crying.

"Give me the phone," the man growled and then I heard him saying, "Judge Covelli, this is Dr. King at Michael Reece Children's Hospital. If you want to see your daughter alive, come immediately."

I fell back to sleep.

Emerging now and then into consciousness, I always found myself in a totally dark place. Children's voices, as if they were coming from a long distance away, whimpering, speaking to one another, calling for their mothers or the nurse, penetrated my awareness.

My whole being seemed to be afloat. Whether my eyes were open or closed made no difference. For me there was no point of orientation, only darkness, babbled confusion and pain, a fierce, white-hot knife blade of pain inside my skull. Letting go of wakefulness and slipping back into unconsciousness was the only escape from its torment.

Gradually, I began to realize that I must be in a hospital, a children's ward, but I hadn't the strength to be concerned about it. Amidst the ward's clamor, I felt very much alone in this totally dark place and shudders of fear rippled through me before I sank away again.

And then something changed. I dreamed or I saw in my mind—I've never known which—a dark-faced boy of about my age. His black hands held a pair of pearl rosary beads. The crucifix was bright mother-of-pearl and clearly visible where it hung just below his fingers. He was gently smiling and all around him a soft light glowed and glittered. He seemed to be clothed in the light itself and the prayer beads wound around his hands shimmered with the same incandescence. He didn't speak, just kept smiling and looking at me with loving, serene, and compassionate eyes. I had never seen him before nor have I ever seen him since, but engulfed in his unearthly presence, his soft, pure light, my fear ebbed away and, despite my pain, I was at peace.

When I finally surfaced from my semiconsciousness, my mother was beside me and we were alone in a different room. The children's voices were gone. There was a needle in the vein of my arm. The air reeked of disinfectant.

"Mom?"

"I'm here."

"Is this a hospital?"

"Yes."

"How long have I been here?"

"Nine days."

I stretched my body. My legs and the arm I could move felt stiff, almost unfamiliar. Slowly I opened my eyes. It was still dark.

I didn't ask about my sight. I didn't have to. I knew it was gone, at least temporarily.

A nurse bounced in. "Oh, she's awake! Really awake!" she exclaimed happily. "Is she talking?"

"Yes," said my mother. "She seems all right, mentally I mean. I waved my hand in front of her face, but she didn't seem to focus on it. Her sight must still be gone."

"I'll let Dr. King know right away, but first I'll give her her shot."

"Already that time again?" my mother sighed.

"Every three hours, you know," the nurse replied, approaching my bed. "Time flies when you're having fun!"

I couldn't remember having had any injections before this one.

"Hi, sweetie," she said loudly as if I couldn't hear her if she spoke in a normal tone. "I'm Nurse Nutly. I have another shot for you. My generosity is only exceeded by my good looks, right, sweetie?" She giggled a girlish giggle as she rolled me over on my side.

I didn't answer. Didn't she know I couldn't see what she looked like?

"Better start eating," she advised. "You need more flesh on your fanny for all this penicillin. You already look like a deflated pincushion back here."

I was glad when I heard the door click shut behind her, but in a moment she burst in again. "There was a young fellow out in the hall," she said. "He said he couldn't come in, but he told me to give you this."

She placed a long, hard-bodied doll beside me on the bed. As I ran my fingers over the stiff, molded legs; the cotton dress; the coarse, tightly curled hair, I heard the nurse's stage-whisper to my mother. "He was crying," she said incredulously, "ran to the stairs, didn't even wait for the elevator."

"I think I know who it was," said my mother.

"This window over here looks onto the parking lot," continued the nurse as she crossed the room. "There he is, see, he's looking up here. He's still crying."

"I thought it must be him," my mother responded quietly. "He's her half-brother."

"Goodness," exclaimed the nurse, "he's getting into that fabulous convertible. I sure wouldn't let a kid drive it if it was mine!"

"It's his own," I snapped. "And he told me it's partly mine, too."

The nurse crossed the room to my bed and patted my leg. "Sure, sweetie," she cooed, "sure it is."

"What are you going to name your doll?" asked my mother, before I could be rude to the retreating nurse again. I heard the door close.

"I'm going to name her Danielle after Dan," I said, and then I remembered the young nurse's words.

"The nurse said he was crying," I said. "Why was he crying? Why didn't he come in?"

My mother put her hand on my forehead. She was waiting for the cycle of raging fever and excruciating headaches to begin again. Several times a day the pattern repeated itself, my temperature sliding up and peaking at 105° or 106° accompanied by the familiar white-hot knife blade of pain that even the sound of shuffling paper drove to unbearable profundity. After hours of cool compresses my mother held to my head and lollipops dipped in water she held to my lips, the fever and pain would subside for a time, only to begin again later.

"Does your head hurt?" my mother asked, stalling for time.

"Not very much yet," I said, not wanting to draw her attention away from the thought that was plaguing me. I repeated my questions, "Why was Dan crying? Why didn't he come in?"

My mother answered softly, cautiously, "I'm sure he's sad to know you've been so sick. He probably finds it too hard to see you like this."

I pulled my brother's gift closer and felt the doll's coarse hair scratch against my cheek. I thought of the dolls my mother gave me every Christmas—beautiful rosy-cheeked babies with pale silky hair and "magic skin" or authentically costumed additions to my storybook doll collection. Just last year she had given me an elegantly coiffed Lenci doll from Italy who wore a strand of tiny cultured pearls on her velvet dress. I had been indifferent to them all. The babies were neglected in their carriage and the other dolls, still in their boxes, lay on a shelf in my closet.

My fingers told me this new doll was not as beautiful as those I already had, but I loved her. Someday when I was better, I thought as stabs of pain began chipping at my head, Dan Jr. would be able to visit me and I would ask him to take Danielle with us for a ride in "our" convertible.

Canvases

Within this stiff and broken brush,
these dull and dried-out paints,
there might have been the praying hands
of angels, even saints.

There might have been a gull in flight,
a storm, a barn aflame;
there might have been a loving face
with or without a name.

There might have been some violets,
a small red fox, new snow;
there would have been a truer me—
That I know I know.

Eleven
Re-entry

*M*y hospital room door was open. A crash that sounded like a cascading tray of dishes clanged through the early morning stillness. Young patients, still sleepy, still adjusting to another day of illness and pain, were dozing.

Until the crash, the whole floor had been hushed except for the familiar squeak of Nurse Nutly's thick-soled shoes, but now I heard a voice I recognized issuing from the ward down the hall: "Hey, Nurse Nutty, what was that? The diamond fall out of your engagement ring or did you drop your false teeth again?"

The young nurse admonished, "Okay, Eddy, settle down. Breakfast carts are coming and it's Nurse Nutly, if you please, not nutty!"

I heard Eddy's voice again and I smiled because I had to agree with him. "Breakfast carts? You mean garbage trucks!"

Although I had never met him, never spoken to him, I felt as though I knew Eddy. Several times a day I heard Nurse Nutly scolding, even threatening.

"Eddy, get back over here. Stop hanging around the elevator and bothering people! Eddy, don't be so noisy. The other children need their rest even if you don't! Eddy, so help me, if you put one more ice cube into one more bed I'll break your arm. God, I hope your blood work comes back good enough for you to go home."

A soft-spoken aide murmured "Good morning," arranged the bed table across my bed and deposited my breakfast tray in front of me. I had begun to feed myself in this new, dark world, but my mother took the spoon from my lagging fingers in an attempt to coax a few extra spoonfuls of food into me. My stomach rebelled at every mouthful of slimy cereal, baby applesauce and the milk that was so nauseating I could scarcely swallow it. Eventually, the aide came back to remove the tray and rescue me.

My mother closed the door of my room. I knew why. It was almost time for the doctors and nurses to change the dressings on the burn victim across the hall. The little girl, Janie, four years old, was scarcely alive. I heard Nurse

82

Nutly tell my mother, "Her brother wrapped her in newspapers and lit a match to her."

Every morning the little girl's tortured screams drove my head under my pillow, but I could still hear her. She didn't die, she just kept screaming.

Each morning I was shifted into a wheelchair and my mother took me for rides up and down the corridor. I hoped not to meet Eddy and become an object of his pranks. I hoped not to hear Janie scream.

"Time to start using those legs again, young lady," boomed Dr. King one morning. "We have to get you strong enough to walk out of this place soon."

My legs trembling with the effort, I steadied myself behind my wheel-chair and took the same route up and down the corridor several times a day. Finally I could manage the trip without having to push the chair in front of me for support.

Now and then mothers slipped out of the ward or private rooms for a chat. Their stories were distressing to hear, but they gave me time to rest as I leaned against the wall and listened. "Yes, your daughter is blind, but she's alive and you'll be taking her home soon. I won't be bringing David home until I have to bury him."

"My Ginger will be permanently brain-damaged. She'll never walk again, never sit up on her own. Your girl can go out with you, go to school, even to college! Look at what Helen Keller's doing and she's blind and deaf both!"

College, yes, not art school as I had always planned, but college, and I could go with one of those beautiful big German Shepherd Seeing Eye dogs. Why not?

Back in my room and resting on my bed, I began to daydream—*my dog and I are striding swiftly across a big university campus. Then I'm in a long black gown and mortarboard and my dog and I are walking sedately down the middle aisle of the university auditorium to a stage where I accept my degree.* Degree in what, if not art? Maybe music. Maybe writing. I played the piano and I wrote poems. One of my verses, a Mother's Day card, was framed and sitting on the piano in our living room. Does that make me a real poet, I wonder....?

"I really want a Seeing Eye dog someday," I told my mother one after-noon as I tried to consume whatever the contents of the tray might be.

As soon as I had pronounced the words, I was expecting her usual Italian retort to my use of the verb "want":

"The plant 'want' doesn't grow even in the king's garden." But instead she said, "You won't be strong enough for a dog like that if you don't eat."

Another forkful of something undistinguishable went down.

And then the day came when I was allowed to go downstairs to the cof-fee shop and order whatever I would like to eat. I graduated from pajamas to the clothes I wore into the hospital weeks before. My mother borrowed safety pins from Nurse Nutly to pin the waistband of my slacks on either side so they wouldn't slip off when I stood up. I put my hand into a pocket and found a ticket stub. The Ferris wheel ride! The carnival! My brother! He never came back to visit me since the day he brought the doll and ran away, but then, my father hadn't come at all.

On the way down in the elevator I thought about what I would order and I decided that a hot fudge sundae might taste good. Too soon I find that it would have been wise to sacrifice desire for convenience.

I slid into the booth. The vinyl bench was smooth and cool under my hand. The clink of dishes and glasses and the buzz of conversations swirled around me. My head felt like a bobbing balloon and I leaned against the tall back of the booth to steady myself.

A blast of perfume and a raspy but friendly voice at my left greeted us, "Hi, girls, what can I ge'chas?"

"Just a black coffee for me, please," responded my mother.

"How's about for her?" the waitress continued.

Why didn't she ask me directly? I mused, but my mother placed my order.

"A hot fudge sundae with all the trimmings."

The realization descended upon me that since my illness struck, I had eaten all my meals in my hospital room, where my mother had cut and arranged the food on the plate. It had been easy enough to stab whatever it might be with a fork or scoop it with a spoon. I was suddenly very much aware that this adventure back into a public, sighted eating place, was a turning point. I sat up as straight as I could. The table was so high that it almost reached my shoulders.

In a few moments the waitress returned. "There you go, doll," she said as she set my sundae in front of me.

I slid the index finger of my left hand up the side of the glass to gauge its height and picked up the long spoon with my right. The glass was tall and the ice cream, whipped cream, nuts, and chocolate syrup soared above its rim—a mountain of mess to conquer. I poked my spoon into the side of the mound. It got stuck. I was afraid to yank it out for fear too big a glob might come with it. My mother saw my hesitation.

"Start at the top; just scoop very lightly," she advised.

As gently as possible, I removed the spoon and started over. The glass was so tall I could scarcely reach up to the toppings, but I tried. The spoon didn't feel any different as I lifted it off the mountain so I assumed there was nothing on it, but then again, whipped cream is soft and light so it probably wouldn't make the spoon feel any heavier.

I knew my mother was watching me and maybe other people were too. I didn't want to make the foolish mistake of putting an empty spoon into my mouth, but I was curious and actually hungry enough to try it. As I moved the long spoon toward my lips, chocolate sauce dripped down my fingers. I buried the spoon back into the mound of ice cream and wiped them on a paper napkin. The syrup was too sticky to come totally off on paper.

I was beginning to get impatient for that first taste of sundae and decided to ignore my gooey fingers and try again. This time I managed to remove a large spoonful and get it safely into my mouth. It was every bit as good as I thought it would be but so, so shockingly sweet. My mother started to hand me a glass of water just as I moved my left hand forward to search for it myself. My hand collided with the glass and water spilled onto the table, onto my hand. I heard my mother flipping napkins out of the dispenser against the wall. She mopped up the water without a word, but I was getting tired of this game. I decided to give it one last try. And in total exasperation, I plunged my spoon into the enemy. Ice cream, whipped cream, and syrup toppled over the edge of the glass onto the table.

"Shall I feed it to you?" my mother offered in a whisper.

"I'm not hungry," I snapped between clenched teeth.

"It wasn't a good choice," my mother said, "not for your first outing, much too messy. I should have realized....Would you like something else?"

My eyes were stinging and I didn't want to add the shame of tears to this already humiliating situation so, struggling for composure, I responded stubbornly, "No! I really don't want anything. Let's go back upstairs."

As we stepped out of the elevator, I recognized a taunting voice. "Hi, brat! What did Mommy buy you? Did you bring me any?"

I had already learned that my darkness could protect me if I used it as a shield against the world outside itself. If I chose not to respond to a person or a situation, not to answer a question, I could pretend I hadn't tuned in, hadn't heard, and no eye contact could prove differently. Soon my mother would begin to strip the shield away with her firm instructions, "Hold your head up! Look toward people when they speak to you or you speak to them! Stand up straight." But that came later.

For the moment, I consciously chose to remain behind my shield and ignore Eddy so my mother answered for me, "Sorry, Eddy, I didn't think of it. Next time we'll bring you some candy, how's that?"

"When are you going back?" he asked eagerly.

"I'm not sure," my mother told him, "but it'll be soon."

We went back the very next afternoon.

"It's like riding a horse," my mother said. "If you fall off, you have to get right back on."

I knew she was right, but all I could think of was the mess I left behind the day before.

Again we slid into a booth in the coffee shop. I was hoping the waitress who had our table yesterday was not working today, but the same husky voice greeted us, "Hi, girls, what can I ge'chas today?"

She still seemed friendly. Maybe she had forgotten she had to clean up after me.

As she spoke, I began to play my new game of matching voices to physical characteristics that I visualized in my mind. This waitress sounded like she must have frizzy red hair; lots of freckles; a large heavily lipsticked mouth, and blue-lidded violet eyes. It was amusing to me to create physical features I could no longer see and match them to voices. I seldom asked if I was correct. It really didn't matter how accurate my imagination was. The exercise was just a new pastime.

"What would you like?" my mother asked.

"I don't feel like falling off another horse," I said. "I'll try a pony this time, like a strawberry cone."

That choice worked well. Busy tongue and turning fingers kept the ice cream in place. It was a far shorter and far less complicated trip from cone to tongue than from tall glass and long, thin spoon to lips.

I was encouraged. Perhaps next time I would order my favorite, a chicken sandwich and a chocolate soda, if we could afford it. My mother had been with me day and night for more than a month so there was no paycheck from her job as assistant administrator at my grammar school. I knew my father was paying my hospital bill, but that was all. An episode, vague as a dream from the early days of my hospitalization, skirted around my memory. My mother had fainted, slumped across the bars of my bed, and then I heard Dr. King's voice, concerned, angry, penetrating my fog. He was ordering, "Make sure this woman gets a tray along with the child's. If bookkeeping has trouble collecting for it, tell them to inform me personally."

The memory was so real that the episode must have happened, I thought as I popped the point of the cone into my mouth. Success! Not a drop on me or on the table! My fingers weren't even sticky!

Eddy was waiting at the elevator. He didn't bother to speak to me. He knew I probably wouldn't answer. "Did you bring the candy?"

My mother handed him the little bag of sweets and Eddy didn't say "thank you" —he did better than that. He erupted into a joyful shout, "WOW! Tootsie Rolls! My favorite! How'd you know?" He hobbled away with an uneven step—clunk, step, clunk—and for the first time I tuned in to the fact that he must be walking with braces on his legs or on crutches.

"By the way," he called back to us. "Dr. King's looking for you, brat. I heard him telling Nurse Nutty you're going home in a couple of days."

Dr. King strode into my room. "Heard you were in the coffee shop," he said, laying a big hand on my shoulder. "Did you leave any food for the rest of us?"

I didn't answer but I smiled. I could only keep my shield partially up in Dr. King's friendly presence.

More seriously he said to my mother, "There's a long hard road ahead of you. She's stable, but fragile. She'll not survive one of our winters. You'll have to move to a warm, dry climate for a couple of years at least. Let us know where you end up and we'll network an ophthalmologist for her, although I don't think there's much hope for any change."

Within the week we were on the way home. My father sent his chauffeur to pick us up from the hospital and take us to our apartment. As we climbed out of the car, Mrs. Brockman, Red, and Mrs. Maise greeted us with enthusiastic exclamations. "Welcome home! So good to have you back!"

Mrs. Brockman and Red had visited us once in the hospital so they were used to my new state of being, but Mrs. Maise hugged my mother and whispered loudly, "I'm so sorry, so sorry. What a tragedy!"

Her emotionally saturated dramatics caught me off-guard, unhinged me, and I couldn't wait to get away from her, but once we were inside the apartment, my spirits revived.

"I know my way around in here," I told my mother as I strolled around the kitchen. I turned right into the dining room, then moved a little to my left and found the long, glossy table. If I followed it all the way down the room, I would be only a few steps away from the archway leading into the living room. The dining room table ended. Concentrating, I moved slightly to my left so that I would clear the wall and reach the archway. Extending my right hand, I found my piano along the right wall as I entered the living room. Our pearl-gray couch with the white plume print, the white and gold silk armchairs, the paintings, the statues, the large rose-colored Venetian lamp all paraded across the mirror of my memory.

"I remember how everything looks and where everything is!" I said joyfully. "I can move around by myself in here!"

Another joy had been waiting for me—something small and warm suddenly jumped at my legs—Teena! I scooped her up and pressed her to my cheek. She was a tiny bundle of happy wiggles. We rubbed noses and her minute tongue licked furiously at my face. Then I realized, "I can't take her for her walks now."

"I'll walk her," my mother said, "and you can come along if you like."

"Who took care of her while we were in the hospital?" I asked, hugging the little creature to my chest.

"Red did," answered my mother. "He enjoyed her."

Red, still the good friend, came to visit daily. Instead of drawing, hitting golf balls, playing catch, or flying kites with me, he sat patiently on the chair opposite the couch where I lay three times a day while my mother applied steaming compresses to my eyes. Sometimes he read my old comic books to me. Sometimes we ate Cracker Jacks and chatted, but he was always there except when his caddying job kept him on the nearby golf course.

"I wish I could ride my bike," I confided one afternoon from my customary place on the couch.

"Let's try it," he said eagerly and after the session of compresses, I followed the banister down the long flight of back steps to the outside door and waited. Red ran down into the basement and retrieved the bright blue Schwinn my mother had bought for my tenth birthday just three months before.

Red steered the bike down the driveway and around to the front sidewalk. I walked along, my hand on the bicycle seat for direction.

"Get on and pedal. I'll run alongside and steer the handlebars."

We labored down the sidewalk in front of our houses, but Red couldn't keep up unless I went slowly and going slowly made the bike wobble and topple over.

"Wait a second," he huffed. "I'll be right back." In a moment he was back with his mom and his big brother.

"You just ride," said Mrs. Brockman, "and we'll aim the handlebars as you go by if you're not going straight."

My mother rounded the corner from the driveway. "I don't think...," she began, but Mrs. Brockman cut her off.

"She'll be fine," Red's mother assured her and in my mind I could see her again, her merry, round face; soft brown eyes; bright little red mouth; and big, strong arms. And so, with this family of neighbors positioned down the long sidewalk, I rode my bike. It was not the same as sweeping down the sidewalks to the deli a few blocks away for gumballs from their shiny silver machine, not the same as rolling across the prairie as fast and as hard as my legs could pedal through the tall grass, but I was out of the hospital, out of bed, on my bike, and that was better than nothing.

My mother had been trying to introduce my old school friends into my new life, but no one accepted the invitations except one classmate, Barbara Peterson. Very tall and very slim and very blond, she had always been a quiet presence both in class and on the playground, hovering on the fringe of our games and lively chatter, watching us with such pale blue eyes they seemed almost colorless. She had always been placidly friendly to me and now she slipped easily and amicably into the modifications confronting both of us if she was to "play" with me.

"Let's roller skate," I suggested one day when we were both bored with doing nothing.

"I didn't bring my skates," she reminded me.

"That's okay," I said. "We can share mine."

I strapped on the left skate and Barbara the right. Hand in hand, we limped along the sidewalk, giggling at our own clumsiness. "Bump coming up," she forecasted and I prepared to lift my skate. "Curb ahead," she warned and I slowed down.

It was not the same as skimming smoothly along, feeling the fluid sailing motion, hearing the click, click, click of the wheels as they rolled over the seams of the sidewalk, but then again, I was "hopscotch" skating, as Barbara and I named our new sport, and that was better than nothing.

Slowly, August crept across the prairie and the days grew hotter and hotter. Since my birth, my mother and I had escaped the Chicago heat at my grandparents' summer home in Michigan, but after the house had to be sold, we summered in Valerie's spectacular home near the beach in Wilmette.

"Why aren't we going to Valerie's this summer?" I asked one suffocatingly hot afternoon. "I'm better now and I could probably even swim a little in the lake."

My mother didn't disguise or soften the truth.

"Grandmamma Renata won't allow Valerie to invite us this year. She's afraid the girls might contract whatever disease you have. We can't even visit for a day."

The words surprised, shocked, and lacerated my spirit. Ghita and Lill were my best friends, my babyhood friends! I suddenly felt unclean, diminished. I never did like that pompous old lady from Trieste, I reminded myself, and took consolation from the confirmation that my opinion was valid.

When I didn't respond, my mother went on to fill the silence. "I've been thinking. Let's have a party and invite all your old school friends. They might not mind coming if they all come together."

A handful of children arrived for the lawn party. They might as well have been total strangers. I couldn't recognize them by their voices. I never had to identify them just by hearing them speak. We stood awkwardly in the backyard. They bunched up into two groups, the boys silent at my left, the girls giggling nervously at my right.

What games would we play? I wondered. *What would we do with the afternoon?* Maybe it wasn't such a great idea to have this party.

"Let's play recognize voices," suggested my mother cheerfully. "You talk one at a time and see if Bianca can identify you. Then I'll blindfold you one at a time and we'll see how many voices you can each recognize."

We sat on Mr. Maise's precious grass that he never allowed me to so much as step on before. There was no pounding at the window to get us off, so the game proceeded undisturbed.

One by one my mother blindfolded each child and the rest called out, "Hi, Walter, who am I? Hi, Linda, who am I?" and so on down the list of guests. It pleased me to know that they were no better at recognizing one another's voices than I had been.

The boys were still quiet, the girls still giggling.

"Let's play blind man's bluff," suggested my mother and a little more time passed.

Barbara stepped up beside me and tugged at my hand. "Wanna go hopscotch skating and get out of here?"

"It's a great idea, but we better not," I said, and suddenly I was feeling much better. Whatever it was that had wound itself around my throat all afternoon had loosened its grip.

"Let's eat!" my mother called out as she put a cupcake in my right hand and a paper cup of lemonade in my left. I heard the children milling around the yard, approaching the refreshment table and talking happily among themselves. All at once, I realized with a flash of insight that, like Barbara had always been, I was now on the fringe, on the outside. I didn't like being in this lonely place and I was remorseful that I had never done anything to invite Barbara and many others like her into the school's magic circle of popularity.

"Why didn't you invite Red?" Barbara asked with a mouthful of cupcake as she plopped down on the grass beside me.

"I did and he was going to come," I explained, "but he was called into work at the golf course."

The afternoon ground slowly away and finally the children had all gone home. I climbed wearily up the long flight of back stairs, relieved to be alone.

"Time for your compresses," announced my mother. "You look very tired. Lie down on your bed and I'll bring them to you there."

"I think this party was like falling off another horse," I tried to joke as I stretched out and waited for the first steaming washcloth to touch my eyes. "At least I didn't leave a mess of ice cream behind this time."

"That gives me an idea," said my mother, and the following Saturday Valerie drove us to the stable where I had taken riding lessons before my illness. The car windows were open and as we pulled up to the stable and stopped, I recognized the unmistakable pungent scent of horses. My heart leapt with excitement as I heard one whinnying far off in the field and another answering close by. Rags, the huge, shaggy barn dog, barked a noisy greeting and circled the car.

Without waiting for my mother's permission or assistance, I found the door latch, lifted it and jumped out of the car. Roberta, my instructor, came running up and grabbed my hand.

"Hi, honey. Mom told us you were coming this morning. Nell's out, but I have Old Rosie saddled up and waiting for you."

"Old Rosie?" I asked incredulously as the image of the ancient gray animal with the sweet, patient eyes floated into my mind.

"Yep, she'll be fine for your first time back. You're not going on the trail today. We'll just walk around the inside ring, nice and easy."

My excitement drained steadily away as Old Rosie clumped lazily around and around the ring. I felt as though I was three years old again and being led on a pony ride in Lincoln Park. This outing was definitely not meeting my expectations. I was not on Nell, my regular chestnut mare, not on the trail, not galloping confidently on my own, but I was at the stables and astride this gentle old horse and that was better than nothing.

"Bring her any time," Roberta told my mother as I slid off the saddle and gave Old Rosie's neck an affectionate rub.

"We're leaving the area very soon," responded my mother. "I don't think we'll be back."

Dr. King's words echoed through the conversation—"You'll have to move to a dry, warm climate." I hadn't realized until this moment that our move was truly going to happen.

As the time neared for our September departure, I began to panic. Every day as my mother packed boxes I asked, "If I suddenly get my sight back, can we stay here? Can I go back to my old school?"

"Of course," my mother agreed patiently, although she heard the same question over and over day after day.

September was just days away. "How about if I get my sight back the same morning that school starts? Can we stay?"

"Of course."

Every morning I opened my eyes, but every morning it was still dark. Finally I accepted the reality. The miracle was not going to happen. We were going to leave. So instead of shopping for new school clothes, I started sorting through my possessions. I suspected that bringing my books and paints was a useless expense, but I packed what I simply could not bear to leave behind: all my books, my treasured acrylic paints, my horse statues, and my piano music. I grieved for what I must leave: my old life, my home, Barbara and Red, my piano.

It was the humid, breathless evening before our departure and I was sitting on the steps outside the back door, secretly peeling loose paint from their underside. Mr. Maise would have exploded at me if he had known, but my restless fingers needed something to do now that they were not turning pages of a book or guiding a paintbrush or stick of charcoal into a design. Now and then a breeze floated across me from the stretch of prairie extending behind the house.

I knew Red would be over after his dinner and soon I heard gravel shifting under someone's shoes along the driveway.

"Wanna go for a walk to the dairy and get a cone?" asked Red. "I've got money!"

"Okay," I agreed but I wondered how he expected to negotiate the trip since he had been too shy to take my hand and lead me anywhere.

"Stay right here," he said, starting down the driveway at a run, "I'll be right back."

Maybe he was going to get his mother or big brother to walk with me, I speculated as I waited, but I heard only one set of returning footsteps on the gravel.

"Here," Red said as he ran back to the step. "Hold on to this."

He slipped a short, sturdy twig into my palm. Four or five inches away, at the other end of the stick, was his own hand. Our fingers were not close enough to touch, and with this safe distance of the twig between us, we started out for the dairy.

As we strolled comfortably down the sidewalk, he said, so quietly that I could scarcely hear him, "Be sure you have your mom send me your address as soon as you're settled."

"I will. I promise."

As my sandals touched the soft ground that indicated the end of the sidewalk and the beginning of the prairie, I turned my head to my left and caught the full breath of prairie breeze on my face. In my mind I visualized the expanse of deep, waving green that I knew was, even now, touching the horizon and cradling the sinking ball of the sun.

It was not the same as watching the shifting, shimmering shades of the sunset; not the same as running across this seemingly endless land, a long roll of string in my hand, coaxing a ten-cent kite into the clouds, but I was not buried like David, not confined to a bed or strapped to a chair like Ginger, not burned and screaming like Janie. I was walking along with my friend and even if I was at the end of a stick, we were going for ice cream together, and that was better than nothing.

Twelve
The Palomino Promise

"*A*s soon as we're settled in Arizona, I'll buy you your own horse—a palomino!"

My mother's promise had made dealing with my new blindness and our having to leave Chicago, our apartment, my piano, and my friends a bit easier. I had wanted my own horse for as long as I could remember and the promise of owning a palomino was the pinnacle of expectation.

My love of horses was hereditary. Although I could no longer see it, I could visualize the photograph of my grandfather, who had been a colonel in the Italian cavalry, sitting proud and tall on his great horse, and the memory of that picture still made my heart beat faster.

At the last school book fair I had bought a thick volume that had taken all the money I had budgeted for two or three smaller books. The cover of *The Golden Stallion* leaped out at me from the collection of books on the long table in the school library. It was a drawing of a spectacular animal, a golden palomino, rearing up, front hooves lashing at the air, head tossed back, great white mane, touching the sky. His eyes, wild and penetrating, had stared out at me and held me.

What would it be like to ride a splendid creature like that? Certainly it would be different from the tame pony rides in Lincoln Park. It would even be different from riding Nell, the chestnut mare I mounted now and then for a riding lesson. After my mother's promise, I fell asleep at night with fantasies of riding the palomino across the desert, across parched river beds, up and down mountains. I would be able to nestle into a big, comfortable western saddle instead of perching on a lean English one and it wouldn't matter if my posture was properly straight or my hand position correct. In my mind I could see my palomino, his golden head up, white mane unfurling in the wind as we galloped across miles and miles of western land. In my Chicago bedroom I could smell the unmistakable odor of horseflesh, hear the squeak of the saddle, feel the long rhythmic strides of the horse's legs beneath me. It was a joy just to daydream about the freedom I would

93

gain on such a fearless and sure-footed animal. My horse would lift me out of what had become careful, constricted movement through a newly darkened world.

Our first landing place in Tucson was a motel. *No horses allowed.* My mother bought me a cowboy hat, boots, jeans, a red shirt with fringe across the chest, and a wide carved leather belt with a big silver buckle instead.

"Don't worry," she said, "you'll get your horse. We won't be here long." She didn't know how true that was, or did she? At the end of our first month in Arizona, my father decided he had paid enough and stopped sending money for the motel room. We were asked to leave. Where would we go, a young woman on her own with a sick and handicapped child? I was not well enough for my mother to leave me to look for work, and my father had been sending only the motel payment. We had very little of our savings left for existing, much less for paying motel accommodations.

"I'm going to leave you for a little while," my mother told me one morning. "I have to find a place to live. It's a blistering day out and you wouldn't be able to walk very far in this heat. Don't open the door to anyone. I'll be back as soon as I can. You're not afraid to be alone here, are you?"

"No," I lied as my heart skipped a beat. But then I remembered the promise—"Try to find a place where I can have my horse," I said and sat down to wait for her return, Teena on my lap.

She wasn't gone long. She had walked down the highway and found an unoccupied two-room cabin with a FOR RENT sign on the door—thirty-five dollars a month. It was rustic, primitive, poor.

Along one wall was a double bed and, on the opposite wall, a dilapidated chest of drawers. An archway opened to a kitchen with a rickety, teeter-tottering wooden table and two chairs. The bathroom was comprised of a sink and a pull-chain toilet, no tub, no shower. I bathed in a big, round, tin tub my mother would position in the middle of the kitchen. That was all there was, that and the strong smell of disinfectant and the sound of my mother sweeping and scrubbing with a heavy brush.

Fortunately it didn't rain often that time of year in Tucson because the roof leaked badly. Only now and then was the silence of the cabin punctuated by the sound of raindrops dripping into old metal pots scattered around the floor. The desert winds were more relentless. They blew for clusters of days and nights without stopping. Sand seeped, drifted, flew into the cabin until my mother stuffed the cracks in the walls with newspaper. Under such conditions I knew better than to mention my palomino.

It was this calamitous state of affairs that friends of my father found when they arrived in Tucson for a luxurious vacation at the El Conquistador Dude Ranch. My father, still insanely jealous of my mother, had asked his friend to "check up" on us.

It was midmorning. My mother had been reading to me and had just put down the book to go for a glass of milk she periodically tried to convince, coax, or cajole me to drink. We were startled by a knock at the door. Who would be visiting us?

"Excuse me, madame," said a man's voice. "I was given this address for a Mrs. Covelli and her daughter. There must be some mistake. Please excuse me."

"I'm Mrs. Covelli," said my mother warily. "Who are you?"

"I'm Judge Harrigan," the man introduced himself, "a friend of Judge Covelli's, and this is my wife Pat. We're vacationing in Tucson and...." His voice trailed away.

"Please come in," said my mother.

They stepped inside the cabin and I heard the woman gasp—"Oh, Edward!" The man prayed, "Jesus!"

I was lying on the bed where I spent most of my time. They didn't speak to me but moved quietly into the kitchen. Their voices were hushed. Was my mother crying? No, she wouldn't do that. She was always cheerful. I heard the man's voice again, "Where's your phone? I'm going to call the bastard!"

"There's no phone," said my mother.

"Then I'll go back to the ranch immediately and call from there," he said, his voice angry. "Court's in session now. I'll have his bailiff jerk 'im right off the bench." And then he prayed again, "Jesus, I can't believe this!"

They went out as they had come in, without speaking to me. Was I as invisible to them as they were to me, I wondered?

My father, irritable and silent, arrived within the week. He drove up to the cabin in his rented Cadillac and in a few moments we were skimming along somewhere, Teena and I in the back seat, my mother in the front with him.

"There's a state school for blind children right here in town," I heard him tell my mother. "It has boarding facilities. You can get yourself a job, a room somewhere, and have her visit you weekends."

"You can't be serious," my mother said with a hardness I had never heard in her voice before. "It's out of the question. I won't even consider it. She'll die!"

"Nonsense," he said harshly.

My mother's response was carefully aimed, a bullet that held the decision between life and death. "How many deaths do you want on your conscience?" she asked in a stage whisper. "Isn't Alice's suicide enough for you?"

What did she mean? I knew my half-brother's mother's name was Alice and that she died before my brother was two years old, but that ugly word had never been spoken in my presence before.

My father didn't answer, just kept on driving. The warm little dog on my lap had lifted her head off my knees and her disproportionately big ears were pointed straight up. She was alert, watching, listening. I stroked the top of her silky head, her neck, her back, and she licked my hand. We comforted each other. The car sailed on and on. Where were we going?

"Look," my father commanded as the car screeched to a stop. "That chap is putting the finishing touches on that little house over there." He turned off the motor and got out of the car. "Stay put," he ordered me, as if I could go anywhere on my own. I stroked Teena and waited.

"We have a lovely little house, Bianchina," my mother said when they returned to the car. "The man who built it lives right across the street. Your father wrote him out a check for all the seven thousand dollars and bought it."

The builder's wife was to tell us bitterly many times, "You know, you bought this house right out from under me. I was already packing our stuff to bring over here when Alan come in and said the house was sold to some people from back east with a blind kid. Said he couldn't say no 'cause the father seemed real anxious to get 'em settled in and he give Alan a check for the whole amount. I didn't believe it until Alan showed it to me. I cried and cried, but he wouldn't give the money back. And then he goes out and wastes a chunk of it getting drunk with his hunting buddies."

The afternoon of the purchase we went to Montgomery Ward for the cheapest furniture my father could find.

"I'm Judge Covelli," he announced as we entered the store's furniture department. "I just bought a brand-new home for my daughter. It's completely empty and I want to furnish it and settle her and her mother into it today. I'm going back to Chicago on the evening train. If you can't deliver the furniture this afternoon I'll take my business elsewhere."

"Let me make a phone call, Judge," said the flustered salesman. "I'm sure we can accommodate you."

What he didn't know was that the entire acquisition would entail a double bed for my mother and me to share, one chest of drawers, a kitchen set, and a couch.

Even at ten years old I recognized the irony of the scene and I suddenly thought of a cartoon I had seen in a Sunday comic strip before I lost my sight. The first box showed a woman in furs issuing from a long black limo and walking into a linoleum shop. The next three boxes showed more and more samples of linoleum all over the counters, on tables, spilling off onto the floor. An increasingly harried-looking salesman was trying his best to make a sale for what he thought must be a mansion. Finally the woman selected a pattern, stepped to the door, and signaled the chauffeur, who came into the shop carrying a bird cage.

Remembering the cartoon and recognizing its similarity to what my father was doing, I smiled to myself.

"Look at her face," said my mother, who couldn't know what I was thinking. "You've made your daughter happy."

The house was pleasant enough, a good-sized living room, a large eat-in kitchen, and two bedrooms. By that evening the few pieces of furniture were in place and my father was on his way back to Chicago.

"When do I get my horse?" I asked that first evening over a plate of spaghetti.

"Well," said my mother slowly. "I'm not sure we live in a zone that permits keeping a horse on the property and besides, the yard is too small for a stable."

"But you promised," I reminded her.

"I don't think you're strong enough for a horse yet anyway," she said.

"I rode once after I got sick, just before we left Chicago," I protested.

"That was just a half-hour's circling around a corral with a trainer," said my mother. "Caring for a horse full time is different. But you're due for a physical and we'll see what the doctor thinks."

Doctor Andrews was not encouraging. "You're such a frail little peanut," he laughed condescendingly, "the first gust of wind that blows off the mountains would knock you right off the saddle. Put on a few pounds and we'll talk about it."

I was disappointed, annoyed at his attitude, but I had to admit to myself that he was right. I still suffered from tremendous headaches. There were entire days I lay face-down on my bed, my head jammed hard against the pillow in an attempt to dull the searing pain.

Dr. Brown, the ophthalmologist who had been attending me since our arrival, suggested casually one day, "She probably has a brain tumor. Hasn't anyone mentioned the possibility before?"

"No," my mother responded faintly, "but she had all kinds of tests in Chicago. Wouldn't it have shown up then?"

"I suppose," the doctor admitted.

Neither my mother nor I realized that the devastating diagnosis he was toying with had issued from a fog of alcoholism.

In November Dr. Brown gave us a prescription for what were proposed to be miraculous new eyedrops. My father was sending us ten dollars a week, the minimum child support the law allowed, and money was scarce, but my mother took the prescription to the town pharmacy immediately.

The place was busy, buzzing with holiday shoppers. Above the clamor I heard a mellow, crooning voice, "I'm dreaming of a White Christmas, just like the ones I used to know...." The familiar song reminded me that the holidays were close upon us. The dry, warm weather with its constant sunshine was somehow not conducive to the spirit of the season. I was suddenly terribly homesick for the snow, for the snowball fights with the boy next door, for the stinging wind off the prairie that meant Christmas was not far away.

I don't think my mother even heard the music. She was intent on getting my eyedrops. "I'll have to write you a check," she said. "We're new in town and you don't know me, but I assure you there's money in the account to cover this. You can telephone the bank if you wish."

The clerk left the counter to make the call.

"I'd better get some aspirin for your headaches, too," she said and stepped away for a moment, leaving the eyedrops on the counter. When she came back I heard her gasp, then panic. "Bianca, do you have the drops?"

"The drops? No. I don't have them." My mother began to cry. I stood stone-faced and silent in my embarrassment.

"Somebody stole them," she sobbed. "They were wrapped in holiday paper! Someone must have thought they were a lipstick or a perfume. They cost nearly forty dollars."

The pharmacist must have taken pity on us. I don't remember the conversation but I know we went home with a second set of eyedrops for which he didn't make us pay.

"Maybe these drops will stop my eye pain and headaches," I said as my mother and I settled onto the bus for the ride home. "And then," I ventured, "I can get my palomino, right?"

"We'll see," replied my mother. "We'll have to find a stable we can afford. As soon as you're well enough, you can go to the school for blind children in town a few hours a day and I can get a job."

In just weeks the infection was so diminished that my strength and even my sight were creeping back. We had managed a small Christmas tree and a few ornaments and I could just make out the bright multicolored tree lights blinking through my darkness.

"Stop the drops," Dr. Brown said in mid-December. "She has improved to the point where it's safe to discontinue them." But in January, the infection, uncontrolled by medication, flared with such desperate fury that I was once again flung at death's door and my returning sight was gone. A new ophthalmologist was obviously called for.

My mother telephoned Dr. King in Chicago and she was soon packing a few clothes into two suitcases, locking up the house, and we were boarding a train for California. I was so ill I couldn't stay awake for long periods of time. The soothing motion and music of the train clicking over the rails put me almost immediately to sleep. The last thing I heard before I drifted away was my mother's voice, "As soon as you're strong enough and we can come home, you'll start school, I'll get a job and we'll see about your palomino. Don't worry! It'll happen. It's a promise."

Thirteen
Pottinger Sanitarium

Dr. Lloyd Mills, the new ophthalmologist, was soft-spoken and concerned, but as my mother recounted the chronicle of my course of treatment with Dr. Brown, his tone of voice changed. I could hear the contempt in his words: "Irresponsible! Incomprehensible risk! Folly! License revoked!"

None of us could know at the time what tragic fate Dr. Brown was racing toward even as we spoke.

My illness had been a mystery from the beginning. This new doctor in Los Angeles meant new tests and another misdiagnosis.

"The only clue we have is the positive tuberculosis test," Dr. Mills told us. "Before we can consider eye surgery, the child must be admitted to a tuberculosis facility for a year, perhaps longer."

"A year?" my mother echoed incredulously. Dr. Mills was an illustrious specialist. We would have to trust his judgment, follow his advice, but "a year"?

"I would recommend Pottinger Sanitarium in Monrovia," Dr. Mills went on. "It's only forty miles north of L.A. so as soon as she's strong enough, you can bring her to my office for periodic examinations."

The sanitarium was nestled in a valley of citrus groves. The perfume of orange, lemon, and grapefruit blossoms hung in the air like a fragrant curtain opening to welcome us as my mother and I stepped out of the taxi.

We walked into the main building where the doctors' offices, labs, administration office, and dying patients were housed. My mother was escorted into an office and, as I stood alone in the corridor waiting for something to happen, a brisk, efficient woman swooped around the corner and took my hand.

"I'm Nurse Kelly," she said, leading me into a room a few steps down the hall. "You're going to pose for some x-ray pictures in here. I'll leave you with Hilda. You'll be fine." And with a whirl and whisper of her uniform, she went out the door.

A bird-like technician with a high, chirp-quick voice hopped around preparing the machine, placing me in position and throwing the lever for one picture after another.

The sound of the x-ray machine jarred my memory, propelled me back to Chicago and Marshall Field's Department Store. There, in the children's shoe department, stood a big square machine with two steps for mounting and two tunnel-like holes for the child's feet. The salesman hit a switch and a green glow swallowed the feet, leaving only an ugly, skeletal picture of a multitude of little bones and the outline of the shoe being fitted.

"Perfect fit," the salesman would say, smiling, knowing that the new technology would convince mothers of his efficiency. I remembered my last trip to the shoe department before my illness struck. My feet were being examined in brown suede slip-ons, quite grown-up, that matched my brown felt-brimmed hat with the maroon feather.

"Your father said he'd buy your winter coat this year," my mother had said. "Let's go and find one we like before he takes you shopping so you'll know which one to make him buy."

We had selected a lusciously soft camel-hair coat with deep patch pockets and a brown velvet collar. The shoes and hat we were buying that day completed the outfit.

"Now don't forget which coat it is," my mother warned, "or the hat and shoes won't be right."

On the following Saturday when my father took me shopping, I knew exactly where to find the coat.

"She certainly knows what she wants," the silver-blond saleslady with the suspicious green eyes had cooed, batting her too-long, too-dark eyelashes at my father.

I had studied the rack of coats until I spotted "the coat" and I had walked over to it, held out the sleeve, and said as innocently as possible, "This one, please."

I avoided my father's eyes. My mother would be so proud of me when I brought the right coat home. Her pleasure would be worth the deception.

Now, thousands of miles from that department store, I wondered if the bones of my rib cage and whatever else was being x-rayed that day in California were as ugly as the bones of my feet had been in Chicago.

"Negative—her lungs are clear," reported the radiologist, "but she'll receive the same treatment as the positive patients—a weekly injection, bed rest, and fresh air."

I didn't know how much fresh air until we followed Nurse Kelly to one of the fifty cabins that dotted the lanes branching off the citrus groves.

"There are no walls," said my mother in dismay as we mounted the three steps onto a tiny wooden porch and walked into our cabin.

"Fresh air is one of the most important elements of treatment here," replied Nurse Kelly. "It's a smidgen cold now in January, but you'll get used to it."

Actually, there were some walls—two feet of wood extended up from the floor, at which point screening reached to the ceiling.

100

"At night and in bad weather," went on Nurse Kelly, "you can let the roll of canvas down from the ceiling to cover the screening."

My mother said nothing and Nurse Kelly continued, "This is a great cabin. Walter Pigeon stayed in this one, sat in this rocker right here, month after month until he got well."

I tried to remember what the film star looked like. Vaguely I could recall his face, but I couldn't make myself respond with much enthusiasm.

"I guess I can't have my palomino in here, can I?" I asked.

"A palomino?" echoed the nurse, laying her hand on my forehead. "That's a kind of horse, isn't it?"

"Just a joke," I said wryly.

"Oh, all right," she said but she didn't sound convinced. "Get into your pj's and hop into bed," she dictated as she pulled the bedspread down and fluffed the pillow.

"Now?" I asked, surprised. "It's daytime."

"Rest is one of the other most important elements of the treatment here. Patients are in bed for six months before they get any walking privileges. You'll get used to it." She closed the screen door of the cabin behind her and was gone.

"It's freezing in here," said my mother. "You'll be more comfortable under the covers anyway."

In a few minutes I was in bed and the year of treatment had begun.

My mother sat on the other bed. "I have to find a job," she said. "Your father's paying the bill for the sanitarium. He can take your medical expenses off his taxes. He's also paying for me to stay with you and have my meals here, but he's not giving us any money for anything else. You'll need more pajamas and we'll have to take the train into L.A. to see Dr. Mills. We'll need ticket money and a few dollars for lunches." Her voice was strained, full of anxiety as she said, "I hate to leave you here alone."

I hated it, too, but I didn't respond. What was there to say? At dinnertime her fears were magnified. A man walked into the cabin, set two trays down on the table at the foot of my bed, and left without a word.

Nurse Kelly darted in just after him. "You're in bed. Good, all settled in?"

"That man," said my mother warily, "the one who brought in the trays...."

"What about him?"

"He looks strange, rather ominous." And then, her distress overriding her faultless politeness, she said, "like someone you'd see in a police line-up."

"You're absolutely right," replied Nurse Kelly. "He just got out of prison."

The only sound I heard from my mother was a tiny gasp.

"Dr. P. employs the newly released men as tray boys, gives them a second chance in life." When my mother didn't answer, Nurse Kelly said almost belligerently, "Very charitable of him, don't you think?"

"Very," my mother was forced to agree.

"I'll have to find a job that allows me to be here for meal times," my mother said when Nurse Kelly had gone and the tray boy had come back and silently removed the dinner trays. I sensed her fear. Life at that moment was grim.

I heard someone run up the porch steps and Nurse Kelly bounded in. "I'm going off duty," she said, "but I have a message to give you before I go."

"A message for me?" asked my mother.

"Yes," the nurse went on, "your mother just telephoned and said to tell you not to despair, that everything would work out for you and your daughter."

"You must be mistaken," said my mother. "It couldn't have been my mother who phoned."

"Oh, yes," insisted Nurse Kelly. "I spoke to her myself and she specifically said to bring the message to her daughter with the blind child. There's certainly no one else here who fits that description. In fact, Bianca's the only child in the whole place, blind or otherwise."

"Thank you," said my mother rather tremulously. "I appreciate your bringing the message, especially since my mother died of cancer in Italy many years ago."

There was a deep silence in the little cabin for what seemed a long time.

"Glory be to God!" Nurse Kelly finally managed to whisper. "Jesus, Mary, and Joseph, protect us from all evil." She went out the door still calling on the saints and mumbling to herself....

Each cabin held two beds, a table, two straight chairs, and a rocker. Between the two beds was a door leading to a bathroom with a tub. During the forthcoming summer (by then my mother and I had become a part of the patients' underground communication network) we were to find out that the tubs were used for more than bathing. On hot summer nights they sometimes served as gigantic containers for mixing mint juleps.

Opposite the tub was a large, deep closet. We had managed to smuggle Teena into the cabin and the closet became her home for part of each day. Early mornings my mother would take her for a long walk to tire her so that the tiny dog was happy to snuggle down into an old sweater in a corner of the closet when she returned. Some of the day she spent under my covers and some of the time she had the run of the bathroom. Not many days had passed, however, before her existence became common knowledge, but perhaps because I was the only child in the sanitarium, Dr. Pottinger decreed she could stay.

Every morning Dr. Pottinger, a pleasant, cheery, small man and his assistant, Dr. Fuller, made the rounds of the cabins.

"She won't eat much," my mother told them one morning.

"You have to force the food in," said Dr. Fuller. "Shove it in and push it down. Dr. Mills won't operate until she's eighty pounds."

102

"I have to be here for her meals," my mother told the two doctors, "but I need a job. Would you possibly have an opening in one of your offices?"

"Come to my office at ten o'clock," said Dr. Pottinger. "I think I have the perfect job for you."

"I have a job!" my mother announced breathlessly as she rushed into the cabin. "I even have my own office. I'll be reading manuscripts and articles and organizing information for Dr. Pottinger's new book! They've already started bringing cartons of books and papers up from the basement for me and I start tomorrow."

The only companionship I had at the beginning when my mother was at work was Teena and my radio. I listened to every soap opera offered, hiding the radio under my covers during mandatory nap time, two to four every day.

One afternoon just before dinner, there was a light thump on the porch as though a body had jumped up the steps and a young voice called out, "Wanna paper?"

"No, thank you," said my mother. When he had gone she exclaimed, "What a good-looking paper boy, gorgeous blue eyes!" Although we never bought a paper, the boy came back day after day. Finally, one afternoon he lingered.

"How come she's here?" he asked my mother.

"She's a patient."

"She has TB?"

"Maybe TB of the eyes," my mother explained. "We really don't know."

The boy left but the next day he was back early. I was alone when he arrived on the porch.

"Hi," he called. "Can I come in?"

By now I knew his voice and besides, he was the only young person who came to the cabins.

"All right," I called back from my bed. "Come in."

"My name's Larker Howe. What's yours?" I told him. For a moment he didn't speak and then he blurted, "How come you never smile back when I smile at you, or wave back or anything?"

"I didn't know you were smiling at me or waving either," I said simply. "I can't see." Silence.

"Oh, you can't see!" Larker exclaimed as if he had just solved a profound mystery. "I'm glad. I mean...I'm glad you didn't know, not I'm glad that you can't see. I mean...I'm glad it wasn't just because you didn't like me or something that you didn't.... Well. Anyway...."

I had to laugh. He was so flustered and so pleased at the same time. "It's okay," I said. "Relax."

"Blind people like music, right?"

"I suppose," I said. "I don't know any blind people except me and I liked music even when I could see. Why?"

103

"I play the violin," Larker told me. "Would you like me to bring it and play for you sometime?"

"Sure," I said. "That'd be great."

He banged out the screen door and, whistling, jumped off the porch to peddle his papers.

Larker became a daily visitor, sometimes arriving with a strip of rock candy, sometimes with a peppermint stick or a flower he had pulled off a bush on the sanitarium grounds. Once he ran in with rattles from a rattlesnake he said he had killed in the mountains. The moment he bounced into the cabin with that gift, Teena went mad. She yelped in terror and ran circles around the floor, finally scurrying under my bed where she hid, whining and trembling, in as distant a corner as she could find.

"Thanks," I said, sliding head and all under the covers, "but Teena and I don't want those awful things. Please get them out of here, please!" He couldn't have known, of course, of my phobic fear of snakes, but he obliged, although I knew he was disappointed.

"Girls," I heard him mutter as he left with his rejected treasure.

Every Sunday afternoon Larker came with his violin. He would unpack it, make tuning noises on it, pace up and down between the two beds with it in his hands, chat, tell jokes, but there was never a time that he actually played the instrument. I began to doubt that he could really play and then I began to doubt other things he said. The rattles I decided had probably come from a snake he had found already dead. His imagination was limitless.

"I'm the only undercover kid for the FBI," he said under his breath. "My latest case was just this week. I...." or "I got a part in another movie. I go to Hollywood all the time. I'm going to be in a car racing scene or maybe piloting an airplane!"

I never let him know I didn't believe a word he said. He was the only bright spot in the world of sick and dying adults into which I had been plunged and I appreciated the time and energy he spent entertaining me.

One morning a woman knocked at our cabin door. "Hello," said a soft, pleasant voice. "My name's Vera. I'm a patient, too, but I'm also a teacher. I thought you might like to review some math with me once in a while and I could read to you when your mother's at work."

"I'd love it," I said excitedly. "I really miss school, especially reading, and by now I don't care if Helen Trent ever has another romance or My Gal Sunday finds happiness as the wife of a rich and titled Englishman."

Vera laughed a low, husky laugh. "I know exactly what you mean," she said. "I'll have my husband bring some books on the weekend."

Vera's husband, an officer in the Navy, found her in our cabin when he came to visit the following Sunday.

"Did you bring the books?" Vera asked before she had even introduced him to us.

Bianca, age 11, and Larker Howe, age 11, friend

"I did," he said glumly, "but I'm not sure you're up to this project yet."

"I'll enjoy it," she assured him. "It'll be great therapy for me."

And so, for several months, Vera filled many an otherwise blank afternoon with knowledge and conversation and a warm camaraderie.

One day she didn't come. When my mother came in from work I told her, "Vera didn't come today. Maybe she was just tired."

"I saw her this afternoon," my mother said hesitantly. "She was brought into the main building on a stretcher. She had a hemorrhage during the night."

"She'll be all right, won't she?" I asked, alarmed.

"I don't know," said my mother. "I doubt it, though."

My mother was always totally honest with me and often her truthfulness stung. This was one of the times I wished she would have cushioned the harsh reality just a bit. Neither of us voiced it, but we both knew that patients were brought to the main building to die.

Only once during my year at the sanitarium did a patient die in a cabin. Coyotes slipped out of the surrounding foothills and wandered close enough to the grounds to fill the night's stillness with their nerve-shattering howls. It was July, but their piercing cries made me shiver.

"Someone's going to die tonight," my mother had said. "The coyotes know it."

I wondered if their eerie music accompanied all souls to their destination or just the evil ones. Surely, I thought, the voices of an angel choir and not the coyotes' satanic shrieks would sing good souls like Vera to their rest.

Vera never came back and I missed her, but soon after her transfer, I had gained enough weight to take my first steps out of the cabin. Walking privileges were given in increments of five hundred feet. My mother and I walked to the edge of the citrus grove and sat on a fallen tree trunk so I could rest and breathe in the perfume that so delighted me. Other walking patients greeted us as they went by:

"Walking! Congratulations!"

"Walking! Great! Great!"

"Walking! Fabulous, honey, good luck!"

"Come to my cabin, seventeen. I have a coffeepot and my sister just sent a whole box of brownies."

"Stop in, cabin twenty-six. I have a new waffle iron."

Invitations poured in as if we had just moved into a friendly little community.

"Dr. Fuller has invited us to his home for tea next Sunday afternoon," my mother said one evening. "He's been very kind to me and I think it would be a nice change for you. We can walk to his house. It's right here on the grounds."

"Does he have children?" I asked eagerly.

"No, he's not married," responded my mother. "He lives with his mother."

The only aspects of the visit I remember are the tall straight chair I sat on, an older lady serving tea and delicious tiny sandwiches and speaking in a soft but not particularly friendly voice, and Dr. Fuller acting unlike the jolly, joking doctor I knew. He seemed almost timid, almost embarrassed in his own home. His uncustomary behavior made me uncomfortable.

"I don't want to go back there again," I told my mother when we were back in the cabin.

"Don't worry," she said. "We won't be invited back."

"Why do you say that?" I asked.

"Three reasons," replied my mother, "I'm divorced, I have a handicapped child, and I'm not Jewish."

By late August I had acquired enough of a walking range to explore the sanitarium grounds. My mother and I walked up a rather steep hill and found ourselves at a road behind the main building. It was my first trip uphill and I was breathless. As I sat on a boulder to rest, I heard it—a loud, welcoming whinnying and a stamping of hooves.

"There's a big horse in a pasture across the road," announced my mother, knowing we had just stumbled upon the treasure that would make the rest of my confinement at the sanitarium more than tolerable.

"I hear him," I cried impatiently. "I hear him. Let's go over there! Maybe I can pet him."

We approached the fence just as a car roared up and stopped. A young woman jumped out and came over to us. "Good morning," she said. "I'm Beth Pottinger, the doctor's granddaughter. You must be Bianca."

"How did you know?" I asked.

"My grandfather has told us about you," she went on, "but he must not have told us everything. I see you like horses!"

"Love them," I said. "Someday I'm going to have a palomino of my own."

"Oh, my," exclaimed Beth. "Now we're talking gorgeous horseflesh! Victor here is just a brown-and-white pinto, but we love him. I've had him since I was about your age."

Beth walked up beside me. "Would you like to ride?"

"Ride?" I echoed. "When?"

"Now," she said, and I heard her bolt over the fence like a boy, and like a boy whistle for the horse. The animal stopped grazing and came to her.

"I don't think...." began my mother.

Beth reassured her, "We'll stay in the pasture. You'll be able to see us every minute and I won't keep her on long." She took my hand and placed it on Victor's neck. "Victor," she said, "this is Bianca and Bianca, this is Victor."

I heard a giggle, a strange, unfamiliar, little-girl sound. Had it really come out of me?

"Now you've been properly introduced," Beth said, affecting a serious, finishing school voice. "You are formally and officially friends."

107

She grabbed my hand again and put it on the top rail of the fence. "Put your foot on the bottom rail and climb up." I did as I was told, my heart thumping. Beth steadied the horse so close to the fence that his side touched the wood. "I'll hold him next to you. Swing your leg over his back and we're off."

"You don't use a saddle or a bridle or anything?" I asked apprehensively.

"Bareback's more fun. Swing over now."

I felt the big, sturdy body of the horse beside me, smelled the tangy smell of the animal, heard his snorts and his hoofs impatiently pawing at the ground. I followed Beth's instructions and before I knew it, I was on his sun-warmed, bare back. Beth swung on in front of me.

"Put your arms around my waist and hold on," she said as she clucked the horse into a slow, steady pace. I was dizzy with joy and excitement. Was this all a dream? Would I wake up and find myself in bed?

"I'm leaving to go back to college in a few days," Beth volunteered. "You'll have to come and keep Victor company."

"I'll come every day," I said.

"Victor's sixteen-and-a-half hands, large for a pinto," Beth told me, "but he's just a big baby, loves attention."

We rode and chatted for only a few golden minutes, but the joy of those minutes, the feel of the horse's muscles rippling beneath me, the freedom of movement, the fragrance of the nearby citrus groves, the warm spontaneity of the young woman who had so generously befriended me, have all lasted a lifetime.

"I'll ask my grandfather if it would be okay for you to take longer rides," said Beth as we slid off Victor's back. "Maybe we can do this again a couple of times before I leave."

Every day after that my mother and I visited Victor, but Beth never returned. Maybe Dr. Pottinger didn't want me to ride yet, I thought, and I contented myself with petting and talking to the horse that stood patiently at the fence and seemed to be listening.

At the corner of the pasture at the roadside was a large tree with limbs that stretched to left and right from the center of the trunk. Victor, some-how anticipating our arrival, would stand waiting with his head and neck framed in the limbs.

"I have a horse friend," I told everyone I knew, and soon other patients accompanied us on our daily walk to the pasture, some with cameras to catch the waiting horse so dramatically framed in the tree limbs.

"That horse gets as much attention and as many pictures taken as President Truman," commented a groundskeeper on one of our group visits.

Victor's favorite treat was simple for us to find and afford. We would pick a grapefruit from any of the many abundant trees along the road and cut it in half with a knife kept from a meal tray for the purpose. Gently, his big teeth surrounding the fruit, Victor would carefully lift it off my palm and then, as he bit down on it, thrust his head up and shower me with juice.

Bianca, age 10, and Victor, pinto pony

"That horse is a comedian," laughed my mother. "He looks like he's enjoying the prank as much as the grapefruit. He's actually laughing."

With Victor, Larker's visits, the friendliness of the other patients, and our occasional trips to L.A. where we ate homemade ravioli in a casalinga Italian restaurant as part of our adventure to see Dr. Mills, the months slipped pleasantly by. We had fallen into a comfortable routine of sanitarium living and, as Nurse Kelly had assured us the day of our arrival, we "got used to it." Spring, summer, and fall had faded into one another and Christmas was approaching.

I knew such things as a Christmas tree, books, bright oil paints, pastels, reams of art paper, ice skates, and ski sweaters with snowflakes and reindeer patterns were, at least temporarily, just memories, but my mother had been researching for Dr. Pottinger's book and had some money stashed away.

"What would you like for Christmas?" she finally asked.

"Jeans and a jean jacket," I replied without hesitation. I had decided on my gift weeks before.

"I think we can arrange that," she said. "I'll take a bus into town some morning."

Evenings were mild that December and the ceiling canvases were not rolled down until bedtime. A week or so before Christmas I thought I caught the sound of singing. Slowly the voices drew nearer and we recognized Christmas carols. My mother and I stepped out onto the porch and listened. Eventually a group of Girl Scouts and their leader rounded the corner and stood before the cluster of cabins on our lane. My reaction was incomprehensible to me. I wanted to run away, to hide inside the cabin where no one could see my inexplicable distress. The Girl Scouts sang and sang and I stood like a statue, frozen in an emotion I could not explain even to myself.

All at once from a neighboring cabin a voice lashed through the Girl Scouts' shaky "Silent Night."

"Shut up," a man sobbed. "Go away! Go away!"

As strange as it seemed, his cries comforted me. They made me realize that I was not alone in my sadness.

"Sleep in heavenly...." the scouts broke off their caroling in mid-phrase and moved quickly and quietly away. A heavy silence hung in the night air. The only sound was the creak of canvases rolling down in each nearby cabin.

• • •

It was Christmas Eve and our cabin was crammed with fellow patients. Mr. Black had brought his waffle iron, mix, and syrup; Juanita, her coffeepot and coffee; Beverly, a box of decorated Christmas cookies; James, an entire case of Coke, and he wouldn't tell anyone how or where he got it. Donna had come to visit her husband Ronnie and they brought his guitar and a two-gallon tin of popcorn. We were having a real party and, without Christmas carols to stir up memories of healthier, happier holidays, everyone was quite content. I felt almost nostalgic knowing in less than a month I would be leaving for Good Samaritan Hospital in L.A. and the first of my eye surgeries.

Every one of our friends had a gift for the only child on the premises. A fuzzy yellow sweater with big wooden buttons, honeysuckle bubble bath, a beaded Indian belt, a whole box of Bazooka bubble gum, a stocking full of candy, and from many more of the patients together, my first Braille wristwatch with the inscription: *To Bianca from her friends at Pottinger's. Xmas, 1948.*

"What a great present," I exclaimed with genuine enthusiasm as I unwrapped the box and reached inside to find the watch.

"It's a Braille watch," my mother explained. "The lid opens and there are Braille dots next to the numbers. You can feel the position of the hands and tell the time yourself."

"Thank you very much," I said, "I love it!" but what I was really thinking was that it would soon serve only as a fond souvenir of these kind people because after my surgery, I wouldn't be needing a Braille watch. I had no doubt whatsoever that in a month I would be able to see again.

Oranges

Unpacking groceries, opening the sack of oranges,
it's more than forty years ago and I am ten again,
holding to my mother's hand, walking through
the impenetrable new darkness that has swallowed me—
but I am not afraid.
The scent of flowering orange groves lifts me up
and I ride on the shoulders
of a valley of fragrant promises.
I am entering another hospital,
this one nestled among the fruit-thick citrus trees of California.

For a year I lie on a high, narrow bed,
while doctors pump the needles in
and Mother pumps the food in
fattening my frailness, readying me for the knife,
not unlike a lamb, a sacrifice.
Whose sacrifice?
For what purpose?
To please or to appease which god?
The knife descends and I am
swathed and ethered in the promise of the oranges.

Bandages, three weeks of my head held prisoner
between immovable, fat sandbags on my pillow;
the bandages are removed, the sutures snipped.
The doctors and my mother wait.
Shall I lie? Shall I say, "I can see!"
The room is very still. The only sounds
are the surgeon's words, "No change," and his footsteps fading down the hall.
I blink and blink but I cannot coax the light into my eyes,
and in that sterile, lifeless place there is no sun.
There are not even oranges.

Fourteen
Crossing Bridges—Challenges and Compromises

After the first of many unsuccessful eye surgeries, my mother and I and Teena returned to Tucson. We were scarcely in the door before neighbors ran over with the town's hottest news item—mine had not been the only mistake Dr. Brown's struggle with alcoholism had caused him to make. More and more misjudgments had ruined his reputation and ultimately impelled him into putting a bullet through his head.

It was good to be back in our little house again and to be well enough to attend the school for blind children, although the first few weeks there were a trial by fire.

"Nobody's going to lead you by the hand around here," Cora, a brilliant, totally self-sufficient older student had told me. "You have to learn to get from building to building independently."

Cora took it upon herself to be my personal coach for this new sport of traveling alone in a new place in the dark. She would take me to different areas of the grounds, the school building, dining hall, shop, gym, infirmary, primary hall, and dormitories and leave me stranded with an airy, "Okay, find your way back to the girls' dorm."

Stumbles, falls, crashes into fences, bushes, and other obstacles resulting in many bumps, bruises, and cuts prescribed my daily wardrobe. Fortunately, ankle-length skirts were popular then and I wore them to hide a multitude of injuries to my legs that would have certainly provoked my mother's questions and investigation. I didn't want her to know what was going on at school. To be honest, I don't know if I hid my wounds to protect her feelings or my pride. There were accident related consequences I could not keep hidden. One in particular spanned a two month period of complete bedrest waiting for the hemorrhage in my right eye to subside.

Changes had been made to the physical education program in the school and, while the boys were fortunate enough to remain with the wrestling coach who had brought them and continued to bring them to state championships year after year, the girls acquired a new teacher who had an ambitious agenda.

113

Miss K decided we should engage in more strenous exercise than gymnastics on mats and dancing the schottische. Our first time out with her she wanted to see us run in competition against one another. Because the Tucson sun was extremely bright, she stood at the finish line, elbows up, hands shielding her eyes. It was so exhilarating to be running freely and, I assumed safely, that I poured every ounce of energy into the race. The only thing that stopped me was my right eye slamming into her left elbow. "I thought you had enough sight to see me standing here," she exclaimed. And although I didn't reply, I wondered why someone with 20-20 vision hadn't seen me coming. Eventually the pain and hemorrhaging became so severe that the only feasible treatment was enucleation and replacement with a prosthesis.

I was so relieved to be liberated from the intense pain and the con-finemnet to bed that I introduced a touch of levity to the situation by nick-naming the prosthesis, "Eye junior." Occasionally irritation to the eye sock-et required attention and on one of our trips to the doctor, he administered drops and told us to wait in the waiting room for a time to see if the med-ication would be effective. After an hour, my mother asked, "How is Junior feeling now?" A woman standing beside us cried out in a horrified tone, "Don't tell me that poor child is pregnant!"

Back at school, my fear soon changed to humiliation at every failure and I became stubbornly determined to move as independently around the cam-pus as the rest of the "blindies." Eventually I managed it, but I never did acquire the same facility in mobility as the children who had been born blind or who had lost their sight at a very early age. They seemed to have a more sophisticated system of radar built into their brain, onto their skin, and into their sense of spatial orientation.

Mike, a senior the year I entered the school, was famous for his expertise. He could leave something on a table or a desk and when he came back for it, he could walk directly to the spot and place his hand immediately on the object without groping for it. He and many other students traveled alone in town without assistance from a dog or a cane.

The school housed another group of pupils, the deaf. We each lived in our own separate worlds of different dormitories and classrooms, crossing the threshold of our handicaps only when one of the partially sighted chil-dren could see well enough to distinguish the sign language of the deaf or one of the "deafies" could read lips or hear well enough to communicate with us. Some of the blind bridged the gap by learning sign language. By feeling the position of the deaf student's fingers, we could identify the sign language alphabet and read their spelled-out words. For other bigger motions, the deafie would take our hands and show us the gestures being made. A partially deaf boy surprised me once as he guided my hands through the pattern he was making—a finger on his chest, a crossing of his hands over his heart, and a finger pointing at me—"I love you."

Those of us who knew the deaf alphabet code often used it among ourselves for privacy. It was useful everywhere. We signed messages into each other's hands and no one else would know what we were communicating. It usually worked out very well except when Larry, a newly blinded teenager, and I were sitting in the back seat of a car on our way home from a picnic. Larry tried several times to sign something into my hand, but I, for a reason unknown to me at the time, simply could not decode his finger patterning and understand what he was trying to tell me. In frustration, he pulled his hand away. "Forget it," he said gloomily and refused to speak to any of us for the rest of the ride home.

The incident haunted me for days. It disturbed me that I had hurt his feelings. From the moment Larry had entered the school it was obvious that he was profoundly unhappy and I certainly didn't want to add to his misery. Somehow we all knew that not only did he have to come to terms with his new blindness, but also with his mother's abandonment when he had suddenly lost his sight. Finally, I confided my concern to my mother. "The firecrackers that blinded Larry also blew off his thumbs," she told me. "It's impossible for him to form the sign language alphabet without them." Mystery solved—conscience cleared.

Like normal children and teenagers, we sometimes took advantage of one another. We commented none too kindly if a deafie needed deodorant or made gruesome noises trying to speak, but their unkindness was more pronounced than ours. Many a small blind child issuing from the dining room with a treasured apple or orange was left empty-handed and crying because a deafie had snatched the fruit and run away with it. Or, worse still, one of their favorite tricks was to extend a foot or anything they might have available in our path to trip us.

Both groups of students came together in the dining hall where a deafie, who sat at the head of the table, was assigned to dish out the food onto the blind children's plates. Since I went home every day, I wasn't compelled to eat the foul-smelling horsemeat, liver, and other more undistinguishable food. I seldom consumed more than my slice of bread and the fruit of the day.

I was also immune to Mrs. Morgan, the deaf woman who supervised the dining hall. She had decided it was her responsibility to break some of the blind children's habit of slouching, head down, at the table. Quietly she would walk up behind the child's chair and jab the prongs of a fork into the small of any back that was not sitting up straight. Thanks to my mother's daily reminders—"Sit up straight. Stand up right, put your shoulders back! Hold your head up—" I was never one of Mrs. Morgan's victims. She always passed me by with a friendly pat on my shoulder.

The partially sighted girls were enlisted to help at the tables. Clare, a quiet, frail youngster, suffered from double vision and from Mrs. Morgan's daily wrath. It was Clare's job to pour the milk which, because of her double imaging, she would often aim at the glass that wasn't there.

"Why don't you hold the glass in your left hand as you pour with your right," I suggested one day when she had been slapped for pouring milk onto the table. "That way you know where the real glass is and you won't try to pour into the double."

When mashed potatoes, turkey, an edible vegetable, and ice cream were served at lunch, we knew the state legislators were scheduled to make their annual visit that day.

Despite the daily unpleasantness at school, it was good to be with other young people, to establish friendships that would last a lifetime and to learn Braille and be able to read again.

Best of all, it was good to be well enough for my special Saturday morning outings. Every week at eight o'clock my mother drove me to a riding stable. George, the owner, had decided I should ride with Ben, an elderly stable hand who was the perfect personification of the stereotypical silent cowboy. Actually, I preferred the lack of conversation because I could pretend I was riding alone on my own golden palomino.

"Put her on Cleo," George had told Ben the first morning, and for a few weeks we rode around the stable grounds or down tourist paths. Cleo was old and plodding, and I was beginning to grow impatient with what seemed to be little more than the riding I had done in Chicago.

And then one Saturday Ben announced, "You're getting a different horse, Lady-Sassy. She's real perky, but we'll handle her. You ain't never gonna learn to ride on a horse that's already half-dead."

With the change to Lady-Sassy, Ben's personality also changed dramatically. "Sit up," he would bark. "The saddle ain't no bed," or "Let go the saddle horn, Missy, it ain't meant to be your hitching post," or "Shorten the reins. You're givin' her too much head. She's gotta know you're in control or that black devil'll take you clear to the moon."

And slowly, my fantasies were being realized. With Ben riding close at my left, I began riding across the desert, across dried river beds, up and down the mountain foothills.

"You ride good enough to start jumpin'," he said after a year of Saturdays. "You game?"

"Oh, yes," I said eagerly. "I've always wanted to jump. How will I do it?"

"I'll let you know when we're getting close to the gate—figure, maybe five or six strides away—pull her head up when I tell you and grip hard with your knees, lean into her neck. Ain't hard. We'll start low."

"Now," he would shout above the pounding of the horses' hooves and I would pull up on the reins to lift Lady-Sassy's head and prepare myself and the horse for the jump. Up we'd go over the gate. I would feel her legs rise off the ground and for a matter of seconds we were in flight, suspended in air...free! It was glorious! It was everything my daydreams had promised.

"You ever square dance?" Ben asked one afternoon as we rode along.

Bianca, age 12, riding Lady-Sassy

"No," I said. "I never have, but I like the music. It sounds like fun."

"The stable runs a horseback square dance club," Ben explained. "Lady-Sassy knows most of the steps already. All you gotta do is ride. You game?"

"Sure," I said, drawing Lady-Sassy to a stop. "Let's try it right now."

"Okay," said Ben. "But it ain't gonna be easy with no music. The music's what gets 'em going, believe it or not."

He began to sing in a high-pitched whine, imitating a fiddle. I laughed in surprise. Ben stopped the song and laughed, a deep rumbling sound in his chest. It was the first time I had heard him even hint at jocularity.

"What do I do?" I asked.

"Just ride. Lady's gonna do all the work. First off she's gotta start circlin'. She's been a-doin' it with the class so she knows what to do."

He reached over and tugged hard at the horse's reins to start her moving in circular motion.

"Yeow-yeow!" he shouted. "Son of a...."

"What's wrong, Ben?" I cried. "What happened?"

"She bit my knee, that ornery brat! We gotta go back so I can tend to it. We'll try the dancin' again next week with the record."

But the next Saturday, Ben wasn't there. George greeted me as my mother dropped me off for my weekly adventure.

"Ben passed," he said gruffly. "Couple days ago, heart attack, but we got a young fella for you to ride with, girlie. This here's Jake coming with Lady-Sassy."

Ben's replacement came forward with the horse. Mechanically I grasped the saddle horn, slipped my boot into the stirrup, and swung onto the saddle. I was numb. What would it be like to ride without Ben? I had grown fond of the taciturn old man. He had taught me so much over the two years we had ridden together. I would miss him.

I lifted the reins, tested the length of the stirrups against the arch of my boots, settled into the saddle, and gave Lady-Sassy my clucking signal. We didn't need a dig of the heel to communicate.

"Hold on there," said Jake. "Don't go nowhere yet. I gotta tie this here leader rope to Lady-Sassy 'fore we ride. She's a spunky one, gotta make sure she don't do nothing wild with you aboard."

"Tie a what?"

"A leader rope. You know," he said as he stood beside Lady-Sassy, "so I can keep a holt of you."

I bristled. "I don't need any leader rope! I never had one when I rode with Ben," I argued, feeling my face getting hot.

"Sure you did," said Jake and there was laughter in his voice. "You didn't never know it?"

A great weakness flooded over me and I had to grip the saddle horn to keep myself from swaying. With an enormous effort I gathered my sense of

118

balance and composure and spoke to the offensive young oaf who had replaced my friend.

"I'm not riding today." The words were simple, my voice calm, but I was trembling uncontrollably. "Would you call my mother and ask her to come back for me please?"

I was shaken, disappointed, angry. I wanted to cry, to throw something, but I slid off the horse, stroked her beautiful velvet nose for the last time, and leaned against a nearby fence to wait.

"You sure you don't wanta ride just a little ways?" asked Jake.

"I'm sure."

He dismounted and I heard him walking the horses back toward the stable. George came out to meet him. "What's wrong? Why ain't she ridin'?"

"I ain't sure, Boss. Maybe she don't wanna ride without Ben," Jake was explaining. "She was shakin' something fierce up there on the saddle, must be scared without the old man. Tell Molly to call her ma."

The betrayal was bitter, scarring. And as I stood there stroking the colt Valentine who had come over to search my shirt pocket for the cube of sugar I always brought him, a gnawing question began seeping into my mind. If I had been deceived about the leader rope, could it be that the palomino promise had also been a lie? I held the sugar on my palm and the colt swooped it up and nuzzled my shoulder. I rubbed his soft neck. I would miss him, too.

"What happened?" asked my mother as she walked me to the car.

"Did you know Ben had a leader rope on me all this time?" I demanded.

"Yes."

"Why?" I almost shouted.

"Think about it," my mother said reasonably. "You want to ride. You enjoy it, but it could be dangerous. What if the horse decided to bolt?"

"I know how to ride," I said defensively.

"I know you do, Bianca," said my mother, "but George wanted to use the rope for his own protection as well as yours and I agreed."

We had reached the car and I slid into the passenger side. I didn't want to ask the question that churned and boiled in my being, but I did.

"And the palomino promise?" I asked wearily. "That was a lie, too, wasn't it?"

"Not a lie exactly," my mother's voice was sympathetic. "More a hope, a motivation for living, a compensation for loss."

As she turned on the car motor, George walked up to my open window. "See you next week, girlie," he said. "Jake's real good with horses. You don't need to be scared or nothin'."

I didn't answer. As we pulled away from the stables that had brought so much joy into my life, I knew something within me had changed, some spark had been snuffed out by the deception, no matter how well-meaning and practical it might have been. "I'm never going back there again," I said.

My mother protested, "That's silly! You enjoy it. What's the difference if you have a rope on the horse or not? It's the same ride."

"No," I said vehemently. "It's not the same at all." I knew she knew better, and she knew I knew.

We drove home in silence. What was there to say? I had just been abruptly tumbled off a comfortable plateau of what I had believed was a fulfillment, an achievement. From the depths of my disillusion, the climb to the next level of reality with its limitations and necessary compromises loomed before me, as elusive as the ride over mountains had once been. At fourteen, challenges didn't daunt me. Compromises did.

Fortunately, new challenges on which I could concentrate would fill some of the Saturday morning void. My life was brimming with plans for the university and a trip back east to Morristown for a Seeing Eye dog. Writing the valedictorian address I was to deliver and practicing the Chopin "Fantasy Impromptu" for the commencement program wouldn't leave much time for brooding.

When the following Saturday morning arrived, my mother rose at the usual time and went into the kitchen. I knew she was waiting to see if I had changed my mind and if she would be driving me to the stables.

"We have to use Saturdays for walking now," I said as I sat down to breakfast. "I have to get in shape for my dog training. I should be hearing from the Seeing Eye any day now. You game?"

I heard the echo of Ben's husky bass asking that old familiar question and I felt my bitterness already beginning to ebb away. In time I would treasure fond memories of Lady-Sassy and the elderly stable hand. Eventually, I would be grateful for the deception that allowed his encouragement and discipline to enrich my early teen years. Above all, time would enable me to recognize and appreciate the wisdom of my mother's palomino promise.

Fifteen
"Nothing to Hit Out There but a Cactus!"

I heard the familiar squeak of Charlie's Buick at the curb, a slam of the car door, his quick footsteps along the walk leading to the front door. He was whistling. He swung open the screen and bounded, all energy and cheerfulness, into the living room.

I was at the piano, practicing a Chopin étude with its myriad clusters of runs and jumping octaves.

"Come on, kiddo, you're going to get your first driving lesson!"

I was nearly fifteen. Charlie was twenty-two.

"You're joking, right?" I asked, still concentrating on the fingering pattern for one of the many chromatic passages that swarm through the piece like hundreds of working bees.

"I don't joke. Only girls from Chicago joke. I kid, but I'm not kidding. We'll head out to the desert. There's nothing to hit out there but a cactus."

I stopped practicing and shut the piano lid down to keep the ever-drifting fine Tucson sand off the keys. Charlie had definitely introduced an exciting prospect. "I'll have to call Mom at her office....," I began.

He interrupted. "Okay, but just tell her we're going for a drive. You don't have to mention who'll be driving."

We slid into the Buick. Although it was not new, it smelled of leather polish. Charlie had bought the car just last month after the engine on his motor bike exploded one day on his way to our house from the university.

A ten-minute ride took us to the Catalina foothills, wide-open desert. Charlie stopped the car and jumped out. "Move over under the steering wheel," he called out to me as he ran around to the passenger side of the car.

"I suppose I should show you how the gear shift works first," he mused. "Think of the capital letter 'H.' Do you remember what a print 'H' looks like?" and the lesson proceeded. I practiced positioning the floor stick shift until he was satisfied.

121

"The gas pedal is all the way to the right. The brake is next to it. Keep your left foot on it very lightly just in case. Some of these cactus are as big as an apartment building in Flatbush. Now, turn the key."

I reached for the dashboard and found a clump of keys dangling down. I took hold of the one in the keyhole and turned it.

Suddenly a ton of living steel and rubber and motor was vibrating and roaring beneath me. We lurched forward. My heart was in my throat and I gripped the steering wheel hard. "It would be convenient to know where I'm going," I exclaimed and Charlie just laughed.

"Clear road ahead," he said. "Feed her a little more gas. Keep the wheel straight."

My head was pounding with exhilaration and fear.

"I'd rather be in a saddle. At least I'd know what I'm doing!"

"You're doing fine," Charlie assured me but I knew he must have been a bit rattled because his next sentence was all Brooklyn. "Wouldn't you rather have 110 hosses unda yeh than just one old nag?"

"I don't ride old nags," I said in my defense, shifting my position on the car seat. My foot inadvertently pressed down on the gas pedal and the car lunged forward.

Charlie shouted, "Turn right, right, right, quick!" He reached for the steering wheel and cranked furiously. "Man," he breathed, "that cactus came very close to meeting its maker and I don't mean its mother!"

After I had taken my foot off the gas altogether and we had caught our breath, he said good-humouredly, "Good lesson, kiddo, but I think I'll drive home today if you don't mind."

It was a week later. "Come on, kiddo, never mind driving lessons today. I'm teaching you how to shoot. I've got my .22 in the car. That's a good light rifle to start with. By the way, how'd you like that venison I brought a couple of days ago?"

Charlie and I were buddies. I didn't want to hurt his feelings, but I didn't want any more wild deer meat either, so I decided to be honest. "Well," I began, "even the dog wouldn't eat it. If you absolutely have to shoot something, stick to chickens."

He was a little hurt but undaunted. "Let's go out on the desert," he said. "There's nothing to hit out there but a cactus."

Ten minutes and we were back at the Catalina Foothills.

"Hold the rifle like this, up on your shoulder. I guess we don't have to concern ourselves with getting the target in the sights for you. I'll throw some rocks at a tin can I brought and you shoot at the sound."

Ping bang. Ping bang. Ping bang.

"This is fun," I said, lowering the rifle, "but this thing's really heavy!"

"Don't point at your foot, for God's sake! You want to shoot it off?" Charlie exclaimed as he took the rifle out of my hands. He continued more calmly, almost apologetically, "Your mom's not going to be happy with me if I bring you home with only your left foot."

Charlie's sister Flora came from California for a visit and she, Charlie, my mother, and I decided to play pioneers and share an overnight camp-out on Mt. Lemon. We spent the afternoon hiking and climbing, resting and descending. My mother and Flora needed a prolonged rest midway down to our camp site. Charlie and I, hand-in-hand, went exploring.

"Can I walk on my own?" I asked, "or would I fall off a cliff?"

"Sure you can. This is a good-sized plateau. It's safe enough—no sharp drop-offs—plenty of sagebrush and cactus though, go slow."

He released my hand and I moved quickly away, reveling in my freedom.

"There's some strange-looking tracks along here, big ones," Charlie said, "I wonder if they could be bear tracks." And in that moment of distraction when he was studying his discovery, my right foot jammed into something, something solid and sharp—a cactus. Fortunately my thick leather cowboy boot was the only victim and I was giddy with relief. "Oops," I giggled, "there's nothing to hit out here but a cactus and I just did."

Charlie spun around from his contemplation of the tracks. He was mumbling words under his breath which I pretended I didn't hear.

"Sit down," he said unhappily. "Let's see how much damage we have to deal with." We sat on the ground and he took my foot on his lap and carefully began pulling out the long penetrating spines. Their sharpness had scarcely scraped my foot, but he kept mumbling to himself.

"It's a good thing you had enough sense not to tangle with a hook cactus," he said. "We would have really had a problem."

"I use my head," I said.

"Maybe you do," he said, disgruntled, "but obviously I don't."

The operation complete, we stood. "I'm holding on to this," he said, grabbing my hand, and we started back to where we left my mother and Flora.

Charlie built a fire and cooked hamburgers and corn on the cob over the open flame. We talked away the evening and as darkness began to wrap the mountain chill around us, we unloaded our sleeping bags from the car.

"Let's bed down here next to this big log," Charlie suggested. "I'll stretch a rope in a circle around us to keep the snakes away."

I froze in my old terror. "I'll sleep in the car," I said, "with the windows rolled up and the doors locked."

He laughed. "Trust me. I guarantee you, a rope will keep us all safe. Snakes don't crawl over ropes. I read it somewhere."

I lay stiff with fear in my sleeping bag between Charlie and my mother.

Not even the bats that poured out of the dead log at our heads frightened me as much as the thought of that other unmentionable thing.

"Maybe I shouldn't have bedded us down next to a hollow log," Charlie said thoughtfully as the clouds of bats rose out of the dead tree and squeaked their way into the night.

"But what do I know about camping in Arizona? I'm just an Italian guy from Brooklyn whose mother got asthma and dragged us all out here."

After a moment his naturally happy disposition surfaced and he resorted to an old joke of his. "As a matter of fact," he said confidentially, "I came to Tucson for my arthritis and I'm not leaving until I get it."

I knew Charlie's comedy was aimed at relieving my apprehension, but it did nothing to dispel my rigid terror.

"Can snakes smell fear like dogs can?" I asked.

"Sorry," Charlie said, yawning, "I don't know what snakes can smell. The article I read didn't deal with their five senses."

"Come on, Charlie!"

In the darkness he recognized not only my annoyance but my panic. He turned over in his sleeping bag and planted his palm on my cheek.

"Come on yourself," he said soothingly. "Stop being silly. Snakes don't even have decent noses." He pressed his thumb against the tip of my nose. "They certainly don't have a nose like yours that can smell the moon when it hasn't showered."

I lay sleepless for what seemed a millennium, listening to my fellow campers' steady breathing, listening for any unusual rustling or rattling sounds. I burrowed deep inside my sleeping bag, allowing myself just enough exposure to the cold night mountain air to breathe. Now and then the incredible stillness vibrated with the echo of an owl's unearthly cry. Whose crazy idea was this camp-out anyway, I wondered, longing for my neat, warm, secure bedroom.

Finally, morning dawned and we climbed back into the Buick and started down the mountain for home.

Charlie and I had met in a radio station where my grandfather was conducting a series of programs. My mother's father had come from Florence and had moved into our little Tucson house with us. With him he brought Old World arrogance and intolerance and an autocratic military bearing inbred in him by years as an officer in the Italian cavalry.

Our quiet, pleasant duet of a life was abruptly and forcefully disrupted by a demanding man with a temper and an old-school European education and attitude.

He was a complex human being, intelligent and multifaceted, dictatorial and gentle, resentful and loving. He stormed at the incompetence of American politicians who, in his eyes, compared miserably to his beloved Mussolini. My grandfather had been not only a follower but also a friend to the dictator. One of his most cherished possessions was a photograph of himself in Mussolini's open car, both men standing and waving to the

Bianca's Grandfather, Comandante Guglielmo Maggini

crowd. That photo was a great source of anxiety to my mother. It had made its way to the front pages of newspapers and eventually into a chapter in a textbook.

"I hope no one ever finds out that the man with Mussolini in that picture is my father," she would worry.

"The war's been over for years, Mom," I would try to reassure her, not realizing how far the fingers of hatred can reach.

My grandfather was consumed with bitterness at the fall of the Fascist regime and the ignominy of Mussolini's death. He raged at and wept over accounts and photographs of his leader hanging from his feet at the hands of his own countrymen, "*i partigiani,*" a name which my grandfather seemed to spit from his mouth like a venomous substance.

Great music could also make him weep—Mimi's death scene in *La Bohème*, the Mozart Requiem, and much more. His irritability often gave way to moods of great tenderness when he would stroke my hair with tremulous and affectionate hands every time he came near me. Often he would poke a bit of apple into my canary's cage and say more to himself than to me, "This tiny creature soothes and refines the soul."

No doubt his naturally volatile temperament suffered torturously at the harshness of his months in a concentration camp. At the fall of Fascism, his own personal chauffeur had reported him to authorities and he had been arrested and tossed into one of the many camps that had sprung up around the country. There he waited, scheduled to be shot. By bribing a guard with a pack of cigarettes, he managed, with the man's help, to hide himself in an outgoing refuse wagon. Reeking but alive, he rolled out of the camp under potato peels, coffee grinds, and worse.

Despite the fact that he was safe and comfortable with us, he perpetually attacked with scathing criticism and contempt the new lifestyle and environment my illness had forced on us.

"Doesn't anyone know how to say good morning or good afternoon in this godforsaken country?" he would roar after taking a walk down our road. "Everybody I meet says 'HI' as though someone were stepping on their toes.

"Where's all your crystal? I was looking for the shrimp cocktail cups with the hollow stems for crushed ice. I thought you might buy some shrimp one of these days."

Times were hard, but even he hadn't realized how hard. My mother hadn't been able to buy shrimp since she and I left Chicago.

"The radio programs are abominable in this part of the world. I can only find cowboy or Mexican music. Doesn't anybody around here know what 'real' music is? When are you going to buy a record player so I can play my own records?"

It soon became evident that we had to find something to occupy his time and enormous nervous energy. One evening as he was turning the radio dial and complaining, my mother suggested, "Why don't you write a proposal for a classical music program? There aren't any, as you well know, and maybe the local station would let you host the program."

The next afternoon when my mother returned from work, the three of us drove to the local station and my grandfather, an outline of a series of programs in hand, asked for an hour a week of air time. To our joy and relief, the station manager was happy to grant it.

Masterpiece Hour aired Fridays at seven P.M. and my grandfather spent each week happily selecting which of his records he would play and preparing notes for his commentaries.

Letters of appreciation from listeners waited at the station for him every week. One evening a family was also waiting for him, Mr. and Mrs. Lombardo and their son Charles.

"Congratulations and thank you," said Mr. Lombardo. "Listening to your program we feel as though we're back in civilization. We had to move out here from Brooklyn because of my wife's asthma. This is our son Charles," Mr. Lombardo continued. "He graduated from Annapolis and is working on his masters at the university."

"We especially enjoy your opera selections," Mrs. Lombardo had said in her breathy whisper. "Our daughter Flora studied opera at Juilliard, but unfortunately, she couldn't perform—terrible stage fright, just froze. She's a chemist in California."

As we waited for my grandfather's program to finish, we settled on a long leather couch in a room outside the studio. My mother and the Lombardos slipped immediately into a comfortable Italian conversation.

"Can you speak that?" Charlie asked as he sat down beside me.

"Yes," I said. "Can you?"

"More or less," he muttered. "Mostly less."

The hour sped by and when my grandfather joined us Charlie jumped up and flipped his car keys out of his pocket.

"Let's go for pizza," he suggested and we followed the family to La Cucina, the only Italian restaurant in town.

"You teach me to read and write Braille," Charlie had bartered as we ate our pizza, "and I'll teach you the Morse Code. I have some extra equipment borrowed from the Navy—I'm in the Reserves—and I can set you up with a ham station."

And so the friendship had begun. Like a sudden burst of warm weather after a brutal winter or a cooling evening rain after an oppressive summer afternoon, the laughter and good-natured *joie de vivre* that emanated from Charlie permeated my own too-serious spirit and reminded me that I was still young.

The phone rang and Charlie, as always, was at the house and answered it. "Hello, this is Covelli's luggage shop. Which old bag do you want to speak to?"

Charlie's energy was limitless. He was always ready to do something, to go somewhere.

"Let's go for ice cream."

"Let's go to the movies."

"In the mood for a picnic? We can swing by the blind school and pick up as many kids as we can cram into the car and go up to Mt. Lemon. I'll grill hot dogs for the gang."

Charlie, brimming with enthusiasm, imagination, and fun, was also practical. He was eating soup with us one evening when he suddenly got up from the table, opened the drawer that held the flatware, and retrieved a tablespoon. He stood still for a moment and then handed the spoon to me.

"Try this," he told me. "I've bent the handle so the soup won't be so likely to spill out when you tip the spoon."

It was a Friday afternoon in April. "I know you like the violin and there's a violin concert at the U tonight. Wanna go? I also know it's close to your birthday. Let's go for hamburgers first and celebrate!"

I dressed up. In 1952 a concert meant a nice dress, possibly a suit. Hanging in my closet was a new white linen suit just waiting to be initiated.

At six o'clock Charlie flung open the screen door. He was whistling. "Come here, kiddo, hold still," he said, pinning a clump of sweet peas on the lapel of my suit.

Surprised and pleased, I teased, "My goodness, Charles, is this a real date?"

He laughed. "That remains to be seen."

"We'll just go for a Coke or an ice cream after the concert," Charlie told my mother. "We'll be back early. I have exams tomorrow."

As he and my mother chatted, I began to feel ill. My eyes began to sting and water. Breathing was difficult.

"I don't know what's wrong," I said, distressed, "but I can't go to a concert feeling like this."

Charlie left as I went into my bedroom, removed the sweet peas and suit and got back into my jeans. I dropped onto the bed to steady my breathing and in a few minutes, all the symptoms disappeared. The flowers—of course! My allergies!

I telephoned Charlie. Neither of us wanted to attempt the concert again but he came back to the house. We popped popcorn and listened to my new recordings of Dvorak's New World Symphony and cello concerto. An RCA cabinet record player was now gracing our living room. My mother was buying it on an installment plan to appease my grandfather.

The cabinet also housed a radio and every week laughter flowed into our home with George Burns and Gracie Allen, Amos and Andy, Fibber McGee and Molly. At the other end of the spectrum, grim news from Korea filtered in, but it was not a threat to our quiet, rather isolated existence until the afternoon that Charlie came in the house more subdued than usual and announced, "I'm getting my masters in a few days. You know what that means."

Something in his demeanor alarmed me. Charlie was seldom serious. "My deferment is up. My commission arrived this morning. I'm boarding ship in a week."

"What about graduation?"

"Just a ceremony. Uncle Sam won't wait. The school will mail my sheepskin."

I suddenly remembered that my mother's only brother, a pilot in the Italian Air force, died in a fiery crash in Ethiopia with his discharge papers in his pocket during World War II. I was scarcely two years old when it happened and too young to experience the grief of it, but images of photos of my grandparents taken at Christmas that year filled my mind. My grandmother's face was a gaunt, heavy-lidded mask of herself. Her luminous brown eyes were barely focused. They seemed to float in a dark reflection of the palpable shadow of her sorrow. My grandfather, jaw set, mustache brisk, steel-blue eyes staring, stood beside an adorned Christmas tree with me in his arms. Despite the loss of their only son, they hadn't denied me the holiday.

My only other exposure to war, living as my mother and I did in a quiet suburb of Chicago, had been a series of posters on street corners where the names of the service men and women from that neighborhood were posted. Beside some names a gold star would sometimes appear and, although I knew what it signified, the reality of death had been beyond the scope of my comprehension until a woman in a blue morning glory apron had claimed one of the starred names as her son's. Still, to me, the war meant little more than the stamps we exchanged for meat or shoes or sugar.

Now, years later, another war was truly infiltrating my life. My awareness was sharpened into personal anxiety as my friend, my surrogate big brother, told me he would be a part of the Korean conflict that, until this moment, had been only a part of radio newscasts from a far-distant corner of the world.

"I'm driving out to L.A. to stay with Flora a couple of days and then I'm off to San Diego."

"When are you leaving?" I dreaded the answer, but I had to know.

"Tonight. My mother's already getting raspy, no use prolonging the goodbye ordeal and having her get sick."

He gave me a long, hard bear hug and said in a husky tone of voice I hadn't heard from him before, "So long, kiddo. Be good. Don't hit any cactus while I'm gone."

The silences Charlie left behind were palpable. His merry, disjointed whistling, the squeak of his car at the curb, the bang of the screen door slamming behind him; his buoyant, "Hi, kiddo" had too suddenly and abruptly disappeared. The house seemed to echo without his animated presence and I was aware that I was not so young and alive as I had become in the wake of Charlie's adventurous good nature.

Months passed. No letters came, no postcards, nothing. Finally Mr. Lombardo telephoned my grandfather with the news that Charlie's ship would be docked in San Diego for a few days.

"We're due to go to California for your eye check-up," my mother reminded me. "Flora invited us to stay at her place and we could make your doctor's appointment for when Charlie's in town."

All the way from Tucson to Los Angeles on a rumbling Greyhound bus I was torn between excitement and apprehension. Would Charlie be the same? Would his months at sea, his involvement in the war, have changed him?

We arrived at Flora's apartment at dawn. Charlie was due sometime before noon.

"Have you talked to him?" I asked his sister.

"No, he sent a wire."

"Oh."

"What's wrong? What are you worrying about?"

"Do you think he'll be different," I finally voiced my doubts, "I mean with the war and everything?"

Flora just laughed. "Who, Charlie? Not a chance! Charlie will never change. He'll be the same funny guy when he's a grandfather."

There was a loud knock at the door and without waiting for an invitation, Charlie swung in with a jolly, "Hi, everybody. I'm here!" I held my breath. He seemed the same—energetic, good-humored. His sister ran up to hug him. My mother followed. I stood still, shy, waiting.

He strode across the room.

"Come on, kiddo," he said, grasping my hand in a tight grip hello. "I've rented a day sailor. Thought I'd give you a lesson. Wanna learn how to sail a boat?"

"Sure," I agreed happily. "There's nothing to hit out there but a cactus."

Epilogue

Charlie remained in California after his discharge from the Navy, married his sister's roommate, and fathered three sons. On a business trip through New York he stopped in for a few moments to see me and meet Phil and our infant daughter.

"I must have been crazy," he said, "to encourage you to do all the nutty things we did. When I think of the dangers I exposed you to I cringe."

"I loved every minute of it," I assured him. "You expanded my horizons just when they needed expanding."

We chatted about his job, his wife, and his boys for a time, and then he jumped up from the couch and flipped his car keys out of his pocket. That quick, impulsive gesture turned the calendar back in my mind to the evening we had met at the radio station. "I've gotta run, gotta catch a plane!" He grabbed my hand and pulled me to him for one of his bear hugs. "Great seeing you! You've made a beautiful baby. Congratulations." He turned as he ran down the porch steps and called to me where I stood in the doorway, "Ciao! Don't forget, kiddo, there's nothing to hit out there but a cactus."

Sixteen
On My Way

"What difference does it make how old I am?" I raged as my mother read me the letter of rejection from the Seeing Eye School. The unbelievable words being read aloud to me stung. They rang in my ears with the clamor of the ultimate injustice.

"It is school policy that all applicants be at least eighteen years of age. We regret...."

I was not about to accept the school's decision without a fight. Sitting down at my typewriter, I fired off a letter that crossed the border from forceful to rude. "I absolutely need a guide dog to navigate the campus of the university I'm scheduled to attend in September. I know I'm just fifteen, but what am I supposed to do," I demanded, "put my scholarship, my entire life on hold for three years, sit around and weave baskets while my idle brain turns to jelly?"

The school wrote back a much more civil response than the one it received from me. "If you can provide a letter of permission from your parents, three letters of recommendation from teachers, one from the principal of your school, and a favorable health report from your physician, we may reconsider. Keep in mind that you will be expected to fulfill all the requirements for graduation and that the four weeks of training are extremely rigorous. Our day begins at six A.M. and ends at eight P.M. Our students must groom, feed, and be responsible for their dogs at all times. You must be prepared to walk an average of five miles a day...."

While I waited for my acceptance, my mother and I walked miles on dusty desert roads in preparation. In addition, my high school gym teacher and I swam at the YWCA pool every Sunday afternoon. We swam lap after lap and then went home for a Sunday dinner of pasta and my mother's homemade sauce.

A month into our swimming regime, I fell ill and missed a pool date. The illness persisted—fever, severe muscle spasms, a terrible weakness. The doctor standing beside my bed said softly, "Polio!" The onset was mild, affecting only my left leg. Within a few weeks my mother and I were walking again, strengthening damaged muscles and retraining nerve endings. I ignored the pain as though it were an unpleasant presence, an irritation to be tolerated best by not acknowledging it.

"I'm going walking," I would announce to my left side, vigorously slapping my thigh, "and unfortunately for both of us, you have to come with me whether you like it or not so you might as well behave." I refused to allow a little bout of illness and a stubborn leg to become obstacles to the new life awaiting me at the university.

There was also another issue to be addressed—the fee for the training and the dog: $250. I was consumed by the desire to buy my own dog, but what kind of job could I find? The jobs for so-called normal teens were out of my reach. Who would leave a baby with a blind babysitter? I couldn't walk dogs, couldn't deliver papers.

"Don't worry about the money," said my mother. "We can pay for the dog."

"I know we can," I said stubbornly, "but I want to pay for it myself if I can."

The acceptance from the Seeing Eye had not yet come when my mother arrived at my school one afternoon to pick me up and said, "Guess what I have in the trunk."

"A horse!"

"Not quite," she said, "but I do have the job you need for your dog."

"Really? What is it?"

The office building where she worked as administrator for the Tucson Public School Health Department also housed the Crippled Children's Association headquarters. "Mr. Howenstein, the director of C.C.A., gave me a thousand envelopes to be stuffed and mailed for a fund raiser," she explained. "I'm sure you can do it. He'll pay you the exact amount you need for your dog."

I was young enough and naive enough to believe in the lucky coincidence!

We carried the heavy boxes of envelopes and letters into the house and made a workroom on my bedroom desk. The job was simple and pleasurable. I listened to my records or "Talking Books" and earned money at the same time. There were two sheets to be put into each envelope, one a letter on regular paper, the other a flyer on slick, glossy paper. There was no way I could confuse them. I stuffed and stuffed, sealed and sealed the envelopes every evening after dinner. In my enthusiasm I didn't think about the fact that my mother had to address them all. On the very day the 1,000th envelope was ready for mailing, the letter of acceptance from the Seeing Eye arrived.

"Please get my money from Mr. Howenstein tomorrow," I said as I went to bed that night. "I want to send the check in before they have a chance to change their mind."

Months whirled by. My mother bought me my own set of luggage for the three thousand-mile train trip that would transport me not only from

Tucson, Arizona, to Morristown, New Jersey, but also from the status of a blind school child to a soon-to-be independent university student. Our departure was scheduled for two weeks after graduation.

I wrote my valedictorian address and memorized it without a problem, but the Chopin *Fantaisie-Impromptu* I was to perform at the commencement exercise was a real struggle. The intricate rhythmic and fingering patterns of three beats in the left hand against four in the right had to flow, to imitate a sweep of cascading water. As graduation drew closer and closer, there were still passages that sounded more like rocks flung at a window.

At last, graduation was only a week away and I was taking advantage of every free moment to smooth out the most difficult passages. After lunch every day I slipped into the music room to practice. I was at the task when Mr. Tillinghast, the principal, came to the door.

"Please come into my office," he said quietly. He was a gentle, soft-spoken man. He was also a gracefully smooth dancer who invited me to the privilege of one waltz or foxtrot at every school dance. I looked forward to gliding across the auditorium floor with him, although that one dance only served to accentuate the awkwardness of the boys whose invitations followed his.

I knew students were not allowed to roam the school building unchaperoned when classes were not in session and I had asked permission to use the practice room, so why had Mr. Tillinghast come for me? Was there a problem with my being there?

As I walked down the corridor to the office I thought of another possibility—the incident just that morning with the rosebushes and the groundskeepers. When I had been elected to the Student Council months before, the first thing I had done was create a problem for the administration.

"Planting rosebushes along both sides of the sidewalk leading from the primary hall to the school building was a mistake," I had said at the first council meeting. "One false step and the little kids run into the thorns and get hurt."

"We haven't heard of any problem, sweetie," Miss Russel, the vice principal, had oozed. With the excuse of stroking my long hair, she swept her hand around and tucked my gold Sacred Heart medal into the front of my blouse. For some reason, the students' display of Catholicism disturbed her.

"I have," I persisted, slipping my chain and medal out again. "Every week when the girls come to me for Brownie Scouts, at least two of them tell me they've been scratched. This week it was Lucy on the arm and Bernita on the leg. The roses should really be transplanted to somewhere else on the grounds."

"We'll investigate it," Mr. Tillinghast had promised, and he had followed through.

He hadn't sounded annoyed when he came to get me in the practice room, but I worried that perhaps the groundskeepers might have complained to him about my outburst of that morning. Although the rosebushes were finally being removed, another equally serious hazard was being left unattended.

Since it had become my habit to greet the little girls at the steps of the school building each morning, I had been quickly informed by the buzzing, agitated youngsters of the latest calamity regarding the rosebushes.

"Leroy slipped and fell into one of the holes where the rosebushes used to be," exclaimed Ruth-Ann.

"He hurt his ankle," squeaked Maria.

"Two of the big boys came and had to carry him to the infirmary!" added Ramona breathlessly. "He was crying real bad!" The girls were close to tears themselves.

"Don't worry," I reassured them. "Leroy's tough. He'll be fine." The little cluster of girls shuffled away into the building. I had kept my voice calm so as not to alarm them, but I was anxious about Leroy and angry.

Down the walk I could hear the rapid fire of Spanish being exchanged between two men and the clang of shovels against cement. I approached the sound.

"Excuse me," I said loudly. The conversation and the clanging stopped.

I took a deep breath and plunged in. "Do you know one of the little blind boys fell into one of the rosebush holes you left and injured his ankle?" My face was burning with exasperation and with amazement at my own audacity. I couldn't believe what I was doing, but Leroy was one of my favorites, a bright, spunky, talented eight-year-old warrior who was not only singing with the "big kids'" chorus but soloing. The thought of his having been injured because of carelessness or indifference made me storm on, "Don't you think it would be a smart idea to fill in the holes when you take the bushes out before someone else gets hurt?" I articulated as though I were speaking to hopeless morons.

No reply from the men, but their heavy breathing and body odor, mingled with the smell of cigarettes, hung between us. They were still there and obviously listening. I went on, "It might also be a smart idea to pick up the shovels and not leave them lying around for the kids to trip over, if it isn't too much trouble, that is!"

The bell had rung and I hurried back up the walk to the school building before the men had an opportunity to respond. Had they been offended by my attack, my sarcasm? Had they gone to Mr. Tillinghast to complain?

I was fully aware that my new personality was a surprise to everyone at the school, and that my new attitude probably even grated on some nerves. I had always been quiet, so quiet that I had overheard one of the teachers remark during my first weeks at the school, "I'm convinced she's mentally deficient or if not that, seriously emotionally disturbed."

IQ and achievement tests had been administered which resulted in my being placed, at twelve years old, in the tenth grade. Retardation as the possible source of my silence had been ruled out. In that environment, any emotional problem belonged exclusively to its owner and no one wasted time or effort in exploring or remedying it unless it was causing trouble. Consequently, as I had slowly acclimated myself to this foreign land of the Arizona State School for the Blind, I had gradually emerged from my protective shield of silence and begun to speak, to sing in the chorus and in a girls' trio, to perform piano solos in concert, to conduct a Brownie Scout troop and to tutor my peers as well as the younger children.

"We have to keep the boys off the top three positions of the honor roll by taking the slots ourselves," I would encourage my friends as we sat around the table in the girls' dorm after school and did our homework.

I also bartered with some of the girls. All the students were required to take classes in shop—chair caning for the boys, basket weaving for the girls. I found the procedure intolerably boring. The straw had to be kept wet and pliable by frequent soaks in a large sink of lukewarm water. Around and around the long strips of straw had to be bent and woven, braided in and out of each other to form the basket.

"If you work on my basket," I would bargain with anyone, "I'll help you conjugate your Spanish verbs or help you write your essay for English or help you work out your algebra problems."

Although I was active, I remained placid and respectful until senior year. My plans for the University of Arizona and for my Seeing Eye dog had suddenly given me a new voice and that voice was not always polite. What ramifications were about to spill over on me from the rosebush incident of the morning?

I walked into the office fully prepared for a discussion or a scolding for my assault on the groundskeepers. I was also prepared for the reality that both or either of the possibilities would be accompanied by a wordless confrontation with Miss Russel over my exposed Sacred Heart medal, but I was not prepared for what I found waiting for me there.

The moment I stepped into the office I was accosted by a sense of deep malaise, a sense of foreboding that catapulted into my consciousness on the reek of a cigar. As my eyes began to sting, an old memory assailed me from the earliest days of my blindness. I was suddenly ten years old again and in a room with my parents. My eyes were burning, tearing. I heard my mother's voice again, "Her eyes are very sensitive. The smoke is painful." There was no response from my father, no words of concern, no cessation of his pleasure, only more cigar smoke, more pain.

"Hello, dear," said a deep, strained voice—my father's.

"Hello," I said coolly and waited.

Mr. Tillinghast must have been puzzled by the lack of enthusiasm in both greetings. He asked hesitantly, "Do you know who this man is?"

"Yes," I said. "My father."

And then apologetically he said, "I hope you understand, Judge Covelli, that we can't allow strangers to pick up the children. I had to be certain she knew you and that you were being honest in identifying yourself before I could permit her to leave with you."

"Naturally," said my father. "I appreciate your concern for my little girl." Something in his words and in his fatuously saccharin tone set my teeth on edge.

He grabbed my hand and tucked it firmly under his elbow. Leaning toward Mr. Tillinghast, he extended his other hand. "Thank you, sir," he said amiably.

"You're more than welcome, Judge," the principal responded almost shyly. "We'll see you at the commencement exercises."

My father tugged at my imprisoned arm. "Let's go, dear," he said, taking quick, short steps toward the door.

I pulled away, yanking my hand free from his silk-jacketed arm. "I can't leave. I have afternoon classes," I protested.

"It's all right," said Mr. Tillinghast kindly. "You go right ahead with your dad."

"Does Mom know you were coming here?" I persisted. "She'll be coming to get me after work and I won't be here."

I was fifteen, but I was suddenly afraid, remembering my mother's fear and admonitions when I was very young. "If anyone talks to you on the street or on the school playground or just anywhere and tells you your father sent him, run away, and if he has already grabbed you, scream, scream as loud as you can and somebody will help you."

I made a deliberate effort to quell my anxiety. After all, that was when I had been small. He wouldn't get away with anything like that now. A year ago I had reached the magic age of fourteen, the legal age at which I could choose the parent with whom I wanted to live. My mother and I had waited eagerly for that birthday. We celebrated the special event with a Mexican food party at Pedro's Hacienda.

My father's soft but domineering hand seized mine again and tucked it back under his elbow. "Your mother knows I've come for you. She's waiting at the house. Come on, dear." He was fighting to keep the irritation out of his voice in the principal's presence. I recognized the effort he was making and it gave me a perverse rush of pleasure to realize that my behavior was manipulating him into a situation he was finding annoying.

I walked outside with him and slipped into the car he had parked in front of the school building. My pulse was still racing. I couldn't speak. I didn't want to speak.

The car smelled of new leather. A slam of the driver's door, a jingle of keys, and the motor purred. There was no other sound. We pulled away from the curb, started down the long driveway, through the gates, and were headed to my home, I hoped.

"So," my father began enthusiastically, "you'll be graduating very soon."

"In a week."

"Yes, well, I'm a bit early—came for a vacation and for your graduation, of course."

"Of course," I said dryly. "How nice of you."

There was a long silence.

"Your mother tells me you're top in the class and that you're going to give the graduation address."

"The competition was nonexistent," I said. "There are six of us in the graduating class, only two going to college. The smartest students in the school all graduated last year."

Another long silence.

"What would you like for a graduation gift? Just name it."

In my mind I saw the Chicago apartment my mother and I had lived in for three happy years. I saw my father, who had come to visit, sitting on a gold and white silk armchair and smiling. He had watched my mother go into the kitchen before he had leaned close to me and spoken softly, "If you come and live with me, I'll buy you your own pony."

I had been nine years old, but I recognized a bribe when I heard it. "No, thank you, I don't like horses," I had lied. His marble blue eyes studied my face. Under his relentless scrutiny I had looked away and pretended my shoe needed retying.

Somehow this new offer echoed the same bribery and I was cautious. I had never asked him for anything, but I had once indicated that I did want something.

Another memory flashed into the present. This time I was twelve and I was seated next to my father in a car that smelled and purred very much like the one we were in. Once before, he had come to Tucson for a vacation and had visited us the day before my mother and I were to take the train to L.A. for another of my many eye surgeries. "Your mother tells me you want a collie," he had said.

"Yes, I've wanted one for a long time," I said hopefully.

"Well, I'll tell you what," he went on, "if you're a good girl and can see after this operation, I'll buy you one."

Was he joking? No, he was completely serious. I had been crushed under the burden that his stupidity, insensitivity, or deliberate cruelty was designed to place on me. I had been so stunned by the remark that I had not been able to answer at the time. If he had made the proposal now, my new whip-edged tongue would have found an appropriate response or two. The first one I thought of was—*if I had that kind of power, why would I need you to buy me a collie or anything else?* With just a blink of a sight-filled eye I could have a whole herd of dogs and horses in my backyard.

For a brief moment I wondered if I should ask for the collie now. After his open invitation, he could not refuse, despite the fact that over the years

I had not been a "good girl" and regained my vision. Unfortunately, it was too late for a collie. In just a few days I would have a beautiful, stately, intelligent, and devoted German Shepherd walking beside me.

"I'd like a clarinet," I said. "I've been playing one at school, but I don't have an instrument of my own."

"Done," he said. "I'll buy it tomorrow."

Another long silence.

Where were we really going, I worried nervously. The house never seemed so far away when I was driving home with my mother.

"I understand you're going for a Seeing Eye dog," he said. "I'll give you a check for it when we get to the house."

"The dog is all paid for. I paid for it myself," I said slowly, savoring the words like the first bite of chocolate egg from an Easter basket after forty days of Lent's elected penance.

The words, delicious and powerful, were a shining reminder to myself. I relaxed and leaned comfortably against the smooth, contoured leather interior of the humming car. Graduation, my freedom through canine eyes, the university with its opportunities for exciting classes, and a return to the world of the sighted hovered within my reach. I realized that the new me, outspoken and confident, no longer had to be afraid of this man who was my father or of much else, for that matter. I was on my way to a future brimming with as much promise and fulfillment as I could pour into it.

I smiled inwardly and I rejoiced with the sudden, acute awareness that my own resurrection was at hand.

Seventeen
Norma

$\mathscr{T}$hermometers in Tucson registered 110° that afternoon in August when I stepped off the train with Norma.

Despite the Seeing Eye School's initial apprehension about my age, I had completed the four weeks of intense training and was returning home with my new canine guide companion. Brimming with enthusiasm at my new independence, my eagerness for the college life that was about to unfold for me knew no bounds.

My mother, who had accompanied me to New Jersey, was returning to Arizona with a new development in her own life—an engagement ring sparkling on her finger. While I had been in training, she had stayed in a hotel in New York and had passed the time contacting old friends from years before. One evening as she and a girl friend were dining, she looked up to see her dead brother's best friend, Enrico, standing beside her. He had been dining in the same restaurant and had spotted her from across the room. An old friendship had quickly flowered into romance and their wedding was pending the annulment of her marriage to my father.

Norma and I walked briskly across the platform. The day was hot but the air was dry and clear, pleasantly light compared to the oppressive humidity of the New Jersey summer we had just left behind.

Norma and I stepped into the shade of the train station while my mother found a taxi, woke the napping driver from his siesta, and we were on our way home, Norma in her customary position at my feet. After two days and nights on the train, I wanted nothing as much as a long, long walk, but I decided it would be wiser to stay at home, unpack, and let Norma settle into the house before we struck out into an environment new to her.

The next morning I buckled Norma's harness on her glossy, well-groomed back and announced that I was taking the bus to town. "I'm going to introduce Norma to our shopping district," I told my mother and we both recognized that I was making a statement, not asking permission.

Diplomatically, my mother suggested, "It's so hot. Why not let me drive you?"

"Maybe just to where the bus would drop us off in town," I compromised, knowing that the quarter-mile walk on the desert road to the bus stop would be difficult in the intense heat.

"We'll walk around for a while and take the bus back," I said. And, in an extravagance of confidence, I added, "I'll buy you a newspaper."

A few moments later Norma and I hopped out of our old '37 Chevrolet and with a breezy, "See you later, Mom," I shut the car door behind us.

The old Chevy pulled squeakily away from the curb. Norma and I were in the middle of town on our own—without my mother's protective hand, without a friend's guiding arm, without a trainer's quick instructions—on our own! Could Christopher Columbus have felt any more elation than I?

Months before leaving for Morristown I had studied and memorized the layout of Tucson's main streets and the route I would have to take to the university. It was my responsibility to know the proper commands to give my dog along the way: left, right, forward. It would be her job to keep me safe in traffic, to keep me from bumping into obstacles, or falling down flights of stairs, but it was my job to know where I wanted to go so I could direct our course. Without my commands she had no way of knowing our intended destination until it became routine.

Seeing Eye dogs walk very rapidly. Most Tucsonions do not. Norma and I skimmed past slow, shuffling, sandaled or soft-padded moccasined feet.

Open shop doorways poured lively Mexican or plaintive country music onto the sidewalk. The sounds and smells issuing from each doorway told me where we were.

Fresh popcorn, chatting, giggling girls, the reek of cheap perfume—the five and ten.

Chairs scraping on the floor, sizzling hot dogs, hamburgers, and chili—the diner.

Shaving lotion and men's voices, a raucous laugh—the barber shop.

We came to our first curb and Norma stopped. I made a mental note to be patient and not step off the curb before her. In my mind I heard Ed, my trainer at the Seeing Eye, reprimanding me during a training session when I had anticipated the step and walked off the curb before my dog. "Miss Covelli," he had almost shouted, "that step could have taken you ten feet down into an open manhole, down a flight of stairs or into the path of a quiet vehicle speeding down on you!" Then more calmly he repeated a phrase we students heard several times each day, "Trust your dog!"

I listened for traffic and when I didn't hear any motor sounds approaching, I gave the forward command and waited for Norma to decide it was safe to take the first step into the street. We sailed smoothly across and were soon on the second block of our adventure.

"*Ciega, ciega!*" (blind, blind) a Mexican woman's voice cried out excitedly as I mounted the curb and there was a flurry of slapping sandals. I had to smile at her alarm. Perhaps, I thought, I should ring a bell and cry out "Unclean, unclean" or sound a horn like Roland in Charlemagne's army to warn pedestrians of our swift approach.

A holiday baking smell, fresh breads and pastries, the fragrance of cinnamon and vanilla, chocolate and orange peel—the confectionery shop.

The sound of one of Raphael Mendez's brilliant trumpet recordings soaring above the whirling sound of a stitching machine and the warm, vibrant smell of leather—Juan's shoe repair shop. As soon as we passed it, I knew the bookstore would be next. The clean, stimulating, promising smell of paper and ink still excited and frustrated me after five years of not being able to read the printed word.

Never mind that now, I told myself sternly, concentrate. You have to turn left at this corner coming up, walk four blocks and then cross over to the right and walk ten blocks to the campus. But we didn't stride past Juan's shop. Norma suddenly veered, pulled into the doorway, whimpered and collapsed, furiously licking her paws. Startled, then alarmed and frightened, I knelt down beside her on the hot concrete. Had she stepped on something? Were her paws cut, bleeding? I couldn't tell by touching them because they were wet from her frantic licking. No amount of coaxing or commanding brought her to her feet. Something had to be terribly wrong for her to ignore all the discipline that had gone into those weeks of preparation for our future together.

From the beginning she had been docile and obedient, perfect in the execution of her duties except for a certain weakness concerning squirrels. She simply had not been able to resist darting off a sidewalk after them. Twice during the first week of training I had found myself being pulled across an expanse of grass and landing face to trunk with a tree, Norma looking up, panting and shifting nervously on her paws beside me.

"This is your own fault," Ed had commented dryly after the second episode. "We'll work on it."

And that very evening after dinner when the students, as always accompanied by their dogs, had gathered in the recreation room to chat and compare the day's experiences, Ed's voice sounded from the open doorway. "Come on, Miss Covelli. We're going squirrel hunting."

It had been a steamy summer day. The perfume of grass and flowers hung on the moist evening air. In the distance faint ripples of thunder hinted at a slowly approaching storm. "We're going to the park," said Ed as he held the station wagon door open for me.

As we rode along he had launched into a stern sermon. "If you don't break her of her squirrel chasing, you're not graduating with this class. I'm not sending her home with you until you have complete control of her behavior." I didn't answer. I tried to think of what I could have been doing wrong. "I have just one complaint about your progress," he continued. "You're too soft on your dog. She's beginning to think she's the boss. A dog that doesn't respect your authority won't work properly for you and that could be fatal."

We arrived at the park. I was preoccupied, not careful as I shut the station wagon door behind us. Norma yelped in pain and Ed rushed around to release her tail from where I had caught it in the wagon's heavy door.

"Good job," he whistled. "If you wanted a boxer you should have said so."

I stroked Norma's silky head in apology. She accepted and wagged her great plume of a tail, which didn't seem any the worse for its encounter. With Ed stationed at his customary ten or so paces behind us, we began our lively walk around the park.

Glumly I hoped the squirrels would be nestling in and hiding from the oncoming storm, but all at once, Norma pulled hard to the left. We flew across a stretch of grass and there I was again, face to tree trunk, Norma panting, looking up, and performing her little dance beside me.

"Correct her!" said Ed sharply.

I jerked the leash with the quick snap that vibrated down to the chain collar around her neck. The gesture was intended to bring the dog immediately away from inattention or misbehavior and back to full alert.

"Harder!" said Ed.

I snapped the leash again.

"Harder, say the word!" he commanded.

I hesitated. I hated the harshness he was forcing me to inflict on this gentle, loving animal. Angry at Ed and angry at myself for the tears that were stinging my eyes and about to betray me, I gave the leash a hard snap and blurted the ultimate correction—"Phooey! Phooey!" Immediately Norma hung her head and stood perfectly still. She was a statue of mortification and remorse.

"Better," said Ed, "now give her a right to get her back on the sidewalk. We have more squirrel hunting to do."

Fortunately, there were no more squirrels that evening and no more discipline problems with this marvelous creature that had become not only my guide but my friend.

Now here we were at the brink of our fulfillment as a team and Norma was lying on the sidewalk with me on my knees beside her and not even the hated "phooey" could bring her to her feet. I had to think. How would I get Norma up? How would we get home? I would have to go inside the shop, swallow my pride, and call my mother to come and get us.

The whirling machine sound from inside the shop stopped and Juan came to the doorway. "*Que passa?*" (What's going on?) he boomed as he stooped down beside us.

"She can't walk," I said. "Something must be wrong with her paws."

One by one, Juan took Norma's paws in his hands and examined them. "I don't see no cuts, nothing stuck inside," he reassured me. "The sidewalk's probably just too hot for her. She can't walk on it."

"But I start the university in less than a week," I groaned. "What am I going to do?"

"I don't know, señorita," he replied softly. And then, generously lying, he said, "Listen, I was just about to close up shop. It's too hot for me, too, today. Let me drive you home."

Juan lifted Norma off the sidewalk and carried her into his shop. He set her down on her feet and she remained standing. "There," he said happily, "she's fine, just didn't like the hot sidewalk."

I couldn't believe that a simple thing like the weather would be my undoing. I wouldn't believe that the heat alone would be the enemy that no amount of preparation or determination could conquer.

Without my anticipated spin around town and campus and without my mother's newspaper, the symbol of my independence and competence, I was being driven home. As we approached the house I heard Violetta singing to Alfredo in one of my favorite arias from *La Traviata*. Her magnificent soprano was soaring through our open windows.

"Is that coming from your house?" asked Juan.

"I suppose it's meant to be a signal to help me find my way home," I replied, miserably embarrassed. "My mother doesn't realize yet that Norma and I would have found the house without the opera."

Norma and I went into my bedroom while Juan explained our misadventure to my mother. I sat dejectedly on my bed and Norma rested her chin on my knees. Her gesture reminded me of our first meeting.

We students had gathered in the recreation room the evening of our arrival at the Seeing Eye and Ed had spoken with each one of us and walked us around the room and down the long corridor on a dog harness he held in front of us. He was matching us, our strength, our pace, and our temperament with the string of dogs he had prepared for our class.

"The first thing you have to do," he had said the following morning when he brought Norma into my room, "is win her devotion away from me. That's often one of the hardest aspects of the training, but she's bright and sweet-tempered. The transfer shouldn't take long."

We were to spend the entire morning becoming acquainted with our dogs. I examined her great head. "She has a large bone protruding at the back of her skull," I said in concern before Ed left us.

"That's a smart bump," he said, "lots of brains need lots of space." Then more seriously he confided, "She was bred specifically for intelligence. She'll do everything but read your textbooks." And he was so right, but there would be, as we were soon to realize, an enormous price to pay for

144

that intelligence—a frail physical constitution and early death. She would only live another twenty months.

I had sat on my bed that first day and talked to my dog. "We're going to college," I told her, "both of us. We're going to have a ball together." Norma sat and listened and within the hour she had rested her chin on my knee. She seemed to be saying, "All right, sounds good! I'll work with you."

Now, she was saying something different. She sighed a deep sigh and I knew she was as disappointed with our first trip to town as I was. We spent the rest of the day in the cool house, sulking.

I didn't get much sleep that night. My mind vacillated between despair and a stubborn refusal to abandon my plans. I had overcome the polio that threatened to interfere with my training, I had convinced the school to accept me despite my age, and I had earned the money for my dog, but there seemed to be no solution to this new problem. Even if my mother were to drive me to the university every day, the buildings on the campus were too far apart for Norma to walk the distances between them. The intense heat would persist for at least another month and there was no hope for rain at that time of year. With an exhausted prayer to St. Francis of Assisi, lover of animals, I finally fell asleep.

"Wake up," said my mother the next morning. "I have an idea. We're going to town." We were soon standing in Juan's tiny shop.

"I never made boots for a dog before, but I think I can do it," he said. "I'll order the softest leather I can find so that it'll bend easy." Once again he stooped down beside Norma and one by one, took her paws in his hands. "I got some dye here that won't hurt her," he went on. "I'll take the paw prints on a piece of paper for measurement."

"It's a great idea," I told my mother on the ride home, "but what will I do for orientation days and registration?"

"I'll phone my friend Elizabeth," she said. "Her niece is a senior at the university. If she's not busy and if we pay her, I'm sure she'll help you until Norma's boots are ready."

So, after all my daydreams of independent glory, there I was for the first few days of college, walking along on a stranger's arm.

The most difficult aspect of the arrangement was having to leave Norma every morning. She watched me dress for school and stood expectantly by her harness which hung on the doorknob of my bedroom. I knew how eager she was for me to slip the harness over her head and buckle it on her. When I put her at rest instead, she lay forlornly down beside my bed, her chin on her paws.

At the end of orientation week the upperclassmen hosted a mixer for the freshmen and since it was an evening event and Norma wouldn't have to walk far, I decided to attend. One of my dearest friends from the blind school, Smitty, already a senior at the university, was performing with his combo and I never missed an opportunity to hear his singing and his masterful piano.

My mother dropped us off in front of the student center and we wove our way through the cluster of students at the door. I had familiarized myself with the interior of the building and knew where to find the staircase leading down to "Louie's Lower Level" where most of the social events took place. I gave Norma a "left" and we approached the stairs. We walked several paces and she stopped abruptly. Cautiously I extended my right foot and found only space. We had reached the top of the staircase.

"Good girl, Norma," I said. "Good girl! Forward."

As we descended, I heard the sound of Smitty's intricate flourishes across the piano keys already filling the room with his beautiful music.

A girl put her hand on my arm. "Hi, my name is Janet. I'm president of the junior class. Welcome. Here's an empty place at this table for you."

I let Norma slip under the table where she would be hidden and protected from walking or dancing feet and positioned my folding chair in front of her. She made herself comfortable at my feet and I settled back to enjoy Smitty and his combo. The sound of his mellow, velvet voice and familiar keyboard style gave me courage. I wasn't alone in this noisy mob.

A male voice from my right at the table spoke to me. "Hi, I'm Richard. I'm from New York, a freshman, too. Actually, I should say, a freshman again. My parents sent me here as their last-ditch effort. This is my last chance. That's what they told me."

I was startled by his shared confidences and the onslaught of his conversation until the beer on his breath explained everything.

"I was just in New York," I said. "I spent a few days there on my way back from Morristown."

"I saw your dog," he mumbled. "She's beautiful."

I thanked him and deliberately let the conversation lag. Smitty had begun singing a composition of his own which was one of my favorites and I wanted to listen to it without the distraction of slurred speech and wafts of beer-laced breath. I had told Smitty I would be arriving at the mixer at exactly nine o'clock and I knew his choice of that particular song was his way of saying hello. The blind, unable to share meaningful glances or hand waves, arrange other sources of communication.

I also knew that at ten o'clock sharp he would be playing "Penthouse Serenade." Smitty and I shared a dream: "We're both going to make it to New York someday," he had told me. "I'll be performing on Broadway and you'll be in Carnegie Hall. Remember that and remember, too, that wherever I am, every night at ten o'clock, I'll play 'Penthouse Serenade' as a reminder to us even if you're not there to hear it."

Smitty did make it to Broadway, to top network shows, to recording contracts and albums. I played just once in Carnegie Hall in a private studio

Bianca, age 15, and Norma, Seeing Eye dog

recital, where nervousness drove me to play my Bach selections so fast that my teacher would complain, "I can't fault your technique, but you sounded like a machine gun! The concert stage, Miss Covelli, is not a battlefield."

As Smitty's song ended, a voice, deep and confident, cut through the clamor of hundreds of student voices.

"Hello, I'm Phil Stewart. I always work my way around the room, dance with all the blonds, and you're next."

"All right," I said, suppressing a grin. I was sure that the surprise of my blindness would ruffle his brash arrogance and I was going to enjoy his confusion and embarrassment.

"I'll be glad to be the next blond," I said, "but someone has to hold my dog." I moved my chair just enough to let him see Norma lying under the table.

If he was ruffled he didn't show it. He sat down beside me and looked at her.

"I love dogs," he said more quietly. "She's a pretty one." His questions came almost faster than I could answer them. "Did you just get her?"

"Yes."

"How old is she?"

"Eighteen months."

"How long is the training process?"

I was beginning to feel as though I were on a witness stand but I continued to answer because his interest seemed genuine.

"The dogs begin training at a year. They stay with a trainer for six months and then the students train with them for about four weeks."

"How does she know where you want to go?"

"She doesn't, not at the beginning anyway. I have to direct her with specific commands."

"Can she distinguish the difference between the red and the green traffic lights?"

"No, dogs are color-blind."

His intense interest in the dog had convinced me that once his curiosity was satisfied he would get up and move on, but then, pushing his chair back, he asked, "You dance, don't you?"

"Of course," I said, "my eyes don't hinder my feet in the least."

I put Norma at rest and stay, but I was uneasy. She had never seen me dancing with anyone. Would she think it was her job to intervene and protect me?

"Someone better hold her leash," I told Phil and he took it out of my hand and gave it to Richard. "Can you hold on to this for a little while?" he asked.

"Sure, sure," Richard agreed sleepily.

I rose to dance as uneasy about the solution as I was about the potential for trouble, but Norma only sat up to watch more attentively. "Am I the last blond in the room?" I asked when we had danced several dances and he didn't seem interested in completing his customary tour.

"You are for me," he said. "I'm going back to the dorm and write my girl at home to tell her I just met the girl I'm going to marry."

"Rather presumptuous of you, wouldn't you say?" I asked incredulously. Were all college men boozers or brassy boasters, I wondered? "Did it ever occur to you," I went on, thoroughly annoyed at his attitude, "that I might have something to say about that?"

"Naturally," he agreed. "But as a start, will you go to the campus picnic with me tomorrow?"

"Only if Norma's invited," I said.

"I wouldn't take you without her. She's part of the team."

On Sunday evening Norma and I had just returned home from the picnic when the doorbell rang. When I opened the door, Juan pressed four soft leather boots into my hand.

"Hey, señorita," he greeted me. "Where's the princess? Let's try these on her."

Norma's boots fit perfectly and except for a comic high-stepping stride, they didn't seem to pose an obstacle for her. Monday morning we walked onto the campus totally pleased with ourselves and totally unaware of the rather bizarre-looking pair we must have been.

Restored to our cheerful confidence, we approached my first class, not knowing Norma had another serious challenge waiting for her.

Every music major was obliged to take a second instrument. With piano as my major, I chose violin. There were eight of us in the beginners' class.

Our instructor handed out the violins, demonstrated position, spoke of the care of the instrument, showed us how to apply rosin to the bow, and we were ready to play. On our feet, arm, shoulder, chin in position, bows searching for the note, eight amateurs attacked.

Squeaks and groans, cries of pain from the tormented violins filled the room. Disturbing thoughts surfaced in my mind—perhaps I should have chosen the organ as my second instrument. No, I remembered, it was mandatory that keyboard students take a string, brass, or wind instrument. I had played the clarinet and the trumpet in high school, but I had always wanted to learn the violin. The class would certainly improve with time.

Suddenly Norma sat up, leaned against my legs, lifted her chin, and howled. It was a blood-curdling, prolonged, penetrating, primeval wolf sound. The music, or rather our attempts at it, stopped. Obviously, I had a problem on my hands again.

Kindly but firmly the woman instructor said, "Evidently, your dog won't be able to attend class with you, Miss Covelli. In fact," she continued, "I suggest that you remove her now and make other arrangements."

Now what? I pondered as I packed up my violin, took a firm grip on Norma's harness, and made my way out of the torture chamber.

Phil and I had made a date to meet for lunch. I walked to the student center and the clinking of trays and dishes made it easy to locate the cafeteria. Norma found an empty seat for me and we waited.

"Why so gloomy?" asked the deep, by now familiar voice. I related the events of the violin class.

"I'm free that hour every day," Phil said. "I'll meet you at your violin class and keep Norma outside. I can study and she can relax." PROBLEM SOLVED! Maybe he wasn't so bad after all.

Another little snag surfaced that first week of college. Freshmen were required to take a physical education class and the only sports offered to the women were volleyball, softball, and basketball. I attended the first general class where we were to be channeled into one of the three possibilities. The instructor was young, the kind of young that hides insecurity behind a mask of dictatorial arrogance. I knew I was in for a struggle.

"Obviously," I began, "I won't be able to participate in any of the freshman phys. ed. classes, but I have a solution. I rode at the Counts Stable every Saturday for two years. Will that be an acceptable substitute?"

"How could you do that?" the instructor asked skeptically.

"It was quite simple," I said. "I sat on the saddle, gave the correct signals with the reins, and the horse moved her legs. That's all there was to it."

"I find that hard to believe," he insisted.

Having not only my riding ability but my honesty challenged, I retaliated. "Well," I said, feigning an innocent demeanor, "I know the department offers some phys. ed. classes of individual sports where my lack of sight wouldn't interfere with a team's performance. And," I continued, "I believe you are the instructor for the archery class. Would you like me to sign up for that one? You could stand behind the target and ring a bell and I could aim at the sound."

There was a moment of silence. Then he cleared his throat and mumbled, "Have the stable manager send me a letter." I received the physical education credits.

My first term history class didn't cause me any problems, but I'm sure it was difficult for the professor, who had a reputation for uncontrolled irritability. At the first class session he walked into the room, slammed a book on his desk for silence, and announced, "You will use pencils or capped pens for class notes. There will be no click-top pens. Their sound is unnerving. There will be no coughing in class. If you're a smoker, quit! If you're sick, bring cough drops or stay home! Noisy distractions will not be tolerated."

The students tried to comply with his instructions, but I must have caused him great discomfort. It was Norma's custom to guide me to the first empty seat she spotted and that place was generally directly in front of the

150

teacher's desk. Since I could never be sure that the students I hired to read the assignments to me would actually show up, I took as many class notes as I could.

TAP, TAP, TAP, TAP...my Braille writing stylus punched out pages and pages of Braille code throughout the professor's every lecture. He never said a word to me. I don't know if he took an extra tranquilizer before that class or if he simply learned to cope with the minor irritations of life. I do know the experience taught me one thing—fate can sometimes have an ironic sense of humor.

Norma and I were happy on campus. We settled comfortably into our routine and in October her boots came off.

My mother's annulment had not been difficult to achieve. Enrico came in November and Norma and I attended the tiny wedding at St. Peter and Paul Church. As soon as I had arrived from the Seeing Eye, I had phoned and asked the pastor's permission to attend Mass and other church functions with my dog. "She's welcome," Father Green had said. "She probably has more right to be there than some others of God's creatures who come through that door."

A letter from my father arrived within a week of the wedding. Now that my mother was remarried, he demanded that we immediately vacate the little house he had purchased for us.

"It doesn't matter," said my mother. "At the end of the semester we're moving to New York to join Enrico. He's bought a house for us there."

My heart sank. I would have to leave my friends, old and new, and the college life Norma and I were so thoroughly enjoying.

"Enrico told me that there is a German concert pianist living next door to our new house," my mother said. "Why not work with her for a term and prepare for a Juilliard audition?"

"Me at Juilliard?" I laughed. "That's not even a plausible carrot."

But the more I thought about New York, the more exciting the prospect became. After five years in the monotonous desert, the concept of shifting seasons, crisp autumn days, snow underfoot, and the contrast of teasing warm spring breezes on my face after a frigid winter was definitely appealing. The cycle of the seasons would be a feast for the senses. New York, fast-paced, bustling, concerts, theater, opera, Juilliard? Why not? I could try. The worst that could happen was that I would be refused enrollment.

Goodbyes were wrenching. The friends from the blind school were family. Every Friday afternoon for years my mother had loaded the old Chevy with girls who filled our little house to bursting for the weekend. Sunday afternoons the boys taxied over and we all shared music and heaping plates of spaghetti. Smitty's piano, Frankie's saxophone, Pete's bass, Tarci's guitar, our girls' trio, all our voices, boys and girls together, blended with the same harmony that flowed through our friendship. Or, we might decide to listen to my opera records and although we didn't know the words, sing along to the melodies. The low register of my voice always brought a laugh as I was forced into tenor parts.

I had accepted Phil's high school ring. "Do you want it back?" I asked him as the day of our departure approached.

"No," he said, "I'm going to join the Army. It's only a two-year stint if you volunteer. When I get out I'll be on your doorstep."

As I sorted through my belongings for the move, Norma investigated my decisions. She had her nose in every dresser drawer I opened, in my closet, my book bag. She examined and supervised everything I did.

"Well, Norma," I told her as she sniffed around in the opened suitcases, "as you can see, I'm packing your boots. Winters back East are cold and the sidewalks get icy. It's good to know you'll already have your winter wardrobe."

Norma

The summer I was just fifteen
I met my gentle friend;
We both knew from that first bright day
We'd be a perfect blend.

She shared her soft brown eyes with me
Together we went everywhere—
College, parties, Europe, church,
We were a happy pair.

There was no snow too deep for us,
No storm too threatening.
We wove through busy New York streets,
We hiked Grand Canyon's rim.

Perhaps the best times that we shared
Were those that we spent quietly.
I'd play the piano, study, read,
She'd watch me patiently.

We really had no need of speech,
We understood each other well.
A nudge from her, a touch from me
Left nothing more to tell.

Our friendship flowered through the years;
My life was shadowed by her loss,
But I'm convinced that she'll be there
To greet me when I cross

Into that sphere of giving hearts
Whose love lights up the darkest sky.
For now, she's just beyond the stars,
My friend, my dog, my Seeing Eye.

Eighteen
Heidi

*I*t was August and I was in Yorktown Heights at Guiding Eyes for the Blind. Ed, my trainer at the Seeing Eye School in Morristown, had opened his own training center and I had chosen to attend his facility when I became in need of a new dog. Because I had been through the training just two years before, this class should have been simple, but it was not going at all well. Unlike the slight-framed, docile, affectionate, and obedient Norma, this new dog, Heidi, was large, big-boned, husky, strong, and obstinate.

"She's so stubborn," I complained. "It's the third day of training and she still won't do the basics for me unless you intervene. Norma and I were a team in an hour."

I was glad Ed had been Norma's trainer. He would understand how inferior this new dog was. I went on in a burst of frustration and mourning, "You knew Norma, all gentleness, and so intelligent. As you said the morning you introduced us, she could do everything but read my textbooks. This dog will never be another Norma."

Ed was not sympathetic. "Three of us know that—you, me, and Heidi—but guess what, your attitude is a major part of the problem. You're having the same adjustment difficulty as Fitzpatrick. He doesn't think Hal is as good as his Taffie was. Don't think the dogs aren't aware of your lack of trust and acceptance—they're very much aware. They don't understand your emotional resistance, but they react to it and both Heidi and Hal won't team up with either one of you until you accept them for who they are."

Before I could protest, he plunged on. "Norma's gone! Heidi's here. You either make it work or you don't go home with a dog. Now, put her through her paces again and try to mean it when you praise her."

Praise her for what, I thought, she won't do anything I tell her to do. Come, sit, stay, fetch, heel! It was all useless. Heidi stood like the German Shepherd paperweight on my desk until Ed reinforced my commands.

"No good," he sighed. "Let's call it a day. We'll start fresh tomorrow."

154

Evenings the students assembled in the recreation room to play the piano, strum guitars, listen to records, play Braille Scrabble, and exchange the day's experiences. I joined the rest, but I wasn't in the mood for conversation. I sat on a couch and listened.

"Hup up, hup up!" a man's irritated voice coaxing his dog forward rang in the corridor and in a moment Mr. Fitzpatrick lumbered into the room. He was a tall man in his late forties, elderly to me at seventeen. We sat next to each other now and then at meals and had created a commiserating friendship. Now his wonderful brogue searched me out.

"You in here, lass?"

"On the couch, Mr. Fitzpatrick."

"Room for me?"

"Yes."

He made his way toward me and as he approached, his foot bumped mine.

"Ah," he exclaimed in disgust. "Hal here can't even gauge me feet width. It'll be a cold day in hell that I'll be putting me life on the line traveling with this dog!" He sat down heavily beside me and sighed. Gruffly he gave his dog the command to lie down at his feet. "What kind'a day did you have?" he asked.

"The same. You?"

"Not good at all. We knocked over a parked bicycle, we did. Taffie wouldn't a-come even close." His voice droned on and as I listened, I found myself becoming bored with his lamentations. It suddenly occurred to me that Ed could be just as bored with mine.

"You don't like Hal very much, do you, Mr. Fitzpatrick?"

"He'll never be another Taffie," he said and his response caught in his throat, almost a sob.

An idea flicked on and despite the disparity in our ages, I ventured a suggestion. "Maybe it would help," I said hesitantly, "if you changed his name from Hal to Pal. It sounds enough alike not to confuse the dog and I'm sure Ed wouldn't mind."

"And what then, lass," he snapped, "will you be changing Heidi's name to?"

"Actually," I began, "Heidi's not a bad name. It reminds me of a book I read and reread when I was little."

"A book?"

"Yes, it's a story about a Swiss mountain girl named Heidi. I loved that book so much that I'd eat bread and cheese as I read. I'd even try to swallow a mouthful of milk, which I always found so repulsive, just to be like her."

Mr. Fitzpatrick chuckled. "Well," he said, and I could hear the laughter in his deep, colorful voice, "seems like you'll be fine once your dog learns to yodel."

I left the recreation room early, took Heidi for her outing, and went to the room I shared with Penny, a girl from Brooklyn. I was glad she was still exchanging jokes with Jerome in the recreation room. I needed some time alone to think.

My thoughts were never far from Norma. She had died three months before and her loss still scraped at the core of my being. There were times the pain was actually physical.

My mind drifted back to our early days in New York. Norma had adjusted well to our new surroundings in Queens. Maneuvering the predictable and temperate sidewalks was easier than traveling the sandy roads or blistering sidewalks of Tucson. Our neighborhood was residential and quiet. We could easily walk the eight blocks south to a shopping area or three blocks north to church.

I had spent most of my time preparing for my Juilliard audition and Norma, her chin on her front paws, would make herself comfortable beside the piano and listen.

"I'll take you to your audition," my mother had said. "You're going to be nervous enough without having to concern yourself about getting there. You and Norma have never been on that subway route. Let's leave her home and spare her the ordeal."

My mother and I joined a cluster of tense young musicians and tenser parents in the school lobby. My name was finally called and I sat down at the piano, a concert grand, a Steinway! Was I really doing this or was I still fantasizing?

"No music?" I heard a man murmur some distance to my right. "Is she going to play the entire program from memory?"

How did he expect me to use my fingers to play and the same fingers to read Braille music simultaneously, I wondered? Perhaps he thought I could read the music with the tip of my nose. My visualization of the comic picture untangled the knot in my stomach enough for me to place my fingers on the keys and begin to play the repertoire outlined in the audition requirements.

The final chord of the final piece, Debussy's "Cathedral Engulf," ebbed away. I released the sustenuto pedal and waited. To my right I could hear the rustling of papers, whispering, and then a woman's voice rose above the rest.

"You play well, my dear. We are prepared to admit you on probation. We hope you will be able to keep up with the standard of performance Juilliard students are expected to maintain."

"Thank you," I said. "I'll certainly try."

She continued, "You will be required to play a full new program before a jury every semester."

"Of course," a man interjected, "you don't have to memorize the entire program each time."

I had smiled and nodded. How else would I be able to play?

The moment I met Mr. Freunlich, my piano instructor, I knew he would never consider dictating the material to me a measure at a time as my previous teachers had done. Unfortunately, the majority of music I would be expected to learn was not in Braille in the United States. I would have to order as many pieces as I could from the Royal Conservatory in London, where Braille music was more abundant.

For several months, Norma and I took the subway from Queens into Manhattan four days a week. The crashing noise of the train and the fast-moving, jostling crowds, a far cry from the sleepy Tucson environment or quiet Queens neighborhood, were daunting to both of us. Norma would stand, determined but trembling, as the roaring monster hissed and rattled and ground to a stop. I would listen for the train doors to creak open, give the forward command, and with thumping heart, climb aboard. At the curbs, the screech of car tires, the blare of horns, and the explosive blasts of air brakes from giant buses made her head and shoulders twitch in alarm, but she always stood her ground and took me safely across every street. Adding to the stress of travel was the realization that I was not "keeping up."

My practice time at home was severely limited. The piano room was directly above our tenants' bedroom and my stepfather would not permit me to play before nine in the morning or after eight in the evening. I tried to reserve space in one of the school's practice rooms, but probationary students were last on the list. Mr. Freunlich was growing more and more impatient with my slow progress and his harshness grew in proportion to his impatience. Each lesson was a lesson not only in piano but also in humility.

Together Norma and I balanced on the tightrope until the end of the term, and then we both fell off. Norma's health and mine began to express our turmoil.

My eyes ulcerated. The treatment, cauterization of the cornea, was accomplished under local anesthesia in the ophthalmologist's office, but the pain demanded that I be hospitalized after each treatment to have access to injections of Demerol.

Weeks went by and finally, lying on the hospital bed, floating on the soothing pink cloud of the drug, I made the decision to leave Juilliard. Having to miss so much time at the piano doomed the already faint hopes I had of "keeping up."

I transferred to Queens College, became an English major, and basked in the literary genius of centuries. I hadn't realized how much I missed academics. The moment I read the material in Braille, listened to it on recorded book disks, or paid someone to read it to me, the knowledge was mine immediately, not after days and days of practicing. Although I had failed in music and my blindness had forced me out of art, I was exhilarated by the sense that I truly belonged in this world of words.

Norma and I were happy, although my eyes continued to need weekly cauterizations and Norma was suffering from chronic diarrhea. Despite our every effort, special diets, medications, her natural frailness deteriorated into

Bianca, age 15, auditioning for Juilliard

an almost skeletal appearance. Her gait slowed and finally, she began to limp—diagnosis; bone cancer.

One day in class, she stood up, laid her head on my knee, and whimpered. She seemed to be telling me she could no longer tolerate her suffering. I went to a pay phone, inserted my coins with trembling fingers, and called my mother at her Perugina shop in the city.

"Mom," I said resolutely, "this is it. I'm taking Norma to Dr. Kinney's. It's time. She can hardly walk so I'm taking a cab. I'll meet you at the vet's office."

Dr. James Kinney, gentle and soft-spoken, greeted all his patients with a loving, "Hello, my friend." When he saw us he asked no questions. Quickly he and his assistant lifted Norma onto the table. I put my hand on her head as Dr. Kinney injected her with the blessing of a painless, peaceful sleep.

Norma was buried in the Bide-A-Wee cemetery in Long Island. Her tombstone reads, "Here lies Norma, my gentle and loving eyes."

Not only had I lost my dog, my friend, but also my independence, my freedom. Already many pounds underweight, I plummeted down eighteen more before the end of the month. Food didn't interest me and what my mother forced me to eat didn't remain with me.

Final exams were approaching and despite my grief, I had to navigate the campus without Norma. I had memorized the location of my classes and familiarized myself with the new construction trappings strewn between buildings. One morning, as I was about to cross a plank from one building to another, Dr. Thomas Towers, my favorite English professor, a young and charming Southerner, ran up beside me and put his hand on my arm.

"Miss Covelli," he drawled. "I heard you had been in the hospital for your eyes. I see you don't need your dog anymore! I'm so happy for you!"

I was glad I couldn't see his face when I had to correct his misinterpretation.

During her last week of life Norma gave me her last gift. On our trip home from Queens College, we had to transfer from bus to elevated train and walk several blocks to the house. I had paid my bus fare and thought I had dropped my wallet back into my bookbag. We rode the bus, walked two blocks, went up the stairs to the train, mounted, and rode to our stop. We descended the long flight of stairs to the street and walked home. I reached into my jacket pocket for my keys, unlocked the door, and we stepped inside. Norma nudged my leg and I reached down to pet her. Wagging a proud tail and dancing her unique prancing-in-place dance, she put my wallet into my hand. She had carried it from the bus where I had obviously dropped it to my front door.

I knew replacing Norma would be difficult, but I never expected it to be impossible. Even a summer in Italy with my mother had done little to assuage my sense of loss. Now my grief was blocking my new training with

Heidi. I fell asleep telling myself I would have to try harder to like this new dog. College classes were starting soon and I needed her.

The next morning at breakfast, Mr. Fitzpatrick gave his dog the command to lie down at his side. "Down, Pal," he said and his voice was friendlier than I had ever heard it. Ed came to the table and sat beside me. He greeted everyone and then turned to me.

"You must understand, Miss Covelli," he said, "you're living in New York now. You need a strong dog to protect you. I wouldn't have given a dog like Heidi to you two years ago. You were the youngest student ever admitted to the program and you needed what we in the trade call a 'soft dog.' You and Norma were a perfect match. You're older now. You have to be mature enough to handle a strong-willed dog. She's exactly what you need. What do you say?"

"I'm sure we'll be fine as soon as she learns to yodel," I said and was rewarded by Mr. Fitzpatrick's husky laugh from across the table.

As we finished breakfast, Ed made his customary announcement. "Town in ten minutes. Group one meet me at the station wagon by the back stairs."

At each training trip to town, the trainer was seldom more than ten paces behind the student and dog team, particularly during the early days of training. In my case, Ed had to follow closely so he could reinforce my commands if Heidi chose to ignore them.

"Go three blocks and turn left at the corner for two blocks," Ed directed. Simple enough. I was sure I could complete the first set of instructions even with this uncooperative dog. I would just be forceful.

"Hup up, hup up," I coaxed and we actually took off down the street. We came to the first curb and Heidi stopped.

"Good girl," I said and meant it. We were getting a good start.

I listened for traffic, didn't hear any oncoming cars and gave her the forward command. We trotted across the street and down the next block to the curb. Heidi stopped and again I listened for traffic.

"Heidi, forward," I said and we stepped into the street. Suddenly a car, brakes screeching and horn blasting, swung around the corner. The hot breath of the engine lapped at my legs. Heidi lurched sideways, yanked the harness out of my hand, threw her body horizontally across my knees, and pushed. The impact knocked me backwards onto the sidewalk. I fell in a heap and, still holding on to the leash, rolled away from the edge of the curb. Heidi leaped over me to safety. Gas fumes and the smell of hot tires flew into my face. Shakily, I sat up and reached for the dog. She nuzzled her big fuzzy face against my cheek, and almost shyly, licked my face. My breath was still too tight in my chest for speech, but my hug said it all. I brushed my scraped palms, steadied myself, and stood. Where was Ed? I was expecting him to come up behind me, shouting at my carelessness. And then I heard his voice, warm and affectionate and proud, "Good dog, Heidi, good dog!" He put his hand on my shoulder. "You okay?"

"Yes."

"Sometimes," he said, "we don't appreciate somebody until they've proved themselves in a crisis. Now, complete the instructions."

Years later, when Ed and I had become friends, he confided that the incident had been carefully orchestrated with another trainer to teach both the dog and me a lesson.

In three weeks we were home and I was taking Heidi to my favorite stores or to church to familiarize her with our neighborhood.

A week after our return home, Phil and I went to the neighborhood movie. Heidi remained at home with my mother, stepfather, and grandfather. My grandfather, an octogenarian, searching for a breath of relief from the heat, opened the front door to step out onto the porch. The second the door swung open, Heidi bolted out of the house and down the porch steps. My grandfather's cries, "*Il cane! Il cane!*" (The dog! The dog!) brought my mother running. She saw the big Shepherd loping down the block and took off after her. Heidi, in her typical stubborn fashion, ignored my mother's entreaties to stop. The dog dashed across the street on her way to church. At that moment a police car drove up to the corner and stopped. My mother opened the door, jumped in beside the astonished policeman, and commanded him to "Follow that dog!"

Heidi reached the church, skimmed the steps, and paced back and forth before the closed door. Deciding she would have to look elsewhere, she raced back down the steps and headed toward the shops. She knew where to search and she was determined to find me.

Lights flashing and siren wailing, the police car zoomed after the galloping dog. "Pray to St. Anthony that he makes her run into a place where we can trap her," the officer told my mother. "That's the only way we'll ever catch her."

It was eight o'clock in the evening. The shops were closed. Never slackening her pace, Heidi shot past them. The steeple of St. Joan of Arc's church and school loomed in the distance. The dog kept running and the police car kept up the chase. Heidi reached the school and, although she had never been there, she ran through an open gate onto the school grounds.

"He did it," shouted the policeman as he drove onto the sidewalk to block the exit out of the playground, "St. Anthony did it."

"She's not friendly," my mother said. "I'd better go for her myself." But every time she drew near, Heidi sprinted away. Frightened, worried, and mistrustful, the dog was trapped but unapproachable.

While this drama was being enacted, Phil and I were munching popcorn, drinking soda, and watching Henry Fonda in his conflicts on the high seas as Mr. Roberts. All at once, a man's voice rang out.

"Bianca Covelli? Is there a Miss Covelli in here?" Phil and everyone else in the theater turned to see a policeman, flashlight waving, come striding down the aisle.

"That's a policeman calling you," Phil informed me and immediately a multitude of misfortunes flashed across my mind—my grandfather had a heart attack! My mother had been injured somehow! My stepfather, a two-pack-a-day smoker, had fallen asleep with a cigarette and burned the house down! Something had happened to Heidi!

Following the policeman up the aisle, I was very much aware that we had become more interesting than the movie. What were people thinking?

"Your dog's run away," the policeman told me, "but don't worry. An officer is with your mother and they have the dog trapped, but she won't let anybody near her."

The policeman drove us to the schoolyard and as I stepped out of the car, I called to my dog and heard Heidi's chain collar jingling as she came rushing toward me. Totally out of character and totally against training, eighty pounds of fur and devotion leaped on me, yelping with joy. My mother, Phil, Heidi, and I had the dubious distinction of arriving at our front door in the police car.

Heidi's sense of responsibility, laced with stubbornness, remained her paramount virtue, although it sometimes created problems as well as humor for both of us.

For the first week of each term, Heidi and I had a standing argument. She refused to accept my instructions that would take us to new classes in different buildings. Convinced that she knew better than I where we had to go, she was determined to take me to the classes we had the term before. I had to drop the harness handle, the signal that she was off duty, and walk her on the leash to our proper destination. In a few days she accepted the new schedule and we had no more arguments until the beginning of the next term.

When heavy snows fell and the only route between buildings was a plank stretched across fields of snow, Heidi would make sure she and I had full clearance. She thought nothing of pushing other students off into tall snowdrifts as she brought me expertly down the center of the plank.

Heidi had little patience with people who were in the way of her duties. Often, as we prepared to descend a flight of stairs, a girl who might be sitting on the steps would jump up shrieking in alarm as a cold, wet nose ran up and down the back of her neck to nudge her out of our way. Trying not to laugh, I would excuse us and walk quickly down the stairs, leaving the incredulous victim speechless or cursing.

Arriving early for a class one morning, I stood on the stairwell landing to wait. Footsteps ascending from the stairs below triggered Heidi's lionesque roar. The sound was reminiscent of the Roman arenas.

162

A young male voice asked sarcastically, "So, what do you feed that lion for breakfast?"

"Freshman boys," I said and he retreated back down the stairs.

A new professor, Dr. Marina Kaschko, a brilliant, no-nonsense woman from the Sorbonne, greeted my first class of French with, "A dog in class? Americans bring their pets into a college classroom?"

Students in the class came to my defense. "It's a guide dog." "Guide dogs are allowed everywhere."

"She'll behave," I assured the irritated professor.

Because she was a new instructor, the dean of the romance language department had to appraise her teaching skills and our knowledge. The day he made his appearance, Dr. Kaschko naturally called on the two students who were generally prepared—Stan, a Navy vet, and me. As it turned out, Stan hadn't done the homework and I couldn't remember all the verb forms for the subjunctive mood. As the door closed behind the dean, Dr. Kaschko sighed and said, "Only Heidi didn't let me down. After my best students' miserable performance, I expected the dog to act up and start barking."

In senior year, students were required to take comprehensive exams in several fields of study. Regardless of how high the student's class marks had been, they had to pass the comprehensive with a B in order to graduate.

The professor conducting the French comprehensive settled the students with their exams. He had arranged to leave proctors in charge while he administered the exam to me. Heidi and I waited at the back of the auditorium and soon the professor started toward us. He walked quietly—Heidi must have thought stealthily, because she met his approach with her most menacing snarl. The roar echoed through the silence.

When he felt it was safe to come close enough to speak to me, the altogether intimidated professor whispered, "Miss Covelli, you have had an A average throughout your French studies. It's certainly not necessary for you to take this comprehensive. I personally take responsibility for exempting you."

"Good girl, Heidi," I said as we left the building. "Do that again next week for our history comp."

Heidi's reputation for protectiveness was well known on campus, but my biology professor had the opportunity to witness the softer side of her disposition. Heidi hated having her face wet. She didn't mind the rest of her body being soaked, but as soon as her face was damp, she would rub it furiously against my skirt or slacks to dry it. I began packing a small towel in my bookbag whenever rain or snow was forecasted to spare my clothes. One snowy afternoon as we settled into biology class, I took the towel out of my book bag and Heidi immediately buried her head into it for a rubdown. My desk was directly in front of the professor's desk, but I didn't realize he was watching us until he said, "What a ferocious baby you are, Heidi. Wait until I spread the truth about you around campus."

163

At bus stops no one could share my space. A step too close and Heidi's growl warned prospective passengers to wait their turn. We always had to be first to mount the bus.

The summer before my last year of college, Heidi and I traveled to Europe with my mother and stepfather. Heidi was allowed to stay with me rather than having to be housed on the pet deck atop the ship, but there were places where it would not have been appropriate to bring her.

The dining room, for example, was altogether formal. Gowns and tuxedos would not have appreciated being trimmed in German Shepherd hair nor would it have been considerate to expect waiters to maneuver around the big, unfriendly dog. I had breakfast and dinner brought to our cabin and, with Heidi safely tucked under my chaise lounge, I lunched at poolside on deck.

Naturally, it was out of the question to accept invitations to dance with Heidi watching. Occasionally my mother babysat so I could enjoy the ballroom. Other evenings Heidi lay quietly at my feet as I chatted with fellow passengers in one of the salons or attended string ensemble concerts in the music room.

One of my favorite activities on the ship also demanded that my mother babysit the dog for the hour I spent in the gym every morning. Standing in the middle of the tiled room was an enormous wooden horse which prospective riders had to mount by way of three steps. The reins were soft leather, but the saddle was molded plastic on which a chrome knob waited to activate the motion of the animal. One turn and the motor moved the horse into a trot, another turn and the horse cantered, one more turn and the wooden replica galloped in place. It was a noisy ride and not particularly satisfying, but with some concentrated suspension of belief, my imagination could recapture a hint of western mountains and desert.

When we docked in Genoa, my mother and stepfather went on to Perugia. My friend Anna, who had invited me to her home in San Remo, met me at the ship. We were to spend a day or two in a hotel before leaving for her home.

Relatives of my stepfather lived in Genoa. One of his nephews, Genezio, had befriended me all the summers my mother and I had been in Italy. For excursions on his motor boat; long days on the beach; dinners and midnight coffee stops along the Riviera, Santa Margerita, and Porto Fino; the opera at Caracalla in Rome, Gege was always my cheerful and witty companion.

As soon as Anna and I were settled in the hotel I telephoned him.

"*Ciao, Bianchina, come va?*" (Hi, how's it going?)

I told him of our plans and, as I expected, he offered to drive us to San Remo.

"I'll take the day off tomorrow and drive you," he said, "but how about dinner tonight? Bring your friend."

Bianca, age 15 and Heidi, guide dog

"Thank you," I said, "but I think I'll stay in and let my dog relax tonight. She's had many new experiences to live through this week. We'll see you in the morning."

Gege's familiar quick double knock and his energetic voice announced his arrival at our hotel door the next morning. "*Bianchina, permesso?*" (Can I come in?)

"*Si, si, avanti.*" (Yes, yes, come in.)

With typical Italian fervor, Gege strode into the room, arms out-stretched to hug me. Heidi, a growl rumbling deep in her throat, jumped horizontally in front of me and stared at this arrogantly fearless intruder.

Gege's crepe-soled shoes squeaked with the intensity of effort he put on them to stop. Then he whistled and said good-naturedly, "You could have warned me your dog is more jealous than a Sicilian husband."

Heidi had been with me four years when Phil and I were married. She had been fond of Phil from the beginning and we had no concerns about her attitude toward him, but when we discovered a baby was on the way, we became apprehensive. I remembered horror stories I had heard on radio newscasts about dogs attacking infants but, I reminded myself, those were not trained guide dogs.

My stepfather had an immediate solution which he reinforced daily: "Have the dog put to sleep. After the baby comes, you won't be going any-where. You won't need her anymore."

My mother had a less dramatic suggestion: "Ask the vet to give you some tranquilizers for her until you see how she reacts to the baby."

I bought the medication, stashed it in our bathroom cabinet, and prayed I wouldn't have to use it. I hoped Heidi's devotion would automat-ically transfer to the baby.

The morning we brought our infant daughter home from the hospital, I let Phil carry her into the apartment while I greeted Heidi with as much enthusiasm as she greeted me. Phil placed Theresa in the bassinet and I sat down on the couch to wait for the baby's first whimper and Heidi's reac-tion. Phil remained standing. We didn't voice it, but I knew he wanted to be ready to grab Heidi if he had to.

We didn't wait long. A tiny cry issued from the five-pound, eight-ounce occupant of the bassinet. Heidi stood up. I didn't move. I didn't want to be in the way if Phil had to execute a quick rescue. Heidi stood still, listening. The baby's cries grew more persistent. Suddenly I felt the dog take hold of the hem of my skirt and begin tugging. I stood up and Heidi pulled me directly to the bassinet. She couldn't have said it any more clearly with words: "Get up! The baby needs you! Do something!"

I picked up Theresa and sat down with her. Heidi stood beside the couch and watched. Finally satisfied, she released my skirt and lay down on the floor beside us.

166

From that moment on, Heidi was Theresa's personal guardian. If I didn't respond fast enough to a cry or even a squeaky whimper, my skirt or pant leg would be tugged. When the baby slept, Heidi lay with her chin propped on the rod between the front wheels of the bassinet. When Theresa was old enough to play in a playpen, Heidi was always somewhere in the room and only family members could enter.

Long before Theresa had learned to imitate human speech, we knew she had bonded with her protector. Every time the doorbell rang, a sound Heidi met with a series of great loud barks, Theresa joined in with her version of the warning—a soft but definite "woof, woof!"

Friends and neighbors soon spread the news—the Stewarts have a big fuzzy-faced guardian angel and a barking baby daughter.

Bianca, age 17 with Heidi, second Seeing Eye dog

Nineteen
Vanni

*H*e was eleven years old, small for his age, blond, blue-eyed. Everyone in San Remo knew him, liked him, and made use of him.

The carnation growers liked him because he could pick and sort the flowers from the fields, tie the best ones into neat bundles, and place them carefully on the market carts as efficiently as any adult.

The merchants liked him because if they put a broom in his hands while they went to a nearby cafe for a cappuccino, they knew they would come back to find a neatly swept floor. They knew, too, that the boy could be trusted to do more than sweep. Under his hands the choicest peaches, figs, and grapes were arranged in the baskets to look like the painting of a masterful Italian artist. He could also be trusted with the cash drawer, and that was no small qualification.

The cabana owners at the beach liked him because, although he was short and slight, he was quicker at carrying out umbrellas and dragging out beach chairs than the bigger boys.

Most of all, he was liked because he was an even-tempered, modest child who didn't expect to be paid much for his services.

From the carnation growers he would be pleased to accept a few coins and the less-than-perfect flowers that couldn't be sold. He would run home with the second-rate blossoms and put them in a glass before the chipped and faded statue of the Madonna that stood on the bureau in the bedroom he shared with his grandmother.

From the merchants he brought home bags of fruits and vegetables, an occasional crate of eggs—the smallest ones—and loaves of bread. The only real money he made was the pocketful of tips from the ladies he politely and cheerfully accommodated on their beach chairs under voluminous umbrellas. His ready smile and manliness made him a favorite with tourists and townspeople alike. On days he chose not to go to the beach, the fields, or the shops, people would ask, "Where's Vanni today?"

That was what everyone called him—Vanni, just Vanni. His last name was a mystery. It, or rather the lack of it, was a source of deep embarrassment to his grandmother because it meant that a girl from a hard-working, respectable Catholic family had committed one of the gravest and least disguisable sins.

His name was the first sound I heard as I woke in Anna's house the first day of my three-week visit. Anna's voice was coming from the garden, "Vanni, put your sandals on. There might be broken glass out here."

The scraping of a rake and a child's voice drifted through the shuttered bedroom windows.

"I haven't stepped on anything yet."

Anna, affectionate and exasperated, scolded, "Dummy, why do you want to get hurt before you do what you're told?"

No response. The rake kept scraping.

Anna came into the house. She called back to the child in the garden, "Come in when you're finished. I have breakfast for you."

I opened the lid of my Braille watch and ran my fingers over its dial. Eight o'clock! It must have been hours ago that I had heard a distant rooster. My mind had turned it off like an annoying alarm clock and I had gone back to sleep. Obviously, the activities of the day had begun here some time ago.

I swung my legs over the side of the bed and sat up. The cold dampness of the floor shocked my bare feet. Hurriedly I felt around with my toes for my sandals and slipped them on.

It must be sunny out, I thought. San Remo is always sunny. A blast of that sun would quickly dispel the unpleasant, chilly dampness of the room. I lifted the heavy iron bolt that lay across the shutters and let them swing open into the bedroom. There was no glass at the window, only a screen, and as the heavy shutters swung apart, the sweeping fragrance of sea air combined with the distinctive perfume of acres and acres of carnations flowed in with the warm sun.

"Goo-morny, signorina."

I jumped, startled. I hadn't expected the boy to be working directly outside my window.

"Good morning," I said, and aware that I was clad in scanty, babydoll pajamas, I was not only startled but also embarrassed.

"*Sono Vanni*," (I'm Vanni) he said simply.

Anna poked her head into the room. "Ah, you're awake, good. Breakfast is nearly ready." And then, noticing the child at the window, she said, "Vanni, you come now, too. You can finish later. The eggs will be cold."

The raking began again, furiously for a few moments, and then stopped. I bolted the shutters so I could dress.

As I emerged from my room, Vanni was approaching the back doorway. "*Permesso?*" (With permission?) he asked, and without waiting for an invitation,

170

he pushed through the loose vertical bamboo slats that hung at the back entrance. The hangings served a double purpose. They provided privacy and at the same time allowed the perfume of the sea and the crops of flowers to invade every corner of the house.

The three of us sat over steaming cups of cafe e latte at a long olive wood table. Generous portions of warm croissants, sweet butter and home-made marmalade, scrambled eggs, bacon, and fresh figs and grapes filled large platters in the middle of the table.

"*Prendi, mangia, Vanni,*" (take, eat) Anna coaxed the boy. "Since when are you shy with me? I know you since you were born."

The child was respectfully quiet as Anna and I talked and made plans for the beach, but soon he pushed back his chair and stood.

"I can't eat any more," he said. "I have a stomachache. Thank you, excuse me."

His bare feet slapped against the marble floor and in a moment he swung through the bamboo and was gone.

"He can't eat much at one time," Anna explained. "Too much food all at once makes him sick."

"Does he have a problem?" I asked.

"Oh yes, but not the kind you're thinking of. At his house his mother and stepfather feed themselves and their two little girls first. Vanni gets whatever's left."

I set down the small, aromatic fig I was about to pop into my mouth and tried to absorb what I had just heard. "That's outrageous!" I said. "What kind of arrangement is that?"

"He's the son of an American tourist," Anna said quietly, pouring more coffee into my cup. "That doesn't make him very popular with his stepfather."

"Barbaric!" I exclaimed. "Since when is a child's paternity his own fault!"

"His grandmother keeps him in the summer," Anna went on, "but he goes to school in the town where his mother lives so he's gone all winter. It takes time for him to be able to eat normally."

"I never heard of such treatment," I mumbled. "That's a disgrace."

"We all try to make up for it when he's here," Anna said sadly, "but what I'm afraid of is that this will probably be his last summer in San Remo. He'll be twelve in January and his stepfather will be sending him out to work full time to help the family."

"Isn't there a law about keeping children in school here?"

"Not a very rigid one," Anna said. "Boys like Vanni wait tables in cafes, run hotel elevators, work in the markets or in the flower fields, do all kinds of jobs, and the authorities don't interfere, especially if the family needs the income."

After breakfast, Anna and I strolled the short walk to the beach. As we settled onto our beach blankets (we were too young to band with the ladies on beach chairs), I heard Vanni's amicable greetings.

His "Goo-morny" to the English-speaking patrons and "*Bonjour*" to the French sailed comfortably along with his "*Buon giorno*" to the Italian customers.

"With his personality he could go far," I said, "but what do you think will become of him?"

"Who knows," Anna sighed. "He'll probably never escape his fate."

We were quiet. The sea murmuring at our feet, the hot sun, the hum of voices all around us lulled us into a comfortable passivity, but Vanni's plight haunted me. Something had to be done to save this bright, energetic child, but what?

As we prepared to leave the beach, the boy ran up to us, lifted the beach blanket out of my hands, took it a safe distance away to shake the sand from it, folded it, and returned it to me with another "Gooi-morny."

"Come to the house for dinner," Anna told him. "I'm going now to buy some fresh flounder. It'll be easy on your stomach."

Vanni was a daily fixture at Anna's. Early mornings, mid-afternoons, evenings, his "*Permesso?*" rang through the house as he strode through the bamboo into the back hall.

Anna found or fabricated jobs for him around the house or the garden. He always refused the money she pressed on him, but she would tuck it in his pocket with a mock scolding, "Take this and don't argue with your elders. It's not polite."

His quick and curious mind was a sponge for information. He made our daily time together a perpetual language lesson. "English please, Signorina Bianca," he would say as he went down the list of words he wanted to learn that day—nose, mouth, knee, arm, shirt, sandal, flower....

Evenings, while Anna washed and I dried the dishes, the boy darted around the kitchen putting everything in its place.

"English please, Signorina Bianca," he would ask eagerly as he took plates, glasses, cups, and utensils from my hand and the lesson went on until the task was finished. He began carrying a tiny pad of paper and a pencil in the pocket of his shorts and added new words to his personal dictionary daily. By the end of the first week he was beginning to form sentences.

One afternoon, as we were sitting in the garden sipping lemonade and reviewing his vocabulary, he suddenly asked in halting English, "You like flower, no?"

I smiled and clapped. "*Bravo, Vanni! Bravo!*" I exclaimed and then answered in English, "Yes, I like flowers."

"*Aspetti*," he said, jumping up from the grass where he had been lounging beside my chair, "*ritorno subito*." (Wait, I'll be right back.)

"Don't be late for dinner," Anna called out to him. "Where're you going in such a rush?"

"*Ritorno subito!*" the boy shouted over his shoulder as he ran away down the road.

We were just about to sit down to dinner when his "*Permesso?*" sounded through the clatter of bamboo.

"For you," he said proudly, carefully laying an abundance of perfumed, silky flowers into my arms. He stood back and asked in his best English, "You like?"

"Vanni," Anna demanded briskly, "where did you get all those carnations? They're good ones."

"I know they are," said the child defensively, "Alberto gave them to me for the Signorina." And then he added more quietly, "It's going to rain hard tonight and they'd be ruined anyway."

"Help me get the vases out of the back closet," Anna told him. "We have enough flowers here to fill every room in the house."

"They're wonderful, thank you, Vanni," I said, hoping his gift wouldn't bring him more trouble than he already had.

"I have to eat home tonight," Vanni announced as he helped Anna arrange the carnations in the vases. "My grandmother's making chicken alla cacciatora and polenta, my favorite."

Our meal was conspicuously quiet without Vanni and his eager questions.

As we were finishing the frito misto of artichoke hearts and zucchini and the roast chicken, Anna turned to look out the open window behind her. "It's getting so dark," she said. "The sky's really black."

She sliced some of the brick-hard Italian ice cream, spumoni, onto little plates and set one in front of me. "We're in for a real storm," she said and her voice was full of apprehension.

I had already noticed a change in the breeze that floated through the open windows and the bamboo hangings. A chilly undercurrent had begun skimming in beneath the customary balmy softness of the San Remo evening air.

"I promised to babysit for my cousin's twins this evening," Anna said. "Franca and her husband are going to a friend's anniversary party." She was quiet for a moment, thinking, and she said, "I hate to leave you alone in the house with a storm coming. Why don't you come with me?"

"I'm not afraid of a little rain," I said. "Besides, I brought my typewriter, you know, and I haven't written a line since I've been here. I'll stay home and write a letter to Phil at least. This engagement ring on my finger does come attached to some obligations. And maybe," I said, happy with the idea, "I'll write out some lessons for Vanni."

"We lose electricity every time we have a bad storm," Anna went on.

"And?" I said. "You think I won't be able to function in the dark, is that it?"

Anna laughed. "How silly I am," she said, embarrassed. "I always forget you can't see."

When the storm broke, the rain hurled itself from the sky with an angry fury. It pounded in on a lashing wind that flung my papers off the desk where I had set up my work space, sent one of the vases of carnations that stood on an end table by a window crashing to the floor, and slammed garden furniture against the house. Quickly I went from window to window and struggled against the onslaught to bolt the heavy shutters in place. The Neapolitan song festival on the radio sputtered, crackled, and fell silent. The light must have gone out with it, I thought. No matter, I didn't need it. At a time like this I had the advantage over the sighted, who were totally at a loss in the dark.

The storm had choreographed the bamboo slats at the back door into a frantic Stravinskian dance. They were slamming against one another with a wild clatter. Surely they would break if I didn't pull the outside door closed. I rushed down the hall. The raging wind, the savage rain, and the frenzied bamboo slapped at my face and bare arms as I approached the doorway. I fought through the slats and reached for the doorknob. The chill of the rain surprised me. In seconds I was drenched and shivering.

At the moment I pushed through the hangings and stepped outside, an earth-rending crash of thunder shook the house. The sizzling hiss of lightning sounded what seemed only inches away. I jumped back inside to catch my breath and in the storm's trembling wake I heard a familiar voice just beyond the threshold. "*Aspetti, Signorina Bianca. Non chiuda!*" (Wait, Miss Bianca, don't close.)

I stepped back and Vanni burst through the slats with a swirl of wind and water and pulled the door solidly behind him.

"Anna told me she was going out and I thought you might be afraid here alone in the dark," he said breathlessly, "so I brought a candle." He was talking fast, distressed and apologetic. "I had a shield around it, but the storm put it out anyway and now I can't see to find any matches. I should have brought some from my grandmother's."

"You're very kind," I said. "Come with me into the kitchen. I know where Anna keeps the matches. I'll find them for us. Give me your hand."

I led him down the hall and turned left into the dining room. "Stay behind me," I said, "and we won't bump into any furniture. I've memorized where everything is."

We walked through the room and through the archway into the kitchen. I put his hand on the back of one of the chairs that surrounded the kitchen table. "Sit down," I told him, "and I'll get the matches."

But when I opened the drawer of the sideboard and found the match box, it was empty.

"Well," I said, "I think we'll just have to do without any light for a while. Do you mind?"

"No, I don't," he said, "and you don't have to mind either because I'm here with you."

I was touched, and I was confused. Didn't the boy realize that morning, noon, night, sunny skies, or storm-blackened skies were all the same to me? I decided not to mention it.

174

"I know what we'll do," I said. "Let's have a party!"

I reached into the cupboard above the draining board and took out two bowls. From a drawer in the butcher block I took two teaspoons and set everything on the table. I hoped there was some spumoni left in the freezer. I opened it and reached inside. Knowing that Italian women go to the markets daily for fresh foods, I assumed there would not be a collection of frozen packets to sort through. As I expected, a small square carton lay alone on a shelf. This would have to be the ice cream, I thought, and so it was.

Sitting in the dark, against the backdrop of furious rain and howling wind, Vanni and I ate our ice cream and talked. The boy quickly initiated his favorite game. "Please, Signorina Bianca, English."

We named ice cream, many flavors, and many other foods. His native intelligence and memory were remarkable. How could he not realize and remember that a candle or any other light was totally useless to me, I wondered?

The evening slipped away. By eleven the storm decided to return to the open seas and I, too, had decided something—I would bring Vanni back to the States with me.

In my nineteen-year-old enthusiasm, I blurted out the suggestion without evaluating the consequences of my offer. "Vanni, how would you like to come to America?"

There was a moment of silence and then he erupted into volcanic excitement. "America? America? With you? Yes, yes, yes! When?"

I was immediately aware of my mistake and stalled for time. I took our bowls to the sink and ran the water.

"I'm not sure when," I said. "We have to plan many things—passport, visa—but before we can even start, we need permission from your family."

"But I can come, no?" he asked anxiously, sensing the change in my voice.

"We'll try very hard to make it happen," I said.

"I like," he said in English. "I like."

The radio snapped on with a few crackling noises.

"*Ah, la luce!*" (The light!) Vanni exclaimed. "You'll be all right now. I'll go home and tell my grandmother I'm going to America!"

"Maybe you should wait..." I began, but the boy was already pushing through the bamboo and reopening the back door.

• • •

"Are you crazy?" my stepfather roared. "You're only eight years older than he is and you want to play mother?"

My mother and stepfather had come to San Remo after their travels in other parts of the country and had checked into a hotel. I had been eager to tell my mother about the child and my plans. I knew I would meet with resistance, but I hadn't realized how much.

"It's an impossible idea," my stepfather continued, pacing up and down the terrace outside their room. "Where would he live? Not with us! I can tell you that right now."

"Just a minute, Enrico," my mother said. "Let's talk about this calmly." And then, to me she said, "What about his education? I'm sure he doesn't know enough English to start school in a month."

"We'll bring some Italian textbooks with us. I can keep him current and teach him English at the same time. If he misses a few months, even a year of school, it won't matter. He's very bright and advanced for his age. I'm sure he could be prepared soon. And for where he'd live, I'll ask Phil to let him move into his apartment. I can go there after my classes and...."

"You can't burden Phil with an eleven-year-old boy," my mother protested, "and Enrico doesn't want him to live with us. Besides, I can't take care of a child and run a business like mine. You know I have to be there seven days a week."

"He wouldn't be a burden," I insisted. "He's very hard-working and if you'd let him, he could even help the men in the stockroom at your shop. Wait until you meet him before you ruin everything."

The meeting was a disaster. We dined in the hotel's formal dining room, my mother, stepfather, Anna, Vanni, and I. The boy was quiet and well-mannered, but it was obvious to me that he was very much aware of the tension that crackled around us and that it was eroding his self-confidence. If we had planned dinner at Anna's, I thought, where Vanni would have been more at home and where he could have helped serve and clear away dishes, my mother and Enrico would have had a better introduction to him.

"Why don't you eat?" my stepfather demanded as waiters began clearing the table. "Half of your dinner is still on your plate."

"I'm sorry," Vanni began, but Anna interrupted.

"He doesn't eat much," she explained quickly. "He has a small appetite."

"I bet he'll want dessert, though," Enrico replied without humor.

I cringed, wishing desperately that this evening had never happened.

"Let's have our dessert and coffee at the cafe on the piazza, al fresco," suggested my mother. "We can listen to the music and watch the people strolling by. It's more pleasant than in here."

I was grateful for her intervention, but just as we had settled at a table at the cafe, another crisis surfaced.

Two teenaged boys strolled slowly toward our table and called out, "*Ciao, Vanni, non sei ancora partito per l'America?*" (Hi, Vanni, you haven't left for America yet?)

Anna stood, ready for battle with the taunting youngsters. "*Andate via, ignoranti!*" (Go away, you bad-mannered boys.)

Vanni was silent, but I heard his chair scrape the pebbles beneath it.

176

"Sit down," commanded Anna and there was another crunching of pebbles as he obeyed.

My mother turned to the hecklers. "Come, boys," she said pleasantly, "have some dessert with us, some spumoni, a pastry?"

"*Oh no, grazie, signora,*" they answered in unison, "*no, grazie.*" They were obviously taken aback by the invitation and wanted nothing more than to escape, but my mother was determined to make them as uncomfortable as they were making Vanni. "Don't be timid," she insisted. "Join us." Turning to Vanni she directed, "Vanni, bring two chairs from that empty table over there for your friends."

The boys, unable to refuse again, shuffled forward and helped Vanni bring the chairs to the table. All three boys sat in a brooding silence.

"Spumoni or pastry?" asked my mother.

"*Solo una Coka per me, grazie, signora,*" one boy replied. (Only a Coke for me, thank you, madam) and his friend and Vanni mumbled the same request.

A young waiter, polite and cheerful, brought our order to the table, four *anisets alla mosca* (aniset with a fly—a coffee bean at the bottom of the small glass) and the three Cokes. Would Vanni end up living the same life as this young man, serving tables until he was too old to balance heavy trays? Not if I had anything to do with it.

Gradually everyone around the table began to relax. The adults discussed the quickly approaching day of our departure, Anna's return to the States in a few weeks, my mother's business conferences in Perugia, and her plans for the shop's holiday gift line.

The two older boys had turned their chairs to watch the passersby. Vanni did the same.

"Not bad," one of the teens murmured. "She's not bad."

"Not at all bad," whispered his friend, "but the taller one following is even better."

"You're right," snickered the first boy, "she's much prettier, a good waistline and good legs."

"She's got more than just strawberries growing on her chest, too," mumbled a third voice, Vanni's, "she's well built, must be about sixteen."

I held my breath. Enrico was relating to Anna an incident he had experienced with the Cadillac we had brought over with us from the States. His voice, naturally forceful and animated, grew even louder as he relived his annoyance with the narrowness of some of the streets he had to maneuver. I hoped his volume had overpowered the boys' comments, especially Vanni's. My hearing was more acute than most people's, I tried to reassure myself. Surely, my mother and stepfather would not have tuned in to the sotto-voce appraisals of the boys.

I, and I'm sure everyone else at the table, welcomed Enrico's announcement as he paid the bill. "I have to get back to the hotel. I'm expecting a phone call."

"Thank you for the lovely evening," Anna said and she sounded so sincere I would have believed she meant it if I hadn't known her so well. Not being able to match her performance, I said nothing. Vanni rose and remained almost as speechless as I, but he managed a timid, "*Grazie, signori.*"

The phone was ringing as Anna and I walked into her home. "For you," she said, putting the receiver into my hand. "Your mamma."

"I hope you realize now," my mother began without any preliminaries, "that your idea is totally out of the question. Your 'little boy' is only little in stature. He's not as much a child as you think he is. I know you heard his comments this evening, and let me assure you that the look on his face when he was making them was far from childlike."

"Just a minute," I began, but she interrupted.

"You're too young to know what you'd be getting yourself and the rest of us into."

"I know exactly what...."

"Forget the whole idea," she said. "I'll see you tomorrow. Come for dinner with Anna. I have some business to attend to at the customs office for transporting some shop merchandise. It'll take all day as slowly as the authorities do things here. Good night, darling," and she hung up.

I didn't get much sleep that night. Guilt weighed too heavily upon me. Why had I been so impulsive as to mention the prospect to the boy prematurely? Why hadn't I investigated the possibilities before I had filled Vanni's head with hopes that looked as though they would never materialize? I told myself that I simply couldn't let him down. I would call Phil and if he was willing to have Vanni in the apartment and Vanni's mother was willing to let him go, my mother and Enrico wouldn't have anything to say about it. Of course, I agonized, there was the question of his fare.

Vanni didn't arrive at Anna's until after ten the following morning. He was agitated and his words came in short gasps. "I'm working at the beach today," he told us. "I have to go right back, but I brought a present for your mother." He thrust a soft suede coin purse into my hand.

"She'll like it, won't she?" he asked, but before I could answer he had run out of the house.

"I don't like this," Anna said. "It's not brand-new and anyway, where would he have found the money to buy a new one?"

"I hope he didn't take it from his grandmother," I said.

"It's too elegant for that." Anna sighed. She was obviously troubled.

There is a six-hour time difference between Italy and New York. I waited impatiently for the middle of the afternoon to place my call to Phil. He would be home from his office by seven New York time.

"What's wrong?" he asked the moment he heard my voice.

"Remember the boy I wrote to you about?" I began, but as I finished my explanation, his reasonable, unemotional response erased my last hope.

"I can't take on that responsibility. I'm at work all day. Who would look out for him while you're in class, and anyway, I can't afford to support a child yet, not one that's practically a teenager. We'll be married in a few months. Let's settle into our own lives for a while and then talk about it."

I put down the receiver and sank into the armchair beside the phone table.

"No?" asked Anna, laying a comforting hand on my arm.

"No," I said dully. "Now what do I do? How do I tell Vanni?"

All afternoon I waited for the boy's *Permesso?* to sing through the clamoring bamboo slats, but he didn't come.

"He'll probably come in for dinner, don't you think?" I asked Anna.

"I doubt it," she said. "He doesn't come unless he's invited."

"Well, I'll call the hotel and decline the dinner invitation for tonight, if you don't mind," I said. "He's bound to come sometime this evening and I have to talk to him. Besides, I'm not in the mood to listen to what is sure to be Enrico's boisterous good humor at his victory."

I telephoned my mother. "Some friends of Anna's are giving a farewell dinner for me this evening," I lied.

"How nice, dear," my mother said. "We'll see you tomorrow then. We're planning to drive into Genoa tomorrow evening. Enrico booked rooms at the Excelsior. We have to board ship by eight the following morning."

"This is the only day he hasn't come for at least one meal since I've been here," I said as I set the table for two.

Anna and I ate. We cleared the table, did the dishes, and Anna swept the kitchen floor. Still Vanni did not arrive.

"I have some packing to do," I said and went into my bedroom. The shutters were open. I would hear his footsteps outside my window if and when he came.

Anna came in and watched me for a moment without speaking. Finally she said, "I can't believe he wouldn't come on your last night here."

I couldn't respond. My mind was in turmoil. Actually though, I thought, if he didn't come, I wouldn't have to tell him that our plans were dead, dashed against an impenetrable wall of reason. But why hadn't he come? Did he already know somehow?

"Don't be unhappy," Anna tried to console me. "I'll find out what happened to him. Maybe he just stayed late at the beach. I'll be back as soon as I can."

I was still stuffing last-minute mementos into corners of my suitcases when Anna came in and sat down on my bed.

"He stole the coin purse," she said, "took it from one of the cabins at the beach, from inside a woman's bag."

I gasped, "No, oh, no! He wouldn't do that."

"He confessed when the boss interrogated all the cabin boys," Anna said. "He wanted a gift for your mother, to win her over. He left all the money behind, just dumped it out into the bottom of the woman's bag."

I sat down on the bed. My temples were throbbing. "He can give it back," I said, hastily reaching into my handbag. "Look, it's right here. Take it to him and tell him to bring it back first thing tomorrow morning."

"I can't," Anna replied. "He doesn't want you to know. He made me promise not to tell you. He's too ashamed. That's why he hasn't come."

Morning came, but I was awake long before the distant rooster announced the dawn. I got up, dressed, and went out into the garden. Maybe Vanni would come after all. I was sure Anna would have told him I was leaving before noon. I sat on a stone bench against the house and waited.

"He won't be coming," Anna said from the doorway. "I can assure you of that. Come in and have some breakfast, some coffee."

I pushed through the bamboo slats. Their music reminded me of so many of the boy's comings and goings, of the golden afternoons of English lessons in the garden, of the meals, the storm, the candle that had blown out despite Vanni's good intentions, how like that candle my own feeble and useless endeavor had been, I thought bitterly—worse than useless, destructive.

I couldn't resist stepping outside again as I waited for Anna to phone her neighbor, Mario, who had volunteered to drive us to the hotel where my mother and Enrico would be waiting. Perhaps Vanni would go by the house and see me and stop just long enough for a brief good-bye.

I heard footsteps on the gravel walkway into the garden and for a moment I stopped breathing to listen. The footfall was too heavy, too slow to be the child's.

A woman's voice, quiet but full of venom, fell on my ears. "I'm Vanni's grandmother," she almost hissed. "I just want you to know that before you came to fill his head with nonsense, with crazy dreams, Vanni was a good boy. He was not a thief!"

"I know that," I said miserably. "What can I do to...?"

"Leave him alone," the old woman warned me. "Don't write. Don't try to contact him through Anna. You've done enough damage already." She stopped for breath and continued, "Would you believe that he was even talking about trying to find that American bum who is his father?"

"I'm truly sorry," I said. "I meant him no harm."

A car whirled into the driveway and a comical horn played a popular tune. "*Ciao, Bianca, sei pronta?*" (Hi, Bianca, you ready?) Mario called as he unfolded his long frame from the tiny car, and then, seeing Vanni's grandmother, he said warmly, "*Bon giorno, signora, come sta?*" (Good morning, madam, how are you?)

"Very well, thank you," the old woman responded brusquely.

"I'll get the luggage," offered Mario and he swung through the bamboo with the traditional, "*Permesso?*"

And then, to my surprise, Vanni's grandmother took my hand into her own small, dry grasp. "*Ariveder-La, signorina*," she said more gently. "*Bon viaggio.*" She let my hand drop and walked slowly away. As I stood alone in the warm morning sunshine laced through and through with the poignant fragrance of nearby lilac bushes and crops of carnations, I realized that what could have been a significant chapter of my life was ending before it could begin.

There was scarcely enough room in the compact little car for Anna and me and my two suitcases, but we settled in and Mario turned on the sputtering engine. We pulled away from the house and had started down the road when Anna suddenly shouted above the clanking motor, "Stop, Mario. Stop!"

"Goo-bye, Signorina Bianca, goo-bye!" came the voice I knew so well. Vanni, breathless from running, was at the open car window. "For you," he said in English, reaching in and pressing a clump of carnations into my hand.

"Thank you," I said and before I lost my nerve I said, "I'm so sorry our plans haven't worked out."

"I know," he said, "Anna told my grandmother and she told me, but if I can, I'll come when I'm older, on my own. Will that be all right?"

"Of course," I said, "come any time you can." I forced my mouth into a smile although in the back of my mind I heard the prophecy Anna had muttered on the beach that first day of my visit: "He'll probably never escape his fate."

I was beginning to acknowledge the truth of her words. I could only be glad the boy had never heard them.

Italian Summer — Vanni

Wrapped in the spray and scent of the sea,
bleached blonder by the sun,
the eager child molded words
unfamiliar to his tongue.

He nearly twelve and I nineteen
in that village by the sea—
he picked carnations in the fields;
his heart was song and poetry.

He brought a candle in a storm
and armfuls of fresh flowers.
We formed the bond of timelessness
in just three weeks of hours.

I taught him English every day.
He was cheerful, modest, mild.
I taught him words and he taught me
what it means to love a child.

Twenty
I Thought I Could

One of my favorite children's stories has always been "The Little Engine That Could." The engine, heavily burdened with toys, is supposedly too small and weak to carry the load up the mountain that separates him from town, where the children are waiting. Overcoming obstacles, huffing and puffing, the little engine trudges up the impossible mountain inch by inch. As he reaches the top and races down the other side, he exclaims in unison with the rhythm of his wheels, "I thought I could. I thought I could. I thought I could."

If I were asked to choose the phrase, the words that did the most to shape my destiny, strengthen my will, stimulate my stubborn perseverance, I would have to admit they were not words from Scripture or even from any of the great writers. In fact they were not even words of encouragement or approval. Rather they were the two simple but explosive words: YOU CAN'T. Some of the YOU CAN'Ts I ignored or sneered at with the bravado of youth. Others reflected circumstances over which I had no control, but which, through chance, fate, or prayer, resolved themselves in a spectacular denial of those hateful words.

It all began when I was fourteen, thoroughly enamored of Chopin's music and burning with the desire to play his *Revolutionary Étude*. There were other composers I enjoyed playing, especially Mozart and Bach.

Mozart's lyrical rondos and sonatas were full of sunshine and light-hearted excitement. Playing them was like running barefoot through a meadow of summer flowers. Bach's clean, sharp, disciplined two and three part inventions and fugues were a mathematical as well as a musical feast. I respected his artistry and hoped I would someday be proficient enough to play an entire piece without a breath of hesitation to mar the symmetry of the composition. Playing Bach was like riding on a faultlessly smooth track in a luxurious train, wheels humming and clicking along in perfect synchronization.

But Chopin's sensitivity and fire surpassed Mozart's joviality and Bach's intellect. Chopin's spirit dove directly and profoundly into the core of my own.

183

I approached my piano teacher at the school for blind children. "Mr. Owen," I said enthusiastically, "I'd like to learn the *Revolutionary Étude*. I think I know enough Chopin waltzes, preludes, and nocturnes and I'd like to move on to the études."

Mr. Owen didn't say no. He just laughed and the condescension that rang through his "My dear child, YOU CAN'T play that piece yet!" was my first catalyst into new dimensions of endeavor.

When I entered the school, I learned Braille music. I also learned to take dictation, a slow, painstaking process, memorizing one measure at a time. Despite its dependence on a teacher, I preferred the latter method because I could rely on its accuracy. With a cluster of eight or ten measures in my mind, I spent the days between lessons perfecting the new music. Gradually the measures fit together and became a whole. This technique was not only mistake-proof but also the only way to learn material that had never been transcribed into Braille.

"I wouldn't even try dictating that étude to you," went on Mr. Owen. "It has millions of notes. I can scarcely see them myself." Mr. Owen was legally blind, which meant he could travel without assistance and read large print. The tiny and profuse notes of the étude were too much of a challenge to his weak eyesight, but I was not about to allow his limitations to douse my ambition.

"I need a sighted piano teacher," I told my mother. "I'm ready to learn pieces with more complicated formats than Mr. Owen can read."

Somehow, within the week, my mother found Eugenia Bromberg, a serious but kind and encouraging teacher. No piece was too hard or took too much time for her to teach me. Whatever I asked of her she was willing to attempt.

After a month of lessons, she offered, "I'd like to give you a second lesson a week, a scholarship lesson. No charge."

All summer we worked on the étude. When the going was snail-paced and arduous, she remained placid and patient. The only time she expressed anything but a positive reaction was not at the difficult passages which swooped up and down the keyboard in a frenzy of notes, but in my delivery of a particular section of the left hand which was a simple pounding bass.

"I don't believe YOU CAN'T count to four!" she exclaimed in exasperation when the pattern in my left hand refused to coordinate with that of the right.

"CAN'T count to four! CAN'T count to four!" I heard as I drove the pattern of notes into my brain. It was not a problem for long. By the end of the summer I had the piece memorized and ready to play.

When school started I could scarcely wait for my first piano lesson.

"Mr. Owen," I said, trying not to gloat as I settled myself on the piano stool. "I have something to play for you."

184

Mr. Owen was a small man, short and frail. His voice was high-pitched and nasal. It was his habit when he was excited to draw breath in through his teeth until he achieved a whistle, all the while rubbing his child-size hands together. The whole gesture would terminate with a forceful expulsion of breath and the prolonged exclamation, "BY JIMMINY!"

As the crashing concluding chords of the étude died away, there was a moment of silence and then his familiar whistle, his excited, "BY JIMMINY! Those young fingers can do it after all!"

Although Tucson was a small town then, in the early fifties, its one concert hall offered monthly performances that were on a par with those enjoyed in more culturally sophisticated cities. For each concert, the theater manager sent our school a block of free tickets. My mother and I never missed a performance.

One morning during our chorus rehearsal, the secretary came in to take a head count. "How many of you would like to attend the Rubinstein concert Friday evening?"

Artur Rubinstein, my idol, to me the greatest pianist who ever lived, greater than Horowitz, greater than Kapel, greater than anyone, was actually coming to Tucson! I would be in the same auditorium with him, hear him play in person, not just on the recordings I bought with my saved-up allowance!

I sat mesmerized throughout his performance, a traditional program interpreted by a genius. I reveled in his perfect Bach, his powerful and passionate Beethoven, his rich and delicately tapestried Chopin, his fanciful Debussy. When the curtain came down, my mother asked, "Would you like to go backstage?"

Mr. Rubinstein's manager was standing just inside the open backstage door. He was obviously about to close it before the eager fans could disturb the pianist. My mother and I walked quickly up to him. "Excuse me, sir," she said, "my daughter plays the piano and she'd like to meet Mr. Rubinstein."

The manager halted long enough to say politely but firmly, "I'm sorry, miss, but YOU CAN'T do that. Mr. Rubinstein cannot meet everyone who would like to meet him."

Just then, the pianist himself approached our little group. There was a hushed exchange of words between the two men and then the fingers that enchanted and thrilled the world were grasping mine.

"Hello," he said in a deep, lightly accented voice. "Thank you for coming. I hope you enjoyed the concert."

The next time I heard YOU CAN'T was when I had decided to leave Juilliard School of Music and attend a liberal arts college. I met with the dean of students, whose first question was, "Why would you want to leave Juilliard to come to us?"

"I miss academics," I explained. "I would prefer to spend my life with the great writers and thinkers of the world rather than on a piano bench. I plan to major in English and American Literature."

"Do you have any idea how much reading that will entail? How many term papers? YOU CAN'T possibly do all that work without your sight."

Despite the dean's dire predictions, I enrolled in the division of my choice. Typing class had been a daily occurrence at the blind school, so term papers were not a problem, and by hiring students as readers and enlisting my mother to read as well, the reading assignments were accomplished. I took abundant Braille notes, often Brailing many pages of text. Some of the classics were in Braille or recorded on talking book discs and available on loan from the State Library for the Blind. Others I purchased from the Royal Institute for the Blind in London.

The Jewish Guild for the Blind of New York brailed a French grammar and a sixteen-volume survey of French literature for me, and a recording club from inside the walls of a prison taped several French books on open reel-to-reel tapes. The day of the cassette had not yet been born and these open-reel tapes were, at best, inconvenient, often a disastrous mess if they had been damaged in the mail or happened to fall and tangle. But whatever the inconvenience, I was grateful for the hours the men had spent expertly and fluently reading centuries of poets, plays of Molière, works of Voltaire, and other authors who would otherwise have been unavailable to me. Their voices were cultured and pleasant and only the occasional sound of a distant whistle, the shout of a guard, or the clang of a far-off cell door reminded me that these readers were incarcerated.

With all this help, I maintained an academic average that entitled me to a slot on the Dean's List and a possible membership in the Phi Beta Kappa National Honor Society.

Only one class threatened my membership in the society—a mandatory science class.

The school for blind children in Tucson taught the bare basics. Consequently, I had no background for complex college-level material in the sciences. As yet there were no talking calculators and, although I understood the concepts, it was impossible to keep complicated formulas in my head to do the problems at the end of each chapter in the text. The term was only two weeks old when I realized I was drowning. I spoke to the professor.

"It's still early," she said, totally missing the point. "You'll catch on."

The only thing I caught was frustration and the sinking fear that my grade was dipping into an unacceptable danger zone.

I approached her again. "You have a C average," she reassured me, "quite respectable under the circumstances."

Respectable wasn't good enough. Since long before my first day of college I had coveted a membership in the Honor Society, and a grade of C or below would slaughter that old dream. I approached her again. "Would it be possible for me to write a paper of some kind for extra credit?"

The professor was obviously annoyed at my persistence. "I'll take care of it," she snapped and at the beginning of the next class she announced, "I don't usually do this, but we have a blind student in the class who needs help, so from now on I shall write significant information on the board for her to copy as I lecture."

I walked from the class directly into the office of the dean of the science department and explained the situation. "Miss Covelli," he said, and there was an undercurrent of good-natured exasperation in his voice, "I can see that there is a lack of comprehension here which is not exclusively yours. Therefore, I will personally assign you an extra-credit project which will give you the opportunity to maintain the grade-point average you have achieved in other courses."

The class continued to be a struggle, but the dean's project allowed me to squeak through it with a B and I was back on the road to the little rectangular Phi Betta Kappa Key that I hoped would someday proclaim to the world and, more importantly, to me, that I could excel if I worked hard enough.

One afternoon, a professor friend told me over coffee in her office, "Robert Frost will be our speaker at the Phi Beta Kappa induction ceremony this year."

"I'd love to meet him!" I ventured.

She laughed. "So would the entire student body and faculty. I'm afraid YOU CAN'T do that. He's a very private man and we had to assure him he wouldn't be disturbed for autographs or personal interviews."

After the ceremony, my mother and I were walking across the parking lot when she said in an excited whisper, "Here he comes!"

"Who?"

"The poet! Robert Frost! He's walking right toward us. His car must be parked near ours."

My mother, knowing my heart's desire, called out, "Sir, Mr. Frost, just a moment, please."

Her audacity startled me. I didn't know whether to be mortified or grateful, but there was no time for contemplation. Suddenly and unexpectedly, the unofficial Poet Laureate of the United States, winner of four Pulitzer Prizes, was standing inches away from me.

The meeting was less than lustrous. He was shy or taciturn or annoyed at being stopped and I was speechless, but he did take my hand and managed to congratulate me and I managed to thank him. His strong, labor-roughened hand reminded me of his poems on chopping wood, building walls, mending fences. Despite the brevity of the encounter, the moment has remained unforgettable and, thinking of it, I always recall words from one of his poems: "Happiness makes up in height for what it lacks in length."

The summer I was eighteen, my mother and I decided to include a pilgrimage to Padre Pio, the Capuchin with the stigmata, in our annual Italian travels. We boarded a train in Rome and climbed the mountains to San Giovanni Rotondo. The train was full of pilgrims and we fell into conversation with a young American priest.

"Padre Pio has performed so many miracles," my mother said hopefully. "Maybe he'll cure Bianca's eyes."

"Padre Pio doesn't grant many personal audiences," the priest told us, "and the mobs are so enormous that YOU CAN'T possibly get close to him, but you will take away enough grace from being at his Mass to last you a lifetime."

The next morning at three o'clock we rose in the tiny room we had reserved in a family pensione and, without the thought of breakfast, made our way on steep, stony paths to the site for the four A.M. Mass. Since there was no church that could accommodate all the faithful who gathered, Padre Pio celebrated his daily Mass on an open field. Although it was late July, the predawn mountain air was frigid. We knelt on the hard-packed earth under a sunless sky, shivering.

As the Mass progressed, the priest's wounds bled more and more profusely until he became too weak to stand alone. Two young priests supported him as he finished the Mass and walked slowly and laboriously from the altar toward his dwelling.

His walk brought him past the congregation and, although he was flanked by protecting priests, some of the peasant women, crying out for his blessing, pushed through the crowd in the hope of touching his robes. Their devotion and affection were genuine, but their unbridled ardor only irritated the modest old priest.

"*Via! Via!*" (Away! Away!) he cried, weakly waving his arms in impatient frustration.

Since my mother and I had arrived early, we were in the front row for the Mass. As the women behind us had pressed forward, they had inadvertently propelled me nearly into the holy man's path. As he and his supporting priests were about to pass by, he stopped. Amid the clamor of the congregation, I heard his soft, sorrowful voice and felt his fingertips on my head.

"*La volenta di Dio. Non posso fare niente*" (The will of God. I can do nothing), he whispered and shuffled away.

Although my vision was not restored, a miracle of sorts did occur. I survived the stampede of women who, if they could not touch him, would touch me as the recipient of his blessing. The emotion of being addressed and touched by the saintly man, mingled with the confusion and onslaught of the zealous women, made me too light-headed to stand. Seeing my physical distress, the women shifted into a solicitous mode. Two or three pairs of hands caught me as I was slipping to the ground and sat me on a folding chair someone had brought to the Mass. A large wool shawl was wrapped around me and a small metal cup of water was put into my hand. I tried to raise the cup to my lips, but my hands were shaking so violently that the water only spilled down the front of the shawl. Suddenly I heard a familiar voice and felt a steadying hand on my shoulder. The young American priest whom we had met on the train was standing beside me.

"Well," he said, "as always, we mere mortals never know what God has in store for us. After this morning, I shall remove the word 'can't' from my vocabulary."

At the end of two years in college, it was time to declare a minor and I had decided to minor in secondary education, the first step toward my goal—to be sitting one day where my professors sat, on the other side of a college classroom desk. Without knowing my secret plans, a professor of American Literature asked me to conduct our class for two days when she contracted laryngitis. I lugged my talking book machine (a cumbersome record player that played recorded books from the Library for the Blind) into school and played a portion of the book I had borrowed for one of our assignments, William Faulkner's *The Sound and the Fury*. During the discussion that followed, the students expressed their newfound delight in listening to great literature being read by a professional reader. With my motivation whetted by the experience, I declared my intended minor. This time the dean of the school of education pronounced the tiresome words, "YOU CAN'T minor in education because you won't find a school that will accept you for the practice teaching requirement necessary for graduation. Besides, it will be impossible for you to find a teaching position, since handicapped teachers are never hired by public schools. You might want to visit the New York State School for the Blind and speak with the director before you pursue a course of studies YOU CAN'T utilize."

My dog and I arrived at the New York Institute for the Blind on Pelham Parkway in the Bronx a few days later. Sitting across the desk from us was a middle-aged, dour-voiced director who smelled of shoe polish and mint Lifesavers.

"We no longer hire blind teachers," he said. "We feel it's better for the children to have a sighted instructor."

"Why?" I asked.

"Many reasons," he replied, but he didn't offer any.

Firing my last hope of ammunition, I said, "It would seem to me that a teacher who has already traveled the road the children are on would be a better guide than a person who doesn't know what's necessary for the journey."

"I'm sorry," he said, standing and going to open the door of his office as my cue to leave, "we're just not hiring blind teachers."

With public school doors closed to me and now the blind school inaccessible, I stubbornly minored in education and took the prescribed courses. The only one I didn't enjoy was the History of Pedagogy, four to six P.M. twice a week. By that time of day, Heidi and I were both tired, both hungry, and both eager to hop the bus and start for home. To make matters worse, the subject and the professor were equally dull, dull, dull.

As Dr. Murphy droned on and on, my mind wandered farther and farther away. Remembering Bergen Evan's definition of a college professor—someone who talks in other people's sleep—I didn't feel guilty as my head began to nod, but I knew I had to do something to keep myself awake. I began using class time to write to blind friends I left in Arizona when we moved to New York. Since my writing was in Braille, the professor couldn't glance over and determine what I was actually writing.

As I was slipping Heidi's raincoat on her and buckling her harness over it one snowy evening after class, Dr. Murphy approached my desk.

"Miss Covelli, I am so pleased to have you in my class. I can always judge how good my lectures are by how many notes you take. It has been most gratifying to see how busily you've been writing during the last few sessions." There was so much pleasure in his voice. How could I disillusion him with the truth?

As I completed each class in secondary education, the dean's words, "YOU CAN'T minor in education because you won't find a school that will accept you..." echoed in my mind, but I continued on my designated route, hoping and praying for the best, and the best happened.

I don't remember how Miss Ann Culligan came into my life, but every Saturday morning she arrived at the house at nine o'clock and spent three hours reading assignments and correcting the abominable spelling in my term papers. She was a soft-spoken, merry, middle-aged lady with a special presence. She always carried an enormous shopping bag from which she fished out anything she needed—dictionary, pen, glasses, sweater. I never had an address or a phone number for her.

"It might be wise for me to have your phone number," I had said not many weeks into our reading sessions, "so if I'm sick or not going to be home for some reason, I can let you know and save you the trip."

She didn't refuse the information, but she skirted around my request with a breezy, "I'll come by and if you're not available I'll just go on my way."

The more time passed and the more I experienced her joyful, spiritual nature, the more I became convinced that she was truly an angel in disguise, one who had floated down to me for reading and, as it turned out, for much more.

My college years were golden and zipped by faster than I would have liked. Soon the shadow of practice teaching loomed very near. The last term before graduation had to be spent teaching in a high school. I discussed the problem with Miss Culligan. "I don't know what I'm going to do," I said one Saturday morning as we prepared to read an assignment for an education class in adolescent psychology. "I don't know where to start looking for a school that will accept me."

"I do," said Miss Culligan in her perky, uncomplicated manner. "I have an old friend, Sister Mary Borgia, who is principal of Mary Louis Academy. I'm sure she'll take you." And she did.

Phil and I were married in January of my senior year and my student teaching began two weeks later. Phil worked for IBM in New York and the academy was in the Jamaica Estates. Our apartment lay in between the school and his office. Sister Mary Borgia had accepted me with the understanding that my guide dog would not be welcome. That meant Phil had to drive me to school, drive home, and take the subway to New York. Consequently, I arrived at the academy before seven and my first class was at nine.

"Come to the office," Sister Mary Borgia suggested, "and use the time answering the phone for us. Just type out the names of the girls who will be absent."

I enjoyed the new aspect of my job, but it soon became evident that not all the calls were to inform the school of the day's absentees. Some calls were for the principal, some for the vice principal, Sister Miriam, and some for the nurse or gym coach.

Sister Miriam, at the loudspeaker, began the school day with prayers, announcements, and often such complaints and warnings as: "I hope my eyes were deceiving me and that was not lipstick I saw on some busy mouths that should have been unpainted and silent coming down the halls" or "I saw some unpolished shoes walking into the building! Such slovenliness will not be tolerated!"

Sister Miriam was a tall, robust woman with a solid footstep, but I didn't hear her approaching my desk across the soft carpeting the morning of her shoe complaint.

"Mrs. Stewart," she said in her usual energetic voice. I jumped, instinctively thrusting my feet deeper under the desk where she couldn't see my shoes. The nun recognized the hurried gesture. "Your shoes are fine," she assured me with a deep chuckle, "but there is something you do need to address—the switchboard." She leaned her large frame over my shoulder and, placing the plug in my hand, showed me, "This jack is for Sister Mary's office, this one for mine, down here is for the nurse and the athletic office just beside it." And so my job experience expanded still further.

My classes consisted of an average sophomore group, a slow junior, and an accelerated senior class. Fortunately, my brand new title of "Mrs." went a long way in detaching me from the oldest students, who were nearly my age.

The school's discipline also enhanced the respect I might not have otherwise received. At the beginning of each class the girls stood at their desks and, in unison, greeted me with, "Good morning, Mrs. Stewart," to which I had to reply, "Good morning, girls. You may be seated." With the scraping of desk chairs came another chorus, "Thank you, Mrs. Stewart." The whole exercise made me feel very much older and very professional.

And so, it seemed as though I was quickly and smoothly sailing toward graduation and a teaching career, but by the middle of March there was a new obstacle on the course of my practice teaching—an overwhelming,

Bianca, age 21 and Phil, age 26
Wedding in N.Y., 1959

dizzying nausea. Every morning, armed with an apple and a pack of crackers, I gritted my teeth and set out for the academy, hoping I didn't look as sick as I felt. I was extremely underweight so my gradual weight gain was scarcely noticeable, but I did begin buying larger sizes (sevens, tens, fast approaching twelves) to avoid any hint of snug-fitting clothes. By April, I knew I had to tell Sister Mary Borgia the truth. How did I say it? The word "pregnant" was much too blunt and "in a family way" was too archaic. I stalled, thinking I had plenty of time to make the declaration because I was still thin, even in the stomach.

The rain had been pelting down with a stiff wind behind it and I was hanging up my dripping raincoat in the teachers' lounge one morning when Sister Mary Borgia entered. "Good morning," she said pleasantly.

I had just popped a cracker into my mouth and had to swallow it almost whole so I could respond, "Good morning, Sister."

"Mrs. Stewart," she began, "have you been feeling well? You've been looking terribly peaked lately, especially first thing in the morning." The secret was out. She knew.

"Sister," I said almost apologetically, "I have been wanting to tell you, I'm expecting."

"Expecting," a perfectly proper word. Not offensive, one could be expecting a letter, a check, a phone call, a baby.

She grasped my hand. "Wonderful," she said. "God bless you," and she swooped out of the room, large wooden rosary beads clicking against her long skirt.

In relief I sank down onto one of the chairs surrounding the long conference table. With trembling fingers I dug my pack of crackers out of my briefcase and continued my snack. I was ecstatic. Sister would obviously permit me to finish my practice teaching. This was the one and only opportunity I would ever have and the thought of losing it had been devastating.

Classes continued smoothly. Phil or Miss Culligan read the girls' homework to me and I graded it. Only once did the sophomores try to trick me. I had given an A to an excellent paper until its duplicate and then another and another appeared in the stack. The girls must not have thought I would go to the trouble of having each individual paper read to me. I went back to the first paper, had Phil mark an X over the A and write an F beside it. Each matching paper received the same grade. The problem never arose again.

In the middle of May, a month after I had announced my pregnancy to Sister Mary Borgia, I heard Sister Miriam's voice over the loudspeaker: "Mrs. Stewart, please come to Sister Mary Borgia's office after your last class."

I began to worry. I smoothed my suit jacket over my stomach. It really wasn't protruding very much. She wouldn't send me away now, would she, not with only five weeks left in the school year?

"Sit down, please," said Sister Mary Borgia as I entered her office. "There's something we have to talk about. You'll find a chair in front of my desk."

I sat down and waited, my heart thumping loudly in my ears.

"Sister Miriam and I have discussed it and, in view of your condition," Sister began. This was really it, I thought. I was finished at the academy. My face was burning. I had wanted to wait until after graduation to get married, but a convenient apartment and a Saturday morning opening for the Nuptial Mass at our parish church had become available in January and we had decided to take advantage of both. "I hope you won't mind too much," Sister continued, "but I must ask you..." I completed her sentence in my mind, "to leave," but that was not what I was hearing. I tuned into the principal's words and heard, "To wear flat shoes for the rest of the year. I know flats are not as fashionable as those stiletto heels you wear, but Sister Miriam and I are nervous about your going up and down the stairs in them. Please do us a favor and wear oxfords here."

"Of course, Sister," I sighed, "of course."

The news of my "condition" had flown around the school. Sister Miriam clucked a motherly cluck each morning. "You're looking better," or "You're green, my girl, do you need a bite to eat?"

Even Sister Regina, the nun in charge of the cafeteria, mellowed. Sister Regina was elderly, walked with a limp, and was cross most of the time. The day following my conversation with Sister Mary Borgia, Sister Regina came into the office as I was plugging a call into the proper slot. She slapped a paper towel onto my desk and said gruffly, "Not for you. For the future generation."

A tantalizing aroma floated up from the folded toweling and reaching inside, I found two crisp slices of bacon on a piece of hot buttered toast.

"Sister Regina," I murmured with genuine appreciation, "thank you. I didn't realize the future generation is as hungry as it is."

Every morning after that Sister silently placed some kind of treat from the cafeteria on the corner of my desk and I always thanked her with the same words, "The future generation thanks you, Sister." Often I would hear her thin, high laugh as she limped out of the office.

Just before graduation, I received notification from Recordings for the Blind Inc. (RFB), a new organization that had begun recording textbooks, that I was one of four graduates in the country to be honored by President Dwight D. Eisenhower at the White House. Phil and I took the train to Washington the day before the event and were met at a hotel by representatives of RFB. We had dinner with the other three recipients, all men, the RFB officers, and Mr. L. Quincy Mumford, the head of the Library of Congress.

My stomach problems had calmed by then and I was able to enjoy my meals if they were moderate. The dinner that evening was delicious and abundant. The next morning I dared to order what was, for me, an enormous breakfast—a scrambled egg, toast, and bacon. A horrendous mistake!

After half an hour, as we waited for the cars to collect us for our trip to the White House, I was deathly ill. Waves of nausea swept over me and a cold clamminess clung to my skin.

"YOU CAN'T go feeling like that," Phil said. "You'll never make it! You'll be sick on the president's carpet!"

"If I listened to all the YOU CAN'Ts in my life," I said through clenched teeth, struggling to keep my breakfast where I had so gluttonously put it, "I wouldn't be in Washington today!"

President Eisenhower was warm and gracious to all of us, and as we chatted and posed for photographs, no one suspected that under my new size fourteen suit, another person was attending the ceremony.

Theresa was a month old when we brought her to the Mary Louis convent. The nuns clustered around her, exclaiming and complimenting, cooing and laughing with delight over this pink bundle of new life. Sister Mary Borgia lifted Theresa out of my arms, placed her on their little altar, and invoked a special blessing on our tiny daughter.

Our firstborn was followed by Philip, who was followed by Daniel, Francesca, and Thomas. With each birth I remembered my mother's words when Phil and I began contemplating marriage. "I have something I must tell you and that you must tell Phil before you accept his engagement ring," she had begun. "Doctors told me when you were seventeen and finally diagnosed with Brucellosis that the disease leaves women sterile. YOU CAN'T have children."

Bianca, 1959, accepting scholastic award from President Eisenhower

Borders

The mountain—the reality!
But something there is that needs to soar,
to rise above the peak,
to untangle the footsteps of our stumbling humanity,
from the brambles of the harsh and rock-strewn day.

The canyon—the reality!
But something there is that needs to span,
to cross the emptiness,
the cavernous expanse of loneliness
on the flower-petal bridge of empathy.

The ennui—the reality!
But something there is that needs to stir,
to wake from life's caged sleep,
to ride a dream and lift with its glowing, crimson wings
off the straight steel tracks of
where we are and who we are and why.

Bianca and Phil, 1999, 40th wedding anniversary

Twenty-one

Our Father's Funeral

June 1981

The house looked like a warehouse. Tall wardrobe cartons stood just inside the front door. Boxes were stacked upon boxes and now the baby grand, beneath three heavily breathing men, made its way up the seven steps of the porch and was positioned against the far wall of the living room. The fragments of past generations and of current life were being rolled, shoved, and carried into the present, into the house which stood ready to welcome and unite everything. We were moving into the oceanfront Victorian home that had been, until now, our summer residence.

The phone rang and the sound bounced from wall to wall to wall. My mother picked up the receiver, listened a moment and gasped.

"Who is it?" I asked. "What's wrong?"

Without a word she put the phone in my hand.

"Hello?"

"Hello, honey, this is Dan."

I was delighted to hear my half-brother's voice. He didn't phone often now that he was remarried.

"It's great to hear from you," I said. "How have you been?"

"I have bad news," he said and his words were husky with emotion. "Our father had a cerebral hemorrhage. He's still alive but the doctors say not for long. You'd better plan on coming to Chicago for a funeral. You and Phil will stay in my home, of course."

I was not disturbed by the news. The timing was certainly inconvenient, but death doesn't read calendars and in a week Dan called again.

"He's gone. The funeral's on Thursday. Can you come in tomorrow? We've planned just a one-day wake on Wednesday."

It was already Monday evening so I decided to forego the train and take my first plane trip. With a curious sense of excitement, I made reservations for the following afternoon.

199

"Would you like me to read the ads from the airline magazine?" Phil asked before we had even taken off. I knew he was trying to occupy my mind in order to stave off any possible anxiety on my part as a novice flyer, but I was perfectly calm and savoring the new sounds and smells of the plane as well as looking forward to the adventure that lay before me.

The moment the plane shuddered to a stop on the O'Hare runway Phil gripped my hand. "Well, what did you think of the flight?" There was hope in his voice. My fear of flying had always kept me and the children from accompanying him on his global business trips.

"I loved it! I'm free!" I exclaimed, exhilarated because I was released not only from my fear, but also from the only tenuous tie to my father—his own crippling fear of airplanes.

"I see Dan," Phil said as we stepped off the escalator into the buzzing, bustling airport. "His hair's all white, lots of it still and wavy, but all white!"

The image of my brother as a child, his pale curls wet and dark from the shower or a swim, flashed across my mind. How distressed I had always been until the dark wetness disappeared and restored his beautiful blondness.

Now he engulfed me in an expensive cologned hug and I remembered how, on his last visit to my home, he had taken his place in line as I doled out vitamins to my children.

"I'll have one, too," he had said and I had been touched by his obviously unsatisfied and therefore unquenchable need for nurturing.

I had thought his first wife, a sweet, shy orphan who adored him, would have filled every void in his motherless life, but her affection had not been enough to anchor him and keep him from searching elsewhere and, after several years of marriage, she had taken the four youngest of their seven children and moved to California.

I was now eager to meet his second wife, hoping she had supplied what he had never been able to find except for the summer we lived together under my mother's care when our parents had tried unsuccessfully to reconcile.

"This is Rose," he said and a woman's long-fingernailed, limp hand took mine. "Hi," she said unenthusiastically. Her voice and demeanor already disappointed me.

We walked out into the muggy Chicago evening and climbed into Dan's low-slung sports car. "I had a sunroof put on this baby," he told us as we skimmed along the highway to his house in the suburbs. "Dad said I was a damn fool to spend nine hundred dollars just to have a hole drilled into the roof of a car."

I laughed. "I remember your first car, the red convertible," I said, wondering if he was thinking as I was of how we were inches away from smashing into a truck because he had let me sit on his lap and steer. That was more than forty years ago. I didn't mention the incident because it was also the day he had taken me to the carnival where I began to go totally and permanently blind. The memory might make him uncomfortable.

As we approached his house, Rose announced in a dull monotone, "My son, Jerry, was hit on this road last year. He was fourteen. A drunk driver killed him."

I was caught off-guard. Finally I managed to mumble, "I'm so sorry. What a tragic waste, what a heartbreaking thing to have happen."

Dan changed the subject. "I went to Dad's bank vault and got his cash out of the box—eight hundred thousand dollars—plus all the stocks and bonds. There are also his bank accounts, condos, the new Caddy, and the antiques. Of course, we have to wait for the will to be read to see how he wanted everything distributed."

"Of course," I said, but I was already planning to spread my share over college tuitions, a house for Theresa and her husband Jim, a new car, a family trip to Europe.... I reined in my extravagant imagination. There were three of us, after all. Dan and I had a sister somewhere.

I was ten years old and my mother and I had been in Arizona just a month when a friend sent a newspaper clipping announcing my sister's birth. The article had not followed the customary complimentary track that usually accompanied news about my father.

"Three children, three wives," were the reporter's words.

And then, I remembered, there was also Lee—Lee, my father's chronic, off-and-on wife, his mistress between other wives, the woman my mother refused to accept as part of her life with my father.

It was nearly eight P.M. as we pulled into Dan's driveway. I was starving and hoping Rose had a roast or a chicken or at least a pot of pasta waiting. But as we walked into the house there was no aroma of food. Perhaps they planned to take us out for dinner.

"What do we have to eat, Rosie?" asked my brother.

"I don't know," she tossed in his direction as she settled on the living room couch. "I think there might be some salami left." She didn't stir, didn't make a move to indicate she was interested enough in feeding us to investigate.

Phil left me on the couch beside her and went into the kitchen with Dan. "Can I give you a hand?" he asked.

"Sure, thanks," murmured my brother. "We're not too organized in the food department around here, but there's plenty of booze." He laughed unconvincingly.

My initial disappointment in his wife deepened.

In a moment Phil was handing me a floppy paper plate with a sandwich on it, salami between two stale pieces of bread.

"Rosie." Dan's voice, irritated and embarrassed, came from the kitchen. "Isn't there anything to drink in this house besides whiskey and your damn 7-Up?"

"Don't touch that 7-Up!" Rose cried out in alarm. "That's mine."

"You've got your carton with you, haven't you?" Dan asked, coming into the living room and sitting down beside me.

"Those in the fridge are for tomorrow, for the wake. Leave 'em alone."

With a sigh he didn't try to hide, Dan didn't pursue the question but shifted the conversation. "Honey," he began, laying his hand on my arm, "just to let you know, we're surrounded by dead people."

This whole scene was so bizarre that I was expecting him to launch into ghost talk, but he said, "Photos of Jerry, of Aunt Mimi, of our grandmother Rafaela, and of Dad are all over the room. It's gruesome, depressing."

"Sometimes there's a definite advantage in not being able to see," I said wryly.

He didn't react to my comment, but continued, "You know, Dad couldn't talk after his attack, but he could open his eyes and there was real terror in them. I've never seen such terror. I'll never forget it. I see those eyes when I'm trying to go to sleep or when I'm wide awake! It's awful!" He buried his head in his hands. His words were muffled.

I felt a surge of affection and pity for him and would have liked to reach out and touch him, but for some undefinable reason I couldn't. I sympathized verbally, "I'm sorry for you, Dan, but at least you have the consolation of knowing he didn't suffer long."

"Right." Dan sighed again. "Nine days."

We didn't have a great deal to talk about. Silences kept creeping into the lagging conversation. Rose didn't offer a word. I wanted to inquire about Dan's children, but not knowing how Rose felt about Dan's first family, I refrained from asking. Finally, after this incredible welcoming dinner and strained cordiality, it was late enough to justify going to bed.

"I'll put the cat out and be up shortly," my brother said. "Good night. See you in the morning. We should leave by eight."

Rose led the way up the narrow staircase. "You'll use Jerry's old room," she told us in her monotone. "There's clean towels on the dresser. Good night." And she walked away down the hall.

The room was skeletal: a dresser, a double bed, and a card table and chair were all there were.

"There are holes in the wall where the boy's posters must have been," Phil told me. His words echoed in the terrible emptiness.

"This adventure is more than a little disturbing," I said. "The vibes are frightening, and I'm so disappointed in poor Dan's wife, but she's obviously deeply depressed."

"Not very cheerful around here, I'll say that much," Phil agreed.

I heard him swing our suitcase onto the card table and unzip it. I retrieved my nightgown.

"I feel a little guilty," I confessed, slipping off my dress and preparing for bed. "I suppose I should be grieving."

"You can't force it," he said. "Maybe it'll hit you tomorrow at the wake."

In the morning Rose redeemed herself. One of them, probably Dan, must have gone to the store because Rose was at the stove cooking eggs and bacon.

Dan was at the back door, calling his cat, and there was panic in his voice. "Candy! Candy! Where are you? My God, she's not around anywhere."

"Look in the compactor," said Rose with a sardonic little laugh.

He ignored his wife. "We can't leave until Candy's in the house," he said and went out to search.

"You might as well start eating," said Rose as she slid a platter onto the vinyl tablecloth. "He won't be back till he finds his cat."

A young man came in without knocking and stood just inside the back door.

"This is my son Harold," said Rose and the man muttered a "Hi, how you doin'," but he didn't come forward into the room.

"Why aren't you at work?"

"It's raining, Ma," he said. "Haven't you noticed?"

"He does outside work, gardening," Rose explained, then added, "His sister's in veterinary school, though. She's my smart one."

The young man mumbled goodbye and left. This household was becoming more and more pathetic, I thought to myself, and my sympathy for my brother increased in proportion to the time I spent in his home.

Dan found his cat. Rose armed herself with her pack of 7-Up and we were on our way to Chicago and the wake.

"Susan's coming in today," Dan said as we mounted the steps to the funeral parlor. "Christ, it just occurred to me that both my sisters live in New Jersey and they don't even know each other! What a messed-up family we are."

"Well," I said, struggling for breath as I stepped into what seemed like the entrance to an overstocked flower shop, "we both know who to thank for that."

The funeral director came forward. "Judge Covelli is in the first room," he said with such theatrical grief that I fought a smile. We followed him into the designated room, where Lee and her brother Paul were waiting.

"Thanks for letting him wear his robes," my brother said quietly. "He looks great. Thanks."

From his manner I discerned there must have been some disagreement between him and Lee concerning the judge's coffin attire.

Lee, heavily perfumed, sidled up to me. "Hello, dear," she said in her low, coarse voice which made me think of smoke-filled nightclubs. I remembered that she had once been a cigarette girl. How in the world could a brilliant and successful man...no use trying to solve that old mystery now.

Lee and I sat on a brocade loveseat. My brother took his position just inside the doorway to welcome the stream of people already arriving to pay their respects. A handshake, a few murmured words, and he turned to introduce each person to me and to Lee. "My sister Bianca and my stepmother Lee." So the judge WAS ashamed of her after all. None of his colleagues or acquaintances knew her. Interesting!

Lee had a paper cup in her hand. I heard the ice cubes clicking against one another. Her brother came over to us and asked none too discreetly, "What's in that cup, Lee?"

She hurled her response: "Water, just water. Don't bother me. Mind your own damn business." Her last word ended in a long, venomous hiss that made me shudder.

Dan had told me years ago, "Lee likes her booze and then some, but she cooks and keeps an immaculate house for Old Moneybags and doesn't interfere with his other personal interests."

Lee tried to start a conversation. "How was your flight, dear?"

"Terrific! I enjoyed it."

"And how is your mother?"

"Very well, thank you."

"And your stepfather?"

"He's dead."

She obviously didn't know what to say so I relented and got her off the uncomfortable hook on which her limited intellect had impaled her.

"He died years ago, lung cancer."

"Oh?" she said and the inflection of surprise in the tiny word spoke volumes. I knew she was suddenly wondering if the judge's trips to New York and New Jersey had been to visit me and my family or my widowed mother.

Having exhausted all topics of conversation, she rose heavily to her feet. "I have to sit on a straight chair," she said defensively and moved away.

Susan arrived. Dan brought her to me and introduced us. I remembered Aunt Mimi's description from years ago: "Susie is lovely, a little porcelain doll!"

She was petite. Her hand was small, almost frail, but her voice was loud, shrill, not consistent with her physical person.

"At a time like this I'm glad I wasn't close to him, aren't you?" she asked as she sat down in the place Lee had just vacated. "I think I saw him six times in my whole life, how about you?"

Her questions were such a poignant cry for reassurance that she was not the least loved of our father's children that my response was a deliberate lie.

"Not many more than six," I said, thinking of our father's annual trips to my home for his birthday parties. He had started coming after our first two children were born.

"I refuse to wear mourning for this shindig," Susan informed me, "but I see you're in black!"

Although her words were an accusation, I didn't feel obliged to defend myself and justify my choice of clothing to her so I remained silent while she

204

stormed on, "My mother left him before I was three years old. She had her parents to fall back on. She didn't have to put up with his shi— uh...nonsense."

I smiled at her restraint, but her fermenting anger continued to spill out around us. Her sharp, high-pitched voice was slicing metallically through the still, flower-burdened air and I was beginning to be embarrassed, especially since someone had taken the chair beside my end of the loveseat and was certainly hearing her inappropriate onslaught of words.

When she mentioned her mother, the mental picture of a strikingly attractive redhead surfaced in my memory.

"Did your mother ever work for him?"

"Yes, she was his legal secretary."

"Was—or I should say—is she a redhead?"

"Yes."

"I think I must have seen her in his office when I was a child," I mused.

"You did," confirmed Susan. "My mom told me that you and your mother came to see him when she was still working for him, something about a dog."

"Yes, my little dog had been run over and we needed his help to pay her veterinary bills."

"Did he pay them?"

"He must have. My mother wasn't as fortunate as yours. Her parents were in Italy so we were on our own. Money was scarce in those days."

"He never paid anything significant for me," Susan complained, "nothing I know of anyway."

A tearful, grief-stricken young voice cried out from the person on the chair beside me. "I can't believe you're talking about Grandpa that way. He was the only stable thing in my whole life!" The words ended in a sob.

I turned to the voice and the girl composed herself. "I'm Carol, your youngest niece."

Susan launched into questions. "How old are you?"

"Eighteen."

"Do you live in Chicago?"

"Not really. I live in California with my mother, but I'm studying at Northwestern. Grandpa was paying for my education."

Susan exploded in my direction. "Did he pay for yours?"

"No, I had scholarships," I said, hoping she wouldn't blast the girl with more of her tragic fury. We were all silent.

"I love the rosary of white roses around Grandpa," said Carol wistfully. "I've never seen anything like it. I wonder who sent it!"

"I did," I confessed almost sheepishly and waited for Susan to excoriate me, but Carol asked, "Do you think I could have it, before the..." she choked on the word, "...burial?"

"As far as I'm concerned you're welcome to it," I told her. "But maybe you should ask your father or Lee."

The girl left and the fragrance of men's aftershave replaced the sharp and bitter scent of her sorrowful tears. "I'm Judge Morrow," an elderly voice said gently. "I worked with your father. He spoke so highly of you. He was very proud of your accomplishments."

"Of mine?" I asked in embarrassed confusion, wondering if I had spoken out of turn and he was really looking at Susan, but she needled in, "It would have been nice if he had told you that himself, wouldn't it?"

I was overwhelmed with surprise. Nothing my father ever said or did indicated the sentiments this judge had expressed.

Sometimes I hated my indelible memory. This was one of those times. I whirled back years. I was newly blind, trying to function as I did before I lost my sight. My mother and I were in Arizona and my father had come to town for a vacation and had accepted my mother's dinner invitation. Eager to escape his cigar smoke that made my eyes sting and tear, I rose and offered, "I'll help clear the table."

My father's voice nailed my feet to the floor. "For God's sake," he snarled, "sit her down before she breaks something."

And then, I was graduating from college, Phi Beta Kappa, cum laude, and with an award for academic excellence from President Eisenhower. There was a photo and an article in a New York paper. I sent a copy to my father, who didn't acknowledge it until we had an occasion to speak months later. I understood that his words, "What the hell are you trying to do, push your old man off the front page?" were an attempt at humor, possibly even a compliment of sorts, but I also recognized the undercurrent of hostility in his voice.

The elderly judge moved away and another voice broke into my reverie.

"Hi, Aunt Bianca, I'm Dan the Third," said a pleasant, sociable young man. "The last time we met I was five years old." He gripped my hand and went on, "My brother Steven's with me, too."

I waited to hear another voice, but Steven didn't speak. "There's a great article about Grandpa in the newspaper," my nephew told me. "Has anyone read it to you?"

"No."

"Then I will," he offered, but at that moment Steven began to call out to his brother as if the latter were blocks away, "Dan! Dan! I'm hungry, Dan!"

The second I heard his voice I knew there was a problem. My father never told me my brother had a deficient son. He must have been as ashamed of the boy's mental handicap as he had always been of my blindness. Somehow, the imperfections of any family member seemed to threaten his own stature.

Steven began to cry. "Is that really Grandpa? Dan? Is that Grandpa?"

"Yes, Stevie, come on now. I told you all about it. You promised you'd be good."

Steven's sobs got louder and his brother tried to comfort him. "Grandpa's fine, Stevie. He's in Heaven with God."

"No! No!" shrieked Steven. "You're wrong, Dan. You're wrong!"

My brother rushed over. "Christ, Dan," he growled, "get him out of here. Take him for a hamburger or something, and buy him a dark suit for the funeral. Charge it to my account."

The brothers moved toward the door, but I could still hear Steven's anguished words, "Grandpa told me there is no God. No Heaven, no God, Dan. Grandpa told me, Dan! He told me! Grandpa's just in that box, right there, right there, and he's never going to get out of it, is he, Dan? Is he?"

For the first time since the news of my father's death, I was shaken, not by my own nonexistent grief, but by the suffering my father had inflicted on this innocent, childlike young man.

A hand I recognized grasped mine and pulled me to my feet. "You're very pale," Phil said. "Let's get some fresh air."

Once we were out on the sidewalk he said, "People have been wanting to talk to you, but Susan's scaring them off. I thought you might want to break away."

"You know, Phil," I said, "even after he's dead my father still has the unsurpassable power to inflict pain. Why would he have told that poor soul there's no God? That's evil, evil with a capital E. There's no other word for it. No wonder he had terror in his eyes."

"Nothing you can do about it," my husband replied with that logical, practical attitude that sometimes stabilized and sometimes frustrated me.

A crowd exited from the funeral parlor and a boy in his teens stepped up beside me.

"Mr. Covelli, your brother, he told me you're Judge Covelli's da...da...daughter."

"Yes, I'm one of them."

"My...my...my name's Howey," the boy stammered. "My mom and I have a...a...a newsstand in the courthouse and we know...kne...kne...knew...knew your dad."

I waited. The boy obviously had more to say and suddenly his words tumbled out of his mouth all at once.

"I just wanted you to know that he was so good to us, always friendly and nice and he...he helped my brother Glenn get a job when he got out of jail."

"Thank you, Howey," I said. "It was good of you to tell me."

An excited murmur issued from the group on the stairs. "A long black limo is pulling up," Phil told me. "I don't recognize the woman inside but those people seem to know who she is."

"It's...it's...it's...Mayor Byrne," Howey informed us. "An...an...and I heard Governor Thompson's coming, too." The boy moved away in the direction of the crowd and a sad-voiced woman approached us.

"Hi," she began shyly. "My name's Connie. I was your dad's waitress at his club. He was so generous to me, got me the job and even helped me find an apartment—a real good guy."

She scurried off before I could reply, but once I heard her high heels clicking away to a safe distance, I asked, "Blond or redhead?"

"Actually," Phil chuckled, immediately tuning into my unspoken insinuations, "her hair's shoe-polish black."

The early morning rain had melted into a steamy mist. We walked around the block twice before went back inside.

"Breaking for lunch?" Phil asked my brother as we re-entered the room that had suddenly become chill after the damp heat of outdoors.

"No," he said, unwilling to surrender his one and only position of prominence in the family. "People keep on coming. I should be here to greet them."

Phil took Rose and me to lunch. Susan declined his invitation. We found the nearest restaurant and ordered our meal. I was thinking how strange it must look that a customer walked in clutching her own six-pack of 7-Up. I was speculating on this fetish of Rose's—was it a tie to her dead son, his favorite drink? Why else would she be so ferociously attached to 7-Up? Had she mixed another substance in the soda?

"Just in case you're wondering why I'm not sympathetic about your father's passing," Rose volunteered, "it's because your brother has never showed an ounce of sympathy about my son's death. At the burial he just left me standing alone at Jerry's grave. I had to walk back to the car by myself. I can never forget or forgive that."

"Somehow," I replied in my brother's defense, "I don't think he handles stress very well."

Rose unpacked a bottle of her 7-Up and popped off the lid. "I guess I should ask for a straw," she said. "This is kind of an upscale place."

I wondered why she didn't just pour the drink into the glass already set before her, but I didn't assume it was my place to venture the suggestion.

The more time passed, the more I felt like a spectator at a substandard movie, as if, totally detached, I was watching this whole day roll by across a screen. Except for my reaction to Steven, I was devoid of any emotion but a mild curiosity as one film clip after another went by.

Lunch was a quiet affair. Rose's moroseness and my absorption with Steven's anguish made conversation nearly impossible. At last we returned to my brother. His voice was getting hoarse and Lee's was huskier than before. Her words were slurring and I wondered what she managed to add to her cups of water. Another scene in this movie I was watching slipped across the mental screen of my mind—a woman's legs in shimmering stockings beneath a tiny skirt, thick hands balancing a large tray, and dubbed in I heard Lee's languid hoarseness: "Lucky Strikes? Camels?"

At the end of the long hours of hushed conversations and handshakes, we finally prepared to leave the funeral parlor for the trip back to Dan's home.

Lee's stage-whisper ground through the emptying room, "There won't be space for him in the limo tomorrow. He's not family anyway."

My brother's hushed but angry response was just as audible: "What do you mean he's not family? He's Bianca's husband. He rides with her in the limo and that's it."

"It's a long ride to the muslim," she whined. "We'll be cramped."

"Muslim"? Did she mean mausoleum? I wished I had brought my tape recorder so I could share this whole burlesque with my mother.

Snatches of the day crossed my mind as I lay on the bed in the dead boy's room, but the scenario wasn't worth watching twice so I put it on hold and allowed myself a luxurious slow wafting into sleep.

The morning dawned clear and hot. The ride into the city was quiet. A quick prayer on the kneeler beside the casket in the funeral parlor, a not-so-cramped ride in the limo, and in a few moments we were following the mortal remains of our father down the long center aisle of Holy Name Cathedral. We settled into the front pew and the Requiem began. A somber organ was playing not softly but almost too majestically. The perfect acoustics floated the music around the enormous cathedral.

This was the church my parents were married in, the place where my father's deception began. My mother, believing that his only former wife, Dan's mother, was dead, married in good faith. What my father hadn't revealed was that there were other former wives still very much alive—a fact that made their Catholic wedding null and void.

Now, as the priest launched into his eulogy, I began to wonder if I was attending the right funeral. I heard people actually sighing heavily, sniffling, and I heard the priest's voice proclaiming my father's honesty, his integrity as a judge (that's true), his concern for the underdog (really?), his devotion to his family (what family?), and his boundless generosity to people on every strata of life. According to the priest, every aspect of the community seemed to have benefited from his kind concern and open-handedness.

No matter how strenuously I shoved them away, past experiences stormed into Holy Name Cathedral and dragged me through thornbushes I thought I had long ago left behind:

Tucson—the hovel in which my mother and I were forced to live when, after our first month in Arizona, he stopped paying our motel bill.

My mother compelled to take a job at the town pharmacy and walk home alone a mile across the desert from the bus stop at midnight.

His threat to stop the ten dollars a week he was paying in child support once my mother began working as assistant to the doctor in charge of the town's school health department.

Whispering beneath the organ and the choir I heard the echo of old dialogues:

> *Mother*: "Now that Bianca has learned to type at the blind school, she should have a typewriter. She could write out her poems and correspond with her friends in Chicago."
>
> *Father*: "She needs a typewriter like a hole in the head. If you want her to have one, buy it yourself."
>
> *Mother*: "She'd love to take horseback riding lessons, but they're expensive. Will you help?"
>
> *Father*: "That's the most lame-brained idea you've had yet. I'm not paying any more hospital bills."
>
> *Mother*: "I need a car to drive her to school. There's an elderly couple in town that's selling a '37 Chevy for very little. Can you help?"
>
> *Father*: "I told you a long time ago to let her live at the school. She can come home in a cab on weekends."
>
> *Me*: "Phil lost a finger in a lawn mower accident yesterday."
>
> *Father*: "Next time he'll be more careful. Don't expect me to pick up the tab. I'm your father, not a bank."

The ride to the "muslim" was informative. My brother, suddenly less bereaved than the day before, was sitting beside the driver and chatting amiably with this stranger about the advantages and disadvantages of investing in real estate as opposed to stocks and bonds. Obviously, his grieving spirit had taken a consoling leap from the darkness of our father's death into the glittering sunshine of his inheritance.

We arrived at the cemetery and walked up stone steps into a cool, silent building. With a smooth roll of bearings and a click of the coffin into its slot in the marble wall, our father was tucked neatly away into whatever eternity awaited him. No prayers, no tears, no visible sorrow accompanied him.

We had some time before our flight home, but not enough to go back to Dan's house. Instead we went to our father's town apartment, a spacious, multi-room affair where tall glass-fronted cabinets held priceless European objets d'art and where my feet sank into deep oriental rugs. The lingering stench of cigar brought my father's presence into my consciousness as powerfully as if he were still inhabiting this luxurious palace of his.

"My mother had a portrait done of me when I was two," I told my brother as we settled onto a velvet couch. "I'd love to surprise her with it. How it came into our father's possession is a mystery. I do know she asked for it many times and he would never give it back to her. Do you know if it's here?"

"It's hanging in Aunt Mimi's old apartment down the street," he told me. "We haven't rented the place yet so the painting must still be there. It wasn't wanted here," Dan laughed. "Guess who objected?"

My brother sent his son Dan for the portrait. "Christ," exclaimed my brother. "It's much bigger than I remember! How will you get it home? Should I ship it?"

"I'll carry it," Phil said. "Do you have anything to wrap it in?"

Dan found some brown grocery bags and they spent the rest of the time preparing the precious cargo for the trip home.

Just before we left for the airport my brother said, putting an envelope into my hand, "I thought you might like to have Dad's rosary. It's broken, but Phil can fix it. It was in his suit pocket."

A rosary? My father? The man was more complex than even I suspected.

My mother was so pleased with the painting. "I've been wanting this portrait of you for years," she told me. "How did you get it?"

"Easily," I said. "It's not difficult to get something nobody else wants."

Months passed and when the letter from the attorney handling the will finally arrived, I was shamelessly eager to know how much of the multimillion dollar estate had come to me, but as my mother read through the legalese I was stunned to find that my name, along with Susan's, was on a list of several women who all received the same amount—$10,000. His sizable pension and insurance went to Lee. All the rest went to Dan.

Was I surprised? Not really. My father's cruelty always had a long reach. In reality, I was relieved that my long-term opinion of him was correct. After Judge Morrow's words at the funeral parlor and the priest's eulogy and the rosary, I began to waver, to feel a certain uneasiness that I might have misjudged our father all my life. Now I was grateful that this last deliberate act of rejection of me and spite against my mother confirmed my original opinion. My mother's secretary called with the day's closing cash register receipts from the Perugina Shop in New York and I answered the phone. "The letter just came," I began with false enthusiasm. "Guess how much my father left me?" I teased, knowing she, as a friend of many years, had been as eager as we to know how much my family would be inheriting.

"How much?"

211

"A huge ten thousand dollars."

There was no sound at the other end of the phone line for a brief moment and then her angry exclamation actually made me laugh despite my disappointment. "I'm going to dig your father up and shoot him!"

"I'm going to call Dan," I said to my mother. "I want to reassure him I don't hold him responsible for this farce." But when I made the call, Rose answered and after her quick, muffled, hand-over-the-receiver, "It's Bianca!" my brother's harsh whisper hurled itself across the miles, across the years of my affection for him and into my startled, incredulous awareness; "Christ! She must have gotten the letter! I sure as hell don't want to deal with her. Tell her I'm out of town and you don't know when I'll be back."

And so, not only my father but my brother slipped into oblivion as the reel of film faded black on the conclusion of this pathetically comic, satirically tragic production that was our father's funeral.

Bianca's father, Judge Daniel A. Cavelli
Judge of Cook Co., Chicago

To the Angel at my Father's Tomb

You, of beautiful and solemn face,
Is that a trace
of smugness 'round the mouth and at the eyes?
Sweet guardian of Father's last repose,
Do you suppose
That you shall be more virtuous and wise
Than he who plummeted into his rest,
Unwarned and unrepented, unconfessed?

Do you imagine that the bells of time
Will never chime
Against your perfect form and graceful wing?
Will you withstand the wind, the rain, the cold,
Never grow old,
And never mourn the changes time will bring?
Your wings will chip, your fingers crack and then,
Your halo become refuge for some wren.

For nothing made of man, be it of bone
Or yet of stone
Escapes its end, but you, without a name,
Without a pledge or promise to fulfill,
Without a will,
Shall crumble without fear and without blame
Into a soulless dust, while he, oh he,
Shall weep he is not you throughout eternity.

214

Puppeteers

A stranger came to our door that night
Just as the Westminster clock chimed eight,
Just as Zelffina, frocked in white,
Brought in the cake on a silver plate.
"My truck hit your corner pines," he said.
"Road's iced up bad, but my boss'll pay."
He snatched the knit cap from his head
As though he had been asked to stay.
He could see us well from the entrance hall,
The children at Grandfather's chair,
The boys blue-jacketed and tall,
The girls with ribbons in their hair.
The goblets were filled with pale champagne;
We raised them high, wished the old man well,
And I wondered how much we would gain
At the tolling of his final bell.
"I'll need some help with these candles now,"
Grandfather laughed as he bent to blow.
Eight decades twinkled up at him;
His face was rosy in their glow.
"Did you make a wish? Will you tell me, please?"
Cried the youngest at Grandfather's knee,
And the stranger, fingering his keys,
Stared with such wistful honesty
That I wanted to tell him, this isn't real!
This is a puppet show we've staged.
We work the strings and pretend to feel
What we never felt before he aged,
What we don't feel now, if the truth be known.
Though he seems so honored, so held dear,
Despite our sharing blood and bone,
He is as much a stranger here
As you. He comes every year on his special day
And we all play out our parts—
"Dad, what a pity you can't stay!"
But when his chauffeured limo starts
The children scatter to change their clothes;
I raise the windows to set free
Cigar and bourbon that fall like blows
On the shoulders of my memory.

I watched the stranger go out the door.
He'd never know we'd all been lying.
The puppet shows? There were no more.
My father had been slowly dying,
But he died the master puppeteer
Who will scorn us to the end of time.
He made us nod and bow and cheer
And didn't leave us one thin dime!

Twenty-two
Classic Miniatures

Pet Peeves

Occasionally a product is advertised on television that interests me. I begin to listen attentively to the sales pitch and when I'm altogether convinced and ready to make the phone call to order, the announcer says cheerfully and coaxingly, "Just call the number on your screen!" Naturally, he doesn't read it aloud, which is probably just as well.

• • •

Not only do sighted sales departments frustrate blind buyers and lose potential customers, but many of the organizations that offer us gadgets and tools to enhance our independence also lose sales. In a vivid example of comic irony—their catalogues are in print.

• • •

Other pet peeves revolve around my ego. I heartily resent people thinking that, since my eyes don't work, my brain must also be impaired and it is therefore their responsibility to tell me what I already know.

I always enjoyed dressing up my children. I did it not only because I took pride in their appearance, but also because I knew that friends and neighbors, teachers, classmates, and the public at large would be watching to see if the blind mother's children were as well groomed as everyone else's.

Typical of the explain-it-to-me phenomenon was a neighbor, Audry, who dropped in to visit me one morning. I had just dressed my infant daughter in a lovely white dress with tiny blue elephants embroidered across the hem, white lace-trimmed socks, and freshly polished white shoes. She was every inch a powdered and pampered baby girl.

"Oh, you should see how she's dressed," cooed Audry, "the prettiest white dress with darling tiny elephants on it and lacy socks and ...."

"I know," I murmured, trying not to sound as peeved as I was, "I dressed her!"

• • •

The morning I was to bring our second baby, Philip, home from the hospital, the nurse brought him into my room and left. I proceeded to slip off his hospital gown and dress him in the clothes I had brought with me for his trip home.

When the nurse returned to the room, she was very upset. "You shouldn't have dressed him," she whined. "The head nurse told me to do it because you wouldn't be able to."

"Really," I said, holding a neatly dressed infant in my arms. "He looks properly dressed to me, and, believe it or not, I have a two-year-old daughter who hasn't gone naked a day since I brought her home from the hospital."

• • •

Some people believe that because an individual is blind, he or she is also deaf and must be spoken to as loudly as possible or cannot be directly addressed at all.

When my husband and I would go out to eat, the waitress sometimes asked, "What would she like?" Phil would respond, "I don't know. Why don't you ask her?"

• • •

When my boys were altar boys. I made sure that they were always dressed appropriately for the honor—dress pants, a shirt and tie, and shoes, not sneakers.

The same kind elderly priest was often officiating at the Mass our youngest son served. One morning as we dropped Tom off at the sacristy, I heard the priest say as Phil and I went to our seats, "Whoever is responsible for your clothes certainly knows how to dress you for this job."

• • •

My mother had a stroke and was in pain on her paralyzed left side. I spent each day in the hospital with her. One particular afternoon, she was in great need of pain medication, so I rang the buzzer for the nurse. I waited ten minutes and rang again. I waited another ten minutes and rang again. Finally, I opened the door and stepped out into the corridor. Aides were chatting and laughing loudly, paying no attention whatsoever to our cry for help. Loudly I said, "Excuse me, my mother needs pain medication please."

218

No reaction. I repeated my statement. Still the talking and laughing continued without interruption.

I went back into the room and decided to attack the buzzer again and not release it until someone came. Just then a young man brought my mother's roommate back from x-ray and I appealed to him. "I'm going to have to report these nurses to the doctor if I don't get some attention for my mother."

He promised to alert the nurse and must have told her of my threat because in a moment she was in the room with a suppository. My mother had lost the capacity to swallow with her stroke and hadn't yet regained it.

"What kind of medication do you use?" I asked.

"A Tylenol suppository," the nurse replied.

"Oh, I can get that over the counter," I said. "I'll bring my own from now on since it seems to be so difficult to get medication from the hospital when it's needed."

"You can't do that. It's against the law."

"I'll just have to do it anyway," I insisted. "I can't watch my mother suffer needlessly."

"That's ridiculous," the woman snapped. "How would you give it to her? You can't even see."

Deep breath and slow count to ten. "Well," I replied calmly, "I've raised five children and took care of them when they were sick so I think I could manage it. Besides," I continued, "I lost my sight when I was ten years old and, the last time I looked, everybody's rear end was in the same place."

• • •

Adaptations

My children have always taken my blindness in stride, as just a part of Mom. They have adapted their attitudes and behaviors to cope with the inconveniences arising from my handicap.

One of my favorites of their adaptations was at poolside when they were small. Other mothers encouraged, bullied, and clapped enthusiastically when an offspring achieved a lap across the pool or a smooth dive. Naturally, my children wanted some reaction from me as they performed in the water. As each one approached the diving board the message was—"Watch, Mom, listen. The next splash will be me."

• • •

On summer evenings my mother and I would take the children for long walks on the seaside boardwalk near our summer home. Evenings were often chilly near the water so I had purchased some Billy the Kid jean outfits for my son, Philip, four years old. Each outfit had matching jeans and jean jacket. One was the traditional jean color, one light blue, one tan. So that I could distinguish one outfit from another, my mother sewed Braille color tags onto each pair of jeans and jacket. That particular summer I was expecting our third child and, although I was not feeling at all well, I enjoyed the evening walks.

Because my mother was already waiting by the gate with Theresa and Philip on a very chilly evening, I grabbed a jean jacket for Philip and didn't take the time to read the Braille color tag. I quickly bundled my son into his jacket without being concerned about whether it matched his jeans or not. As my mother and I and my daughter started out the gate, Philip hung back.

"Come along," we coaxed. "Philip, come on. What's wrong?"

Finally, still refusing to leave the yard, he blurted in exasperation—"I can't come. Didn't you read the tag? I don't match!"

. . .

Our third child, Daniel, was an extremely active toddler, the kind who unplugs safety plugs and tries to jam a toy in the socket, the kind who pulls up all the newly blooming tulips to find out what's underneath that's pushing them up, the kind who forces a blind mother to turn off the radio, TV, or music in order to concentrate on hearing where he is and what he's doing at all times. I had threaded bells onto shoelaces for Theresa and Philip when they were babies and that had been a perfect solution for keeping track of them, but Daniel was different. At a very young age, just a month or so after he had learned to walk, he realized that if he moved slowly and carefully, he could keep the bells from making any sound. He loved to tease me by hiding behind drapery, couches, under the dining room table. One afternoon, after I had explored all the usual hiding places and hadn't found him, I began to panic. "Keep your head," I told myself. "This is a baby you have to outsmart."

Picking up a favorite truck the boys loved to play with and often had a tug of war over, I asked, "Is this truck Philip's or Daniel's?"

A tiny voice followed by a jangling of little bells emerged from under the baby grand piano with the customary battle cry, "MINE!"

I gave him the truck, gave him a hug, and gave him a bath, where I could easily keep track of him for as long as I had him in the tub.

. . .

Mouthing Off
The school for blind children which I attended in Tucson had a small but outstanding chorus. One of the students, Howlett Smith, accompanied us, taught us our parts and ran our daily practices whenever our temperamental

220

and seldom-present chorus director failed to appear. Under the sponsorship of the local Lions' Club, the chorus performed for schools and clubs statewide.

One year in the early fifties, the national Lions' Club convention was held in Chicago and we were invited to sing. Two days and nights on the train brought a cluster of excited blind high school students across the country from a sleepy western town to what seemed to the young people to be a bustling metropolis.

The train ride was a holiday in itself, especially for the majority of students who had never traveled before. We played cards with Braille playing cards, practiced our repertoire, chatted, made up mental games, and made the long journey three times a day to the dining car. Maneuvering sixteen blind young people through a line of swaying railroad cars was a challenge. We made a human chain, holding hands and following one another through the swinging train. On one of our passages through the cars a woman cried out in heartfelt and sincere sympathy, "Oh, those poor blind children! How do they find their mouths to eat?"

Johnny, the school comedian, stopped in his tracks long enough to bunch up the chorus members behind him and replied, "Easy, we just talk and follow the sound."

• • •

Visiting the Twilight Zone

My mother traveled to Italy every year on business and I always accompanied her until I married and the babies began arriving. When the children were old enough, my mother brought all of us along. The three oldest, Theresa, Philip, and Daniel, took several trips.

After a five-hour train ride from Florence to Rome, my mother and I decided we needed to shower, change our clothes, and have our hair done. We made separate appointments so that one of us could stay with the children while the other went to the hotel's hairdresser.

"I'll take the children to the park while you're getting your hair done," she said. "Can you arrange to get back to the room?"

"Of course," I said. "I'll just ask one of the beauticians to accompany me and I'll be fine. Enjoy the park. The children need some fresh air and exercise."

My mother dropped me off at the hairdresser's shop and left for the park. I explained to the young lady at the desk that I was blind and I would need some assistance getting back to my room. When I was finished, I made my request and offered an appealing tip if one of the girls would take me up to room 309.

As we reached the door, I was surprised to find it unlocked. Thanking the girl, I pushed the door open and stepped inside the room.

Immediately I was aware that something was wrong. My mother's perfume was not in the air. There was not even a hint of the scent of soap I had used preparing the children for their outing.

I moved around the room and ran my hand over the top of the dresser and desk—all clear, no toys, books, no coloring books and crayons. I slid open the closet door and found only emptiness. I checked the luggage rack, nothing there.

Well, I thought, still calm, no doubt the girl just brought me to the wrong room. All I would have to do is phone the receptionist and tell her to send someone to pick me up and accompany me to the right room.

I moved to the bed, to the night table and found the phone. My heart was racing just a bit, but not as fast as it was when I picked up the phone and found it silent, dead. An old *Twilight Zone* episode in which a man returned to his hotel room to find everything changed, even the wallpaper, clicked into my mind. Unfortunately, there was no way I could verify the wallpaper, but I hoped there was a simpler explanation for the disappearance of my family than the man in the TV show had experienced.

Half-serious and half-joking I said, "All right, if there are any ghosts or aliens in here and if you've kidnapped my mother and children, I'll sprinkle holy water in all the corners of the room and destroy you."

Regaining a more logical thrust, I went to the door and opened it. Coming down the hall were two young women, laughing and chatting and smelling of cleaning fluids—chambermaids.

"Excuse me," I interrupted. "Is this room 309?"

"No, signora," they said politely. "It's room 209."

The twilight zone quickly vanished and with another tip, I finally reached the proper room.

As soon as I opened the door, my mother's perfume wafted into my face. Again, I ran my hand over surfaces—the boys' tiny toy soldiers were still marching across the top of the dresser, Theresa's books were stacked neatly on the desk, the discarded traveling clothes lay where the children had tossed them on the beds. REALITY! Never was clutter so reassuring and so welcome.

· · ·

Just Stop and Think About It

In November, our old furnace cranked out its last puff of heat and we were forced to have a new heating system installed in our home. In February we received a phone call from a cheery-voiced woman who related the happy news that we were entitled to a "free" inspection. Our old furnace had roared along for fifty years with only an occasional check-up and filter change, but my husband decided it might be wise to have the new one looked at, especially since the inspection was "free."

222

Phil accompanied the men downstairs into the basement. In a few moments he was back. "We need new filters. A hundred-nine dollars."

Silently I handed him the checkbook. Was there any point in disputing the reality that a brand new system needed filters?

True to form, the next day, when Phil had gone out of town on business, something dramatic happened to the otherwise smoothly running household. As soon as his plane lifted off the runway, the new heating system began blowing cold air throughout the house. I was assured by the same cheery voice on the other end of the phone that a technician would be at my home within the hour and he was.

"Hi, I'm Roy."

"Are you one of the men who replaced the filters yesterday?"

"Nope, this is my first time here. Show me where all the thermostats are."

"Right here, on the dining room wall."

"Where's the rest of 'em?"

"That's all there are."

"In this whole big house, only one thermostat! That's hard to believe! How 'bout upstairs?"

"No, just this one."

"How come you never had one put upstairs?"

I didn't answer. His incredulity at our stupidity was beginning to annoy me.

"Let me show you where the basement is," I said as I led him down the hall into the kitchen and to the door leading downstairs.

On the second step he turned back to me, demanding, "Are there any thermostats on the furnace?"

"I don't know," I replied, beginning to feel as stupid as he thought I was.

"You're no help," he snarled.

That did it! Truly annoyed now, I retorted, "I'm not the mechanic. Why don't you go down and see if you can find the problem all by yourself."

In five minutes he was back, all smiles, his disposition so radically changed I thought he must have found the wine cellar, but he hadn't been down there long enough.

"There was just a tube dangling," he said. "I don't know what to charge you."

"Charge me?" I said, indignant. "Charge me because the technicians didn't hook the machinery back up properly when they changed the filters? I don't think so."

"I gotta call the office and ask 'em."

I indicated the phone and waited.

"You're right," he said agreeably, handing me a piece of paper, "no charge, just sign your name on the line on this here paper."

Now it occured to me that he hadn't realized I'm blind. This should be amusing. I smiled inwardly as I put the paper down on the kitchen butcher block and said, "I guess you're not aware that I can't see. Please show me where the line is and I'll sign...."

He didn't let me finish but exploded into a sympathetic roar: "You CAN'T SEE! Oh, well, just write John Doe on the line then."

I tried, but I couldn't restrain my mouth from spreading into a wide grin. This was even better than I anticipated. "Oh," I explain, "that's not the problem. I know what my name is and I even know how to spell it, but I don't know where the line is."

A huge, rough-skinned hand covered the paper and a finger pointed toward the bottom of the page. I signed where the finger ended and handed him the paper.

"Thank you, ma'am," he said, suddenly respectful, deferential, amazed. "You did real good."

"So did you," I returned the compliment. "Thanks for the hot air."

• • •

I hadn't had pain in my eyes for many years, so when I began to experience some, I decided it might be wise to see an ophthalmologist. Phil and I arrived at his office, which was packed with waiting patients. I noticed that from time to time a young woman would come to the waiting room, call out a name, and someone would rise and follow her inside. When my turn came, Phil accompanied me into an interior room where the young woman showed me to a small straight chair and directed me to: "Read the chart."

"I'm sorry," I said, surprised that I should have to explain my lack of sight, since she had seen Phil guide me in and had herself shown me to the chair, "I'm not able to do that. I have no vision whatsoever."

"Well," she snapped, "you have to read the chart before the doctor will see you. That's the rule. You'll just have to sit here till you decide to cooperate." Phil didn't bother to suppress his incredulous chuckle, but I suggested in as serious an attitude as I could muster, "Perhaps if I talk to the doctor and explain that I'm totally blind, he'll make an exception and see me without my having to read the chart."

Sighing heavily, the young woman retreated to another room. When she returned, she announced in a less-than-friendly voice, "Okay, you win. The doctor will see you."

• • •

My friend Kathy and I walked the boardwalk almost daily. Even the frantic Nor'easters howling in off the water seldom interrupted our walking schedule, so when Kathy's brother, Jerry, came to town for a visit, he joined our early-morning constitutional. His wit, good-natured conversation, and friendly presence were a pleasant addition to our regime.

Soon after his visit, Jerry invited Kathy to California, where he accompanied his sister to every imaginable tourist attraction, including a national park. As they strolled along the trails, he noticed that some of the plaques describing the plants and trees were in Braille as well as in print.

When Kathy returned to town and we resumed our walks, she related Jerry's thoughtful suggestion: "Take a photograph of these Braille plaques to show Bianca when you get home."

• • •

My friend Barbara knows how much I love the cello. With great enthusiasm, she dropped off a video, the story of the famous cellist, Rostropovich. I slipped the movie into our VCR and listened. There was a moment of cello music and the story began. The only problem was, the dialogue was in Russian. I assumed there must have been English subtitles, but not being able to see them, the story line was totally lost to me. I busied myself folding laundry, knitting, preparing artichokes for dinner as I listened for more cello. Now and then the magic of the instrument would surface between long periods of Russian dialogue.

When Barbara phoned me later that evening she asked expectantly, "How did you enjoy the video?"

"The ten minutes of cello were fabulous," I said, "but I had a bit of difficulty following the plot in Russian."

• • •

Driving the Point Home

When my son Philip was in the fourth grade, the principal of his school asked if I would make a presentation to improve the children's understanding of blindness. As I heard the auditorium filling with excited voices, I was confident that I could easily capture their attention and enhance their knowledge. I spoke to them and explained that I used an ordinary typewriter, that a Frenchman named Louie Braille had invented the touch system for reading, that it was possible for blind people to do almost everything sighted people do if they have the right tools. Then I dispersed a Braille watch, Braille music, Braille maps, Braille writing implements, Braille color tags for clothes, and Braille playing cards among them for hands-on experience.

The children buzzed with interest and enthusiasm as they examined each item and I was sure they had gained an insight into the coping skills I had tried to impart to them. When their teachers had gathered all the materials,

I asked if there were any questions. My assurance that they had grasped the concept of blindness began to diminish with each question they asked.

"If you're on a roof, how do you know when to stop walking so you don't fall off?"

"When you're car pooling, how do you know which house to stop at?"

One little girl burst my confidence bubble altogether. "How do you know which way to turn when you're driving your car and you get to a corner?"

• • •

When my daughter Francesca was in the third grade, she had a part in the school play. Naturally, I wanted very much to attend. My husband and my mother both worked in New York City, some seventy miles from our seashore home, so they couldn't accompany me to the school. We were new in the neighborhood and I didn't know any of our neighbors well enough to invite them to attend the play so I could catch a ride with them. A cab was not practical because when I arrived at the school I would need assistance getting into the building, finding the auditorium, and returning home.

Francesca had played with a classmate a few times and, knowing that I was blind and obviously couldn't drive, the girl's mother had brought the child to our home to play. Perhaps that mother would be going to the program and might not mind picking me up. I phoned.

"Francesca is in the school play and I was wondering if I could get a ride with you if you plan to attend."

"Oh yes, I'm going," she said, "and I'll be glad to bring you to school with me. Just drive over to my house by one o'clock."

• • •

The greatest compliment I can receive is for someone who knows me well to forget my handicap. A longtime friend, Winnie, phoned me not long ago with a request.

"My car won't start and I have to get to my doctor's appointment. Would you mind driving me?"

• • •

Red Ink, No Ink
I had made arrangements to take an English exam with the professor in his office. I explained that I would ask him to read me the questions, which I would Braille, and then write the responses on his office typewriter. That procedure had been successful many times before with other professors, so I didn't anticipate any problem.

We met; he read the questions and I Brailed them. He left to go to his classroom to administer the exam to the other students and I took several sheets of typing paper out of my book bag and went to work. I was pleased with my efforts. The questions had been difficult but interesting and I had pounded out twelve pages of answers. I took my stack of papers to his classroom, put them on his desk, and sat down at my desk to wait for his dismissal. I heard students walking up to his desk, depositing their exams, and returning to their places.

Suddenly his voice boomed across the silent classroom, "Okay, who's the wise guy that handed in twelve sheets of blank paper?"

With a sinking feeling in the pit of my stomach, I realized that his office typewriter must have been on stencil.

"I'm afraid," I said slowly, "I must be the wise guy."

"And I'm afraid," he said, "that you'll have to write the exam over again."

The next morning my mother and I were in a typewriter store buying a small Olivetti typewriter that I subsequently brought to every exam I took from then on.

· · ·

When my mother and I moved from Tucson to New York, I was pleased to find that a German concert pianist lived next door. As soon as we were settled I approached the artist for some review and coaching sessions to prepare for my Juilliard audition. Since she had never worked with a blind student, she was hesitant, but once I had played for her, she agreed to accept me. I thought we would have a comfortable rapport until she said, "Jah, und when you are needing more work somewhere, I am underlining the passage in red so you are seeing it better, *Ja?*"

· · ·

Mistrial for Lack of Information

My friend Cathy invites me to the Garden Club luncheon annually. At the last luncheon she said, "I think that's your new neighbor at a nearby table. I'm going over to say hello."

When Cathy came back she was laughing. "Your neighbor asked if that was Bianca Stewart at my table, and when I told her I had brought you as my guest she exclaimed, 'How did you ever get her to agree to come with you? She's such a snob!'"

"Why am I a snob?" I asked, surprised.

"She said she's been waving at you for almost a year and you never wave back."

In a moment my neighbor was at the table.

"I feel terrible," she began, "I've been telling everybody what a snob you are!"

"Don't worry about it," I told her. "It's a title I have never had before. Perhaps I'll try it on and see if I like it."

• • •

When I was fourteen, I was skating with a girlfriend in a roller rink. We decided to take a rest and have a Coke. Approaching the exit ramp, I put my hand down on the railing to steady myself and stop. The instant I placed my hand on the wooden rail I felt another hand already there and removed my own as quickly as possible with a smile and a "Sorry." A teenage male voice said confidentially, "That's okay, baby. Don't be shy. You can hold my hand any time."

As my friend and I were sitting at the snack bar, the same male voice, now annoyed, sounded behind me: "What is it with you, anyway? First you grab my hand and then you totally ignore me when I smile at you or motion you over to my table. What kind of games do you play?"

• • •

When my mother had a lung cancer operation, I was at the hospital daily. She was in a great deal of pain and it was always a relief when the medications allowed her to sleep. One afternoon, a man stepped into the room while she was comfortably dozing and asked loudly, "Is she asleep?"

"Yes," I said defensively. "Please don't wake her."

"All right," the man answered. "If you think she wants Holy Communion sometime just tell the nurse and they'll let me know. I'm the hospital chaplain."

Embarrassed, I hastened to explain. "I apologize for my rudeness, Father. I can't see. I didn't know you were a priest. I thought you might be another lab technician or...."

He chuckled. "I apologize, too," he said. "I didn't know you couldn't see. I should have introduced myself."

He came every day after that and any time he arrived he was welcome.

• • •

Communication Gap

I teach classes in Italian, French, and creative writing. Most of the time, people hear of the classes through word-of-mouth, but occasionally I run an ad in a local newspaper. Prospective students telephone for information and to register for classes. The students who answer the newspaper ads and don't know of me are always surprised when they come for their first lesson to find that I can't see. Once they recover from the shock and the first lesson proceeds smoothly and pleasantly, they're willing to continue. One gentleman expressed the initial surprise perfectly when he said, "How about that! You didn't sound blind on the phone."

• • •

Because I can't drive, I do the majority of my shopping on the phone. Over the years I have been fortunate to find salespeople who are willing to be helpful and look for the article I need. Now and then I find myself at the mercy of an impatient employee who tells me, "You'll have to come and look for it yourself." When I explain that as much as I would like to, my lack of vision prohibits me from doing so, they usually agree to help. More than once, however, I have been told, "Look in the newspaper. We run ads all the time. You can't miss 'em."

• • •

Victims of Circumstance

Theresa never told me until she was an adult that when she was in second grade at Mt. Carmel School in Ridgewood, New Jersey, the class had been discussing handicaps. Theresa volunteered the information that her mother was blind. Unfortunately, her teacher didn't believe her. When Theresa insisted that what she had said was true, the teacher made her get down on her knees in the classroom, say an act of contrition for lying, and apologize to the class for the disruption. Theresa was wise not to have told me until twenty years had passed because my reaction would have done more than "disrupt" the entire school. The thought of my innocent and truthful child being so humiliated still stings and howls for retribution.

• • •

My handwriting is poor and my son Tom had a run-in with a teacher because of it. It was the policy of the school he attended, St. Catharine's in Spring Lake, to have each test signed to ensure a parent had seen the exam and was aware of the grade, good or bad. When Tom was in the third grade, his teacher would not believe that I had signed the test sheet because the

229

signature was unclear. She accused Tom of signing it himself. Nothing Tom could say would convince her. She had taken him out into the hall to prolong his persecution when another teacher who knew me walked by. Hearing Tom trying to convince his teacher of my blindness, she verified what Tom was saying. Tom's embarrassed teacher allowed him back in the classroom.

• • •

My mother had fallen and hurt her back. It was difficult for her to get in and out of the car or to walk for any distance. One stormy Friday afternoon we had picked Tom up from school and he asked if we could stop and get a movie at the local video rental shop.

I had severe bronchitis and didn't want to venture out into the pouring rain to go in to the shop with him. "Run in and get a movie," I told him. "Just sign my name for it. You shouldn't have a problem."

In a few moments Tom, accompanied by the store manager, was back. The man, obviously abashed, said apologetically, "The kid told me his grandmother can't walk, his mother can't see, and she's too sick to come out in the rain so he's supposed to pick out the video himself. Sorry, real sorry, but I just had to check out his soap opera for myself."

• • •

Beyond the Call of Duty
Total strangers as well as friends have gone out of their way for me. One episode in particular stands out in my memory. When I was fifteen and had just returned from training with my first Seeing Eye dog, I took the bus to the home of a piano teacher in town. I had often ridden that bus with my mother so the ill-tempered driver known as Mr. Grouch to all his steady passengers was not new to me. I worried that he might deny me the ride because of the dog, but he said nothing as we climbed up the steps, paid the fare, and found a seat. By counting the stops, I knew when I was approaching my destination. I rose and worked my way to the front of the bus. As the bus shuddered to a stop, the driver, without a word, climbed out behind me, grabbed my arm with a strong grip and propelled me across the highway to safety. It wasn't necessary, of course, but since he had left a busload of passengers to accompany me, I was not so ungrateful as to let him see my embarrassment or to tell him that my dog and I had been well trained to handle the crossing. As I started down the sidewalk to my piano lesson, I heard a most heartwarming sound, the passengers on the bus clapping and cheering for the driver's act of kindness and I wondered if Mr. Grouch had managed to crack a smile.